The German Parliament

Table of contents

The parliamentary ideal and parliamentarianism in Germany, 1800–1945

Manfred Görtemaker

The establishment of the primacy of parliaments in the political process is one of the outstanding achievements of modern times. Its foundations were laid by the Enlightenment in 18th-century Europe and the rise of bourgeois society during the Industrial Revolution, which enabled the parliamentary ideal to take root. The political systems that proceeded from it were no longer based on the divine right of sovereigns but on the sovereignty of the people. Absolutist monarchs gave way to parliaments with freely elected members, who organised themselves into parties and parliamentary groups on the basis of their general political orientation and assumed responsibility for legislation within a division of powers, that is to say the separation of the legislative, executive and judicial branches.

At the beginning of the 19th century, this development was already far advanced in Britain and France; indeed, in the United States, it had even been brought to completion with the Revolution of 1776 and the drafting of a republican Constitution. In Germany, the process was far more arduous. The spread of the ideal of parliamentary democracy was obstructed by the territorial fragmentation of the nation and by the absence of a central governmental authority and of a central place where schools of political thought could crystallise. Another negative factor was the low level of industrialisation, which delayed the development of a strong middle class that could have become the vehicle of liberalism within society and its driving force. Calls for political freedom and a voice in government, expressed chiefly by poets and philosophers such as Immanuel Kant, Gotthold Ephraim Lessing, Friedrich Schiller, Johann Gottlieb Fichte and Friedrich Hölderlin, therefore fell largely on deaf ears.

After inflicting heavy defeats on the Prussian army, Napoleon entered Berlin on 27 October 1806. Charles Meynier (1768–1832) celebrated the event with this painting, which is now part of the *Musée de l'Histoire de France* collection in the Palace of Versailles.

Prussian civil servant, statesman and reformer Freiherr vom Stein (1757–1831) was one of the main initiators, along with Karl-August von Hardenberg, of the Prussian reforms. Because of his anti-Napoleonic views, he was compelled to go into exile in 1808.

Prince Karl August von Hardenberg (1750–1822) came from an aristocratic family in the Electorate of Hanover. Having served as Prussian Foreign Minister from 1804 to 1806, he became Chancellor of Prussia in 1810, which he remained until his death, and in that capacity he represented Prussia at the Congress of Vienna and the Carlsbad Conference.

Not until the cataclysmic event of 1806 – the fall of the Holy Roman Empire of the German Nation in the struggle against Napoleon – did it become widely apparent that Germany's fate would be sealed if it continued to ignore the need for political unification of the German nation and for liberalisation of its internal political structures. Calls for freedom, constitutional government and national unity therefore became a defining characteristic of the age. Reformists sought to achieve political emancipation of the citizen, to arouse public interest in the state and nation and thus to contribute to the liberation of Germany from French rule.

The Prussian and Bavarian reforms

The most visible transformations were surely those that took place in Prussia and Bavaria. In Prussia there was the 'Berlin Enlightenment', which had been developing since the mid-18th century and whose leading figures were the author and publisher Friedrich Nicolai and many of his literary friends. It became bogged down, however, in polemics with other intellectuals, such as Immanuel Kant. As in other parts of Germany, it had not progressed significantly beyond the mere formulation of reformist ideas. Not until Prussia had suffered defeat at the hands of the French and signed the 1807 Peace of Tilsit did a small group of government officials under the chief minister, Freiherr Karl vom und zum Stein (1757–1831), an imperial baron from Nassau engaged in the service of Prussia, succeed in implementing plans for fundamental reform of the Prussian state. Their aim was a "representative system" which "guarantees the nation effective participation in lawmaking so as thus to implant in it an enduring public spirit and love of the Fatherland".

The October Edict of 1807 in Prussia initiated the abolition of the system of estates and introduced freedom of movement for the rural population, hitherto bound by hereditary serfdom. Together with the Edict of Regulation, it paved the way – once the complex issues of redemption and compensation had been resolved – for an influx of willing and able jobseekers into the emerging industrial metropolises. The administration of the state was reorganised, and the Municipal Ordinance (*Städteordnung*) of 1808 introduced the principle of the participation of the 'citizenry' in public life in Prussia for the first time. Further reform acts entered the statute books, including the Corporation Tax Edict drawn up in the summer of 1810 under the chancellorship of Freiherr Karl August von Hardenberg and the army reforms enacted between 1807 and 1813 under Gerhard von Scharnhorst, Hermann von Boysen and August Neidhardt von Gneisenau.

In Bavaria too, Napoleon played a part, contributing indirectly to the enactment of the Constitution for the Kingdom of Bavaria on 1 May 1808, with which the Minister of the Interior, Maximilian Joseph von Montgelas, tried to thwart Napoleon's efforts to create a common constitution for the 16 states of the Confederation of the Rhine. These states had formally seceded from the Empire in Paris in 1806 and had entered into a military alliance with France, in which Napoleon took on the role of their Protector. The new Constitution, in which Montgelas codified

Following Napoleon's defeat in the War of the Sixth Coalition, representatives of some 200 states, princely houses, corporations and cities gathered at the Congress of Vienna, held from 18 September 1814 to 9 June 1815, to discuss the new European order. This painting by Jean-Baptiste Isabey (1767–1855) shows the following 23 delegates: seated, left to right: Karl August von Hardenberg, Pedro de Sousa Holstein, Robert Stewart, 2nd Marquess of Londonderry (Lord Castlereagh), Johann von Wessenberg, Pedro Gómez Labrador, Charles-Maurice de Talleyrand-Périgord, Gustav Ernst von Stackelberg; standing, left to right: Arthur Wellesley, 1st Duke of Wellington, Joaquim Lobo da Silveira, António de Saldanha da Gama, Carl Axel Löwenhielm, Paul-François de Noailles, Klemens Wenzel Lothar von Metternich, Frédéric-Séraphin de La Tour du Pin, Marquis of Gouvernet, Karl Robert von Nesselrode, Emmerich Joseph von Dalberg, Andrei Kirillowitsch Rasumowski, Charles William Vane, later 3rd Marquess of Londonderry, Richard Le Poer Trench, 2nd Earl of Clancarty, Nikolaus von Wacken, Friedrich von Gentz, Wilhelm von Humboldt and William Cathcart, 1st Earl Cathcart.

numerous reforms that had already been implemented since 1799, provided for the repeal of all of the special constitutions, privileges, hereditary offices and corporations of the estates in the individual provinces. It thus smoothed the way for the unification of the territories subsumed into the new Bavarian order in a state that could be governed on the basis of uniform social and administrative principles. At the same time the King, as an 'institution' of the new state, guaranteed key fundamental rights – equality of all citizens before the law, equal tax obligations, equal access to all offices of state, abolition of serfdom, inviolability of the person and of property, freedom of conscience and religion and freedom of the press within the bounds of certain censorship laws. Bavaria was thus a comparatively early starter on the road from princely autocracy to constitutional statehood.

The new laws, however, remained largely alien to the people affected by these reforms, which, according to a contemporary source, were "received by most with disinterest, by many with diffidence and by some even with reluctance". This was especially true of the many peasant farmers and craftsmen who fell victim to economic liberalisation, while education and property remained the privilege of a narrow caste. Under the 1811 Edict of Regulation, for instance, peasants in Prussia had to compensate their landlords for the loss of former socage and labour dues. This deprived many peasant smallholders of their living and compelled them to sell their debt-ridden land. It is therefore one of the "tragic ironies of Germany's underlying constitutional history" (Ernst Rudolf Huber) that an edict which was supposed to bring about greater freedom led to an expansion of the landless peasant classes, whose dependants now had to hire themselves out as day labourers. Similar problems were posed by the introduction of freedom of trade in 1810, because it caused the increase in the number of tradesmen to outstrip population growth, which meant that the members of some oversubscribed trades, particularly shoemakers, joiners and tailors, slid into the lower classes of society.

Moreover, the reforms did not lend decisive impetus to the liberal constitutionalist movement. On the contrary, after the victory over Napoleon, Prussia as well as Bavaria opted at the Congress of Vienna in 1815 for a return to the old order, upholding the principle of monarchist government. Restoration, monarchical legitimacy and solidarity among the ruling princes began once again to determine political developments, which were guided by the absolutism of the past rather than the liberal visions of the present.

The German Confederation

The German Confederation that was created at the Congress of Vienna was also a source of disappointment in this respect. It was not the federal state for which many had hoped, a state that would unite Germany, but a loose confederation of states under Austrian leadership with 35 sovereign princes and four free cities, which was designed solely to preserve "the external and internal security of Germany and the independence and inviolability of the individual German States". The central organ of the Confederation was the Federal Assembly (*Bundesversammlung*), which met in Frankfurt and remained in existence until 1866. The Assembly, also known as the Federal Diet (*Bundestag*), was

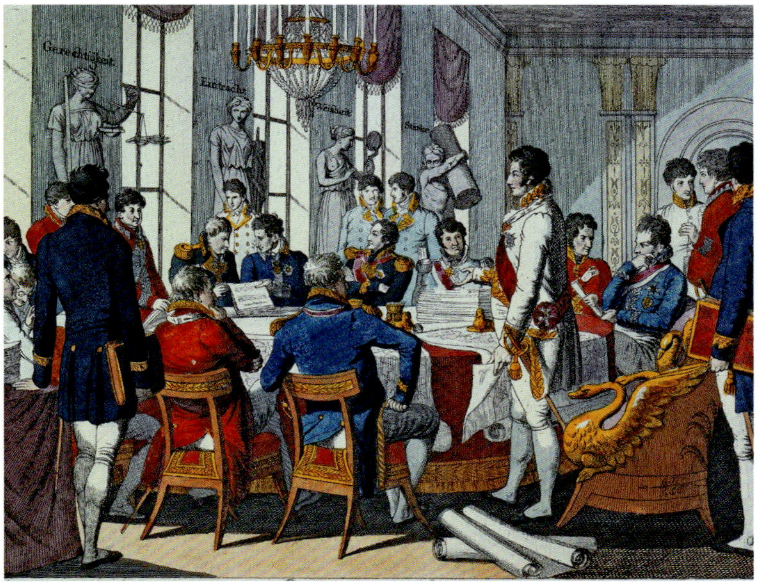

This engraving, entitled *Deutschlands Hoffnung oder der Bundestag in Frankfurt* ('Germany's hope, or the Federal Diet in Frankfurt') depicts the first meeting of the Federal Assembly, a designation soon replaced in common usage by *Bundestag*, held in the Palais Thurn und Taxis in Frankfurt am Main on 5 November 1816. The standing congress of all member states of the German Confederation, modelled on the Imperial Diet (*Reichstag*) of the Holy Roman Empire, met once a week. Its last meeting took place in Augsburg on 24 August 1866.

Aufruf zur Freyheit
Verfassungs Rath
Souverainitaet des Volkes
oder Tyranie einiger wenigen Demagogen
Press Freyheit oder Publikation alles Unraths durch den Druck
Philantropie.
das heißt die Kunst für sich selbst zu sorgen und zwar auf Kosten seines Nächsten
Glük des Volkes.
oder Kumer u. Sorgen für jeden ins besondere und Jamer und Elend für alle
Zeitung und anderer Unrath
Libelle
Dies ist der Kleister
Von einem Quidam
Geist unserer Zeit

not a parliamentary body but a congress of envoys in which the 39 member states of the Confederation were represented by plenipotentiaries who were bound by instructions from their own princes and who could only take decisions on important matters by consensus.

Within the German Confederation, Austria and Prussia remained the principal forces of the Restoration until 1848. Decisive influence was wielded by the Austrian Chancellor, Klemens Wenzel Lothar von Metternich. He played a major part in the formulation of the Carlsbad Decrees in the autumn of 1819, which were designed to curb and eliminate liberal and nationalist tendencies in post-Napoleonic Germany. The Decrees also served as the basis for repressive measures, and institutions of the Confederation – the Federal Assembly and the censorship enforcement authority – were deployed in the effort to crush democratic aspirations. The aim was to allay as quickly as possible the princes' fears of revolution, which had been further kindled by the murder in March 1819 of Russia's Consul-General August von Kotzebue by Karl Ludwig Sand, a theology student and *Burschenschaft* member.

In Prussia, the hopes that authoritarianism would gradually give way to the development of a bourgeois democracy were never fulfilled, not least because King Frederick William III failed to honour his repeated promise of a constitution and clung to the absolute power of the monarchy.

Following the war of liberation against Napoleon, liberal and nationalist movements were on the rise in the states of the German Confederation, as elsewhere, but met with resistance from the ruling classes. This cartoon was a response to the Carslbad Conference, held from 6 to 31 August 1819, at which the most influential states of the German Confederation discussed how best to proceed against the constitutionalist movement. Carlsbad (Karlovy Vary) was chosen as the venue for this secret conference, since it could be presented in the press as a chance meeting of diplomats at a spa town.

The majority of the German population therefore turned their backs on politics in frustration. In the Biedermeier period, this withdrawal into private life was primarily reflected in an apolitical middle-class lifestyle based on homeliness and tranquillity, conviviality and the pursuit of artistic and literary interests and strongly tinged with Romanticism. Politically, it was, in the words of Theodor Fontane, an 'age of stagnation and police', which continued virtually throughout the 1820s and 1830s. Even the July Revolution of 1830 in Paris, which forced the abdication of the French King, Charles X, found few Germans prepared to emulate it.

Germany in the years before 1848

The nationalist and liberal impetus generated by the wars of liberation against Napoleon could not, however, be entirely suppressed. The political opposition that took shape between 1815 and 1848, known in Germany as the *Vormärz* (pre-March) period, because it preceded the Revolution of March 1848, gained ground, primarily among the bourgeoisie and at the universities as well as among merchants, traders and craftsmen. Its quest for a liberal constitution and for economic and social reforms was connected with the aim of a unified German nation state. Among the manifestations of this groundswell of opposition were mass gatherings ('festivals') at the Wartburg, a castle near Eisenach, in 1817 and at Hambach Castle in the Palatinate in 1832, attended mainly by members of the educated classes and of the student *Burschenschaften*.

From 27 May to 1 June 1832, the Hambach Festival took place at Hambach Castle and in the vicinity of Hambach as well as in nearby Neustadt an der Haardt. Today the Festival is regarded as the climax of bourgeois opposition during the period between the Restoration and the revolution of 1848. Its participants protested against the efforts of the German Confederation to restore the old order, calling instead for national unification, freedom and sovereignty of the people.

The Liberals registered successes, chiefly in the states of southern and south-west Germany that had formerly belonged to the Confederation of the Rhine. Under Napoleonic rule, class barriers had already been abolished in those states, their economies had been modernised and their citizens made equal before the law – through the introduction of the *Code civil*, among other things. On the basis of constitutions that were already in force, elected assemblies were established in Baden and Bavaria in 1818, in Württemberg in 1819 and in Hesse-Darmstadt in 1820 on the model of the French constitutional monarchy. Events took a similar course in the Grand-Duchy of Saxe-Weimar-Eisenach in central Germany, where Grand Duke Karl August had promulgated a liberal constitution based on representation of the estates as early as 1816. Saxe-Weimar-Eisenach was thus the first state in Germany to be given such a constitution after the wars of liberation against Napoleon. The state diet, which met in Weimar, lasted from 1816 to 1918.

Although the powers of these 'parliaments', known as chambers, state diets (*Landtage*) or estates, were still limited, since each depended on the ruler of its territory to convoke it and none of them could introduce its own bills, they did nevertheless play a part in the legislative process and had the right to approve or reject the state budget, and so it seems to be no exaggeration to say that the origins of German parliamentarianism are actually to be found in these assemblies. The same process occurred in Bavaria, where King Maximilian I introduced a new constitution on 26 May 1818 to thwart Metternich's plan for a federal constitution. The new constitution reaffirmed the fundamental rights and freedoms that had already been granted to Bavarian citizens under the constitution of 1808 but it also accorded new participatory powers to Parliament. Although the bulk of political power still rested with the King, who, in accordance with the monarchist principle, embodied all governmental authority in his person, the status of the people's representative body was now enshrined in the constitution, even though the state diet could only approve or reject royal bills and taxation proposals and could not take legislative initiatives of its own or attach conditions to its approval of taxes.

The introduction of parliaments in other states, particularly in north and central Germany, followed after the July Revolution of 1830. By the eve of the 1848 Revolution, more than half of the 39 states in the German Confederation already had parliamentary assemblies within the framework of constitutional monarchies, most of them concentrated in the southern part of Germany. The pre-1848 constitutions typically established a bicameral system in which the first chamber comprised representatives of the aristocracy, the churches, the universities and other institutions, while the second chamber was the real representative assembly. The franchise, however, was generally restricted to taxpayers and property owners. Only in the Grand Duchy of Baden were all persons with the right of citizenship automatically enfranchised, but even there the right to stand for election was dependent on a census, as in the other constitutional states.

The Second Chamber of the Baden Parliament therefore served as something of a model for the liberal and nationalist movement in Germany in the period leading up to 1848. Two of its members, Karl von Rotteck and Carl Theodor Welcker, professors at Freiburg University who published a liberal newspaper, *Der Freisinnige*, which was seized several times after its first appearance in March 1832 and ultimately banned, as well as a twelve-volume encyclopaedia of political science entitled *Das Staats-Lexikon*, were among the most notable champions of liberal political and constitutional ideas and mouthpieces of the Liberal movement in the south-west of Germany. After the July Revolution of 1830 in France, the Second Chamber in Baden became the first popularly elected assembly in Germany to call for freedom of the press and the abolition of censorship, and it was also the first parliament in which a motion was tabled for the establishment of a parliament representing the whole German nation.

On 18 October 1817, to mark the 300th anniversary of the start of the Reformation and the fourth anniversary of the Battle of Leipzig, about 500 students and some academics from almost all of Germany's Protestant universities gathered at Wartburg Castle in the Grand Duchy of Saxony-Weimar-Eisenach in modern-day Thuringia. The Wartburg Festival was a demonstration against the reactionary policies of the German Confederation and in favour of a nation state with its own constitution.

The Revolution of 1848

The situation in Germany in the years leading to the March Revolution was thus characterised by opposing trends, the crushed hopes of constitutional progress and the calls for freedom and unity contrasting with inspiring examples of political renewal in south-west Germany that soon began to open up new vistas for the whole nation. Increasing industrialisation, the formation of customs unions that began in 1818 and culminated in the founding of the German *Zollverein* in 1834 and the mobility and modernisation of the country that resulted from railway building went hand in hand with the rise of the bourgeoisie as a political force. Calls for freedom of the press, trial by jury and citizens' militias, as well as for the introduction of constitutional systems of government and even a German parliament, grew louder, and political tension increased. Bad harvests and economic crises accompanying the transformation of the economy gave rise to pauperism and aggravated the situation. Unrest and rioting broke out in many parts of Germany, particularly among the peasant farmers.

In the spring of 1848, when another Revolution in Paris lit the torch of revolt in Europe, Germany was ripe for change too. In the smaller and medium-sized states of the German Confederation, the ruling princes did not even resist but agreed without delay in March 1848 to the formation of reformist cabinets (the 'March ministers') in order to defuse a volatile situation. Even in Vienna and Berlin, the Revolution won an easy victory. Metternich was driven out of the Austrian capital, and, after serious disturbances, particularly in Berlin, the Prussian King, Frederick William IV, was left with no option but to enact orders on 18 March 1848 satisfying demands for which the Liberals in Prussia had been campaigning for many years, namely freedom of the press and the introduction of a system of constitutional monarchy. In addition, he issued a proclamation in which he stated that Prussia 'is henceforth merged in Germany'.

In spite of such rapid concessions, revolutionary unrest and bloody street battles could not be entirely avoided. The fact that, in the face of this pressure from the revolutionary movement, all the ruling princes ultimately declared themselves willing to introduce constitutional systems and to agree to the convocation of a constitutive assembly for the whole of Germany was a great advance. On 5 March 1848, fifty-one politicians from the liberal and democratic opposition in the south and west of Germany had already met in Heidelberg to make preparations for the election of a national assembly. A 'committee of seven' appointed by them invited all "former or present members of the Estates and participants in legislative assemblies in all areas of Germany" along with other figures from public life – a total of more than 500 men – to a 'pre-parliament' (*Vorparlament*), which began its deliberations in St. Paul's Church (*Paulskirche*), Frankfurt, on 30 March 1848.

The debates were disputatious and sometimes stormy. They focused primarily on the principles of the future German Constitution and elections to the National Assembly. In the end it was not the representatives of the democratic Left, led by Gustav von Struve and committed to a federal republic on the American model, who won the day but the moderate Liberals, who sought to achieve a new political order through agreement with the

The railway age began officially for the German Confederation on 7 December 1835 with the opening of the private Ludwig Line between Nuremberg and Fürth. In the early days, however, trains were still frequently pulled by horses, as the procurement of coal initially remained very expensive. This lithograph shows the opening of the Munich-Augsburg railway on 1 September 1839.

Adolph von Menzel (1815–1905) used the workers in a rolling mill in Königshütte (Chorzów), Silesia, as models for his painting *Das Eisenwalzwerk* ('The Iron-Rolling Mill', 1872–1875). While Menzel's contemporaries regarded the work as a celebration of modern technology, it was later reinterpreted as a condemnation of the grim working conditions in that industry.

ruling princes. In collaboration with the old Federal Diet and the governments of the individual states, the requisite electoral laws were adopted. At the end of April, deputies were elected to the National Assembly in all parts of Germany, and they gathered in Frankfurt on 18 May 1848 for their constituent sitting in the *Paulskirche*.

The National Assembly in the *Paulskirche*

The National Assembly comprised 831 full and substitute members (587 excluding the substitute members); initially, only 330 were present, but an average of 400 to 500 subsequently attended the debates. Heinrich von Gagern was elected President (Speaker) of the Assembly. In his inaugural speech on 19 May, he stressed the 'sovereignty of the nation' and its right to give itself a new constitution, but he also laid emphasis on the cooperation of the governments in the individual states. The vast majority of the deputies came from the educated and propertied middle classes. Most of them were senior civil servants and academics, chiefly legal scholars. There were also writers, merchants and landowners but very few craftsmen, no labourers and a single peasant farmer. The aristocracy and the petit bourgeoisie were also sparsely represented in the Chamber.

The mood was dignified and the atmosphere laden with pride, hope and confidence. This was a long-awaited moment, the culmination of almost half a century of laborious and unrelenting effort. Now the history of Germany was set to reach a decisive turning point in the *Paulskirche*. The aim was to make Germany into a modern constitutional state on the Western European model with some elements of the American system too, though without the violent eruptions that had accompanied the French Revolution, and at the same time to resolve the question of German unification.

When the Assembly began to discuss the basic features of the new state, however, a wide diversity of political forces and opinions from all parts of the country and various strata of society collided. Origins, education, property and political conviction all played a part, for most of the deputies had come to Frankfurt as individuals, not as delegates of a political or economic interest group. On the basis of the experience gathered in the parliaments of the Southern German states, however, more stable political groupings gradually developed, which would serve to structure the work of the Assembly more effectively. These groupings met in inns and hotels, organised themselves into 'clubs', whose names did not reflect their political philosophies but identified the hostelries where they met – the *Deutscher Hof*, the *Württemberger Hof*, the *Casino* and the *Café Milani* were just a few of these political clubs. Executives were elected, membership lists compiled and programmes adopted. Some even referred to these clubs as 'parties', which at that early stage was something of an exaggeration.

Procession of the members of the preliminary parliament into St Paul's Church, Frankfurt, on 30 March 1848. The 574-man body met there from 31 March to 3 April for the purpose of making preparations for the Frankfurt National Assembly. Its participants were invited by the members of the Committee of Seven and were drawn from the parliaments of the individual German states.

From May 1848 to May 1849 the National Assembly, elected by the people, met in St Paul's Church, Frankfurt. It established a provisional government and adopted a constitution, the implementation of which, however, was blocked by the larger states, led by Austria and Prussia.

The Casino group was a liberal constitutionalist caucus in the Frankfurt National Assembly, whose members played a key part in convening the assembly as well as significantly influencing its work. The name of the group, which was founded on 25 June 1848, is derived from their customary meeting place, a social club belonging to the Casino Society and located at number 10 Rossmarkt. This image gives some impression of what their gatherings would normally have looked like.

The political orientations of the clubs that emerged there can certainly be described in modern-day terminology: the Republican Left, the Liberal Left, the Liberal Conservatives and the Conservative Right. In addition to these, there were splinter groups, new groupings, regroupings, combinations of lists and associations. Even party discipline, deputies changing parties and indeed expulsions of party members were not unknown phenomena in the political clubs of the Frankfurt Assembly. Robert von Mohl, a member of the National Assembly who represented the Centre Left, remarked in his memoirs that party discipline forced many a deputy to wrestle with his conscience and that many a good proposal was swept under the carpet during preliminary discussions in the clubs; and fragmentation into numerous sections and subsections, he said, hindered the development of large uniform parties – a particular problem in Germany, which was already burdened by an inborn predisposition to particularism and by an obstinate attachment to entirely subjective points of view. Mohl concluded that large parties which were fit for government were 'the foundation and precondition of organised parliamentary life'.

Fundamental rights and the Schleswig-Holstein question

One of the first milestones in the work of the Frankfurt National Assembly was the election of Archduke John of Austria as Imperial Regent. He was not accountable to the National Assembly; after his election, he was recognised by the ruling princes of the individual states and could thus be regarded as the 'legitimate' successor of the Federal Assembly, which assigned its powers to him. The fact that this election placed a member of the ruling House of Austria at the head of the German Confederation would not necessarily make it any easier to decide on the borders of the future Empire. In his address of 15 July to the German people, however, the new Regent promised "freedom, full and uncurtailed, after years of oppression". The main task now, he said, was to complete the drafting of the Constitution for Germany.

Thereafter, the deliberations on the Constitution initially focused on the effort to compile a binding bill of rights based on the examples of the American and French Revolutions. The paramount aim was to guarantee the rights of the individual in relation to the state. In pursuing this aim, the deputies in the Frankfurt Parliament were applying the lessons they had learned from their experiences of police states in the pre-revolutionary period. Germany was to be based on the rule of law, with a uniform imperial code of civil law, the abolition of aristocratic privileges and equality of all Germans before the law. Other articles related to freedom of expression and faith, freedom of association and assembly, freedom of science and teaching, the separation of church and state and the right of citizens to dispose freely of their property.

In August 1848, in the midst of these deliberations on the bill of rights, a crisis flared up over the duchies of Schleswig and Holstein, where the German populations had joined the Revolution and risen against their sovereign, the King of Denmark. When the King responded by trying to incorporate Schleswig, which, unlike Holstein, was not part of the German Confederation, into the state of Denmark, the provisional government of the two duchies sought military help from the German central authority in Frankfurt, in its role as the legal successor of the Federal Diet. Troops of the German Confederation, under Prussian command,

On 28 June 1848, the Frankfurt National Assembly appointed an interim central authority in the form of the provisional German Government. On the next day, it elected Archduke John of Austria as head of state. A deputation from the National Assembly informed the Archduke of his election as Imperial Regent, and he accepted the honour. This lithograph shows his entry into Frankfurt on 11 July 1848.

were then sent to intervene against Denmark. In spite of all the military successes achieved, Prussia yielded to external pressure, especially from Britain and Russia, and signed a ceasefire in Malmö on 26 August, but this did not offer a satisfactory solution for the Germans living in Schleswig and Holstein. The National Assembly was incensed at this climbdown, but, since the Assembly itself did not have the means to steer developments in a different direction, it had no option but to respect the Prussian decision. Those who saw Frankfurt as proof that the Revolution had succeeded were made to think again by the Schleswig-Holstein episode, which demonstrated that real power still lay where it had lain before 1848, namely with the individual sovereign states and their princely rulers.

The failure of the Revolution

The outcome of the Schleswig-Holstein conflict did lasting damage to the credibility of the Revolution and indeed split the ranks of the revolutionaries when the radical Left, in its outrage – not only at the 'betrayal' of Schleswig-Holstein, it must be said – staged an uprising in Frankfurt against the National Assembly on 18 September 1848, which led to the storming of the *Paulskirche* and the murder of two right-wing deputies, Prince Felix Lichnowsky and General Hans von Auerswald. This seriously undermined the authority of the Assembly, especially as the events in Frankfurt were accompanied by a wave of radical insurrections in the Rhineland, Hesse and Thuringia as well as in the Palatinate and Baden.

The diplomatic crisis and the clashes between the majority of the *Paulskirche* Assembly and the radical Left not only prompted many of the middle class to turn their backs on the Revolution but also repeatedly prevented the Parliament from devoting itself to the primary task of formulating the Constitution. A draft had been completed back on 26 April 1848, but the deliberations on it, which began in October, stretched into the spring of the following year. Not until 27 March 1849 did the National Assembly adopt the Imperial Constitution, which was signed by its President and promulgated in the Imperial Law Gazette on the following day. It was based on the 'Little German' solution (*kleindeutsche Lösung*), i.e. the German Empire was to exclude Austria, which had opted for the preservation of its own multinational state ruled by the Habsburg dynasty. The new Constitution provided for an empire with a hereditary emperor at its head and a strong unitary government whose powers would primarily encompass the fields of foreign policy, the army, general legislation and the economy. The Imperial Diet, or *Reichstag*, was to comprise two chambers: the House of States (*Staatenhaus*), composed of representatives of the individual German states (*Länder*), and the House of the People (*Volkshaus*), elected by universal manhood suffrage and secret ballot. Although the decisions of the Reichstag required the consent of the Imperial Government – in other words, of the Emperor – if the Reichstag adopted the same decision unamended in three consecutive ordinary sitting periods, it automatically entered into force, even without the consent of the Imperial Government (section 101). This meant that the Emperor was only granted a suspensive right of veto.

On 28 March 1849, the National Assembly elected King Frederick William IV of Prussia German Emperor (*Kaiser*), with 240 out of 290 votes in favour. However, when a deputation led by Eduard von Simson, President of the National Assembly, travelled to Berlin to convey to the Prussian King, at a reception in the knights' hall of the Royal Palace on 3 April 1849, the decision to "humbly invite [...] the Emperor-elect to consent to accept His election on the fundament of the Constitution", Frederick William IV rejected the offer. The King of Prussia had long since firmly re-established the power he had temporarily surrendered during the events of March 1848. Similarly, the troops that had been forced to withdraw from Berlin on 18 March 1848 had

This lithograph by Adolph Schroedter (1805–1875), *Die Grundrechte des deutschen Volkes* ('The Fundamental Rights of the German People') shows the Bill of Rights that entered into force on 27 November 1848 by virtue of imperial legislation and was reproduced almost unaltered in the Imperial Constitution of 1849. The larger German states, however, rejected the implementing act, which was explicitly declared invalid by the Federal Diet in 1851.

Die Grundrechte des deutschen Volkes.
Gesetz,
betreffend die Grundrechte des deutschen Volks.
Grundrechte des deutschen Volks.
Frankfurt a. M., den 27. December 1848.
Der Reichsverweser:
Erzherzog Johann.
Die Reichsminister:

№ 1453.
Neu Ruppin, bei Oehmigke & Riemschneider.
Empfang der Kaiser-Deputation der deutschen National-Versamlung im Rittersaale zu Berlin am 3. April 1849.
Der Präsident Simson sprach: „Die verfassunggebende deutsche National-Versamlung im Frühling des v. J. durch den übereinstimmenden Willen der Fürsten u. Volksstäme Deutschlands berufen, das Werk der deutschen Verfassung zu Stande zu bringen, hat am Mittwoch, den 28. März des Jahres 1849, nach Verkündigung der in zweimaliger Lesung beschlossenen deutschen Reichs-Verfassung, die in derselben begründete erhebliche Kaiserwürde auf Se. Königliche Majestät v. Preussen übertragen. Sie hat dabei das feste Vertrauen ausgesprochen, daß die Fürsten u. Volksstämme Deutschlands großherzig u. patriotisch in Uebereinstimmung mit der National-Versammlung die Verwirklichung dieser von ihr gefaßten Beschlüsse mit aller Kraft fördern werden.
„Sie hat endlich den Entschluß gefaßt, den erwählten Kaiser durch eine Deputation aus ihrer Mitte ehrfurchtsvoll einzuladen, die auf Ihn gefallene Wahl auf Grundlage der Verfassung annehmen zu wollen. In Vollziehung dieses Auftrags stehen vor Ew. Majestät der Reichs-Versamlung u. 32 ihrer Mitglieder, in der ehrfurchtsvollen Zuversicht, daß Ew. Majestät geruhen werden, die begeisterten Erwartungen des Vaterlandes, welches Ew. Majestät als den Schirm u. Schutz seiner Einheit, Freiheit u. Macht zum Oberhaupte des Reichs erkoren hat, durch einen gesegneten Entschluß zu glücklicher Erfüllung zu führen."

returned to the Prussian capital in November of the same year. When word of the offer of the imperial crown reached him, Frederick William IV declared privately to General Joseph von Radowitz, who represented the Westphalian constituency of Rüthen in the Frankfurt National Assembly and advocated the *Kleindeutschland* solution against the King's wishes, that the Frankfurt Parliament had "no crown to offer" and that "we accordingly have none to refuse or accept".

Although the Imperial Constitution was recognised by 28 German states, almost all of the larger states, including the Kingdoms of Prussia, Saxony and Bavaria, rejected the draft. The bid to create a parliamentary form of government under a constitutional monarch in Germany had thus failed. The *Paulskirche* Assembly had not grasped the opportunity that had briefly presented itself after the March Revolution to compel the weakened princes to establish a new political order. A great chance to effect radical reforms had been squandered. Prussia then recalled its deputies from the National Assembly on 14 May 1849. Many of the other deputies returned home disillusioned or were recalled by their governments. The rump parliament moved at first to Stuttgart on 31 May in order to escape prosecution by the Frankfurt police and subsequently dissolved itself. Resistance in Saxony, the Palatinate and Baden, in which supporters of the Revolution protested against the turn of events, was brutally crushed with the aid of Prussian troops. Rastatt, the last stronghold of the insurgents in Baden, fell on 23 July 1849. Throughout the 19th century the German Liberals and Democrats failed to recover from this defeat. Not least among the reasons for this failure was a schism in the German Progress Party, which split into a left-wing liberal and a national liberal wing in 1866/67 under the influence of Bismarck's policies, thereby seriously weakening the liberal movement in Germany. The unification of the German Empire, too, was to take place in different circumstances to those envisaged by its advocates in the *Vormärz* period.

A deputation from the St Paul's Church Parliament, headed by Eduard von Simson, offers the imperial crown to the Prussian King, Frederick William IV, on 3 April 1849. The latter, however, refused the proffered crown, since he believed in the divine right of kings and therefore rejected the sovereignty of the people.

The constitutional crisis in Prussia

The failure of the Revolution was followed by a period of reaction that continued virtually throughout the 1850s. In all of the German *Länder*, the Liberal ministries were replaced by Conservative cabinets. Numerous parliaments were dissolved and constitutions revised. This was no less true of Prussia, where, in May 1849, King Frederick William IV amended the Constitution that had only been adopted on 5 December 1848, replacing the system of equal universal manhood suffrage with a three-class electoral system. Voters were divided into three categories on the basis of the amount of tax they paid, with the small group of high earners, comprising about four per cent of the population, choosing the same number of delegates and deputies as the

Neue Bilder-Zeitung. — 77stes Bild.

Entwaffnung der Insurgentenbesatzung von Rastatt.

Tollen Muthes hatte die aufständische Besatzung von Rastatt mehrmals die Aufforderung zur Uebergabe der Festung verweigert; da hatten sich zwei von ihrem Kommandeur abgesendete Offiziere durch eine Reise überzeugt, daß das Insurgentenheer vernichtet und ihre Sache verloren sei. Deshalb beschlossen sie sich endlich am 23. Juli auf Gnade und Ungnade zu ergeben und rückten Nachmittags gegen 3 Uhr heraus. Die Belagerungstruppen bildeten ein Quarré und nun erschien der Prinz von Preußen, dankte den Truppen in lauter und fester Sprache für die Anhänglichkeit, die sie dem Könige, ihm und dem Vaterlande bewiesen, für die Tapferkeit, die sie überall gezeigt, für die Bereitwilligkeit, mit der sie sich Allem unterzogen und wies sie mit eindrucksvollen Worten auf die entehrende Demüthigung der fremden, ihren Fahnen eidbrüchig gewordenen Krieger. Die Soldaten nahmen die wichtige und würdevoll gehaltene Rede mit Begeisterung auf, der Prinz entfernte sich dann, das Quarré schloß sich auf und es bildete sich eine Linie, in der zwei Batterien abgeprotzter und geladener Zwölfpfünder aufgestellt waren. Dieser Linie gegenüber stellten sich die aus den verschiedenen Thoren kommenden Soldaten und Freischärler der rothen Republik auf; die Offiziere trugen die Epauletten nicht mehr und den Degen in der Scheide. Als sie so einander gegenüberstanden, kommandirten die preußischen Heerführer das Gewehr zum Strecken und die badischen Soldaten und Freischärler legten dieselben bei sich nieder oder stellten sie in Pyramiden auf. Die Pyramiden wurden mit Helm und Lederzeug behängt, so daß dem Soldaten nichts als die Uniform, die Mütze und der Tornister blieb. Die Offiziere legten ebenfalls ihre Degen ab, Tiedemann überreichte seinen Degen dem würdigen General von Holleben. Im sogenannten Generalstabe waren Tiedemann, Corvin, Sander, Sigel der Jüngere u. a. Bei der Entwaffnung zeigten sich die preußischen Soldaten in der ganzen Größe eines edlen Characters. Kein Wort des Hohns, nicht einmal ein Lächeln gab sich den Feinden gegenüber in ihren Reihen kund, ernst, würdevoll und lautlos war ihre Haltung. In dem Augenblick der verdienten Erniedrigung ihrer Gegner mochten sie ihren eigenen Werth und die innere Belohnung für die Treue gegen den angestammten Fürsten doppelt empfinden und mit Bedauern auf die zerknirschten badischen Truppen blicken. Nach Abgabe der Bewaffnung marschirten die 5700 Mann wieder in die Festung zurück.

Der König ruft dem Volke sein:
Steh' auf, du Volk der Treue,
Steh't auf, ihr wackern Mannen mein,
Bewährt mir heut' auf's Neue,
Daß Preußenstamm und Preußenblut
Und Preußentreu' und Preußenmuth
Frisch in euch grünen bleiben,
Und frische Zweige treiben.

Der König ruft; das Volk steht da,
Läßt keiner zur Eil' sich mahnen;
Sie kommen fern, sie kommen nah,
Hin zu den alten Fahnen.
Wohlauf, du lieber Bruder mein,
Sollst meiner Söhne Führer sein,
Zieh' aus zum heil'gen Streite,
Gott geb' euch das Geleite.

Nun, Gott mit uns! das gute Wort
Half uns in schweren Zeiten.
Gott sei mit uns! der alte Hort
Soll uns auch jetzt begleiten.
Mit Gott umschlingt ein heil'ges Band
Den König und das Vaterland.
Wir zieh'n zum heil'gen Streite,
Gott giebt uns sein Geleite.

Sie haben schmerzlich ihn geschmäht,
Verleumdet seinem Volke;
Nun ist die Schmach hinweggeweht,
Verweht die böse Wolke.
Durch Kampf verkläret steht er da,
Und alles Volk ruft fern und nah:
Er ist vom alten guten Stamme,
In uns die alte heil'ge Flamme!

Und ich, des alten Königs Sproß,
Weis' euch des Sieges Bahnen;
Will mit euch steh'n als Kampfgenoß;
Hoch flattern die alten Fahnen.
Sie rufen uns zum heil'gen Krieg,
Zu bitterm Tod, zu schönem Sieg,
Komm du mein Herr von Preußen,
Ich bin der Prinz von Preußen.

Original u. Eigenthum No. 2235.

Neu-Ruppin, zu haben bei Gustav Kühn.

In March 1848, the insurgency that came to be known as the March Revolution began in Baden. The rebels belonged to the bourgeois-democratic camp and were striving for a unified German state but could not press their demands in the face of the military power of the confederal states. The chalk lithograph shows the capitulation of the fortress at Rastatt on 23 July 1849, which brought an end to the Revolution.

largest category, the low earners, who accounted for eighty per cent of the population. Moreover, in January 1850 the principle of hereditary peerage was introduced in the first chamber, known as the House of Lords (*Herrenhaus*), which consisted henceforth of hereditary members – princes of the royal house and heads of certain aristocratic families – and a smaller number of public figures appointed for life by the King. Both of these changes remained in force until 1918 and were a defining feature of the political system of the Prussian state. In view of the key role played by Prussia, they were not without influence on the general political climate in Germany either.

The basic conservative orientation of the Prussian state under Frederick William IV continued under his successor, William I, even though the handover of royal power as a result of which Prince William became the monarch of Prussia on 9 October 1858 after ruling for a year as Prince Regent seemed initially to herald the start of a 'new era'. The Conservative ministry of Otto von Manteuffel was replaced by a Government of Liberals and Conservatives. In a keynote address to the Ministry of State, William himself announced far-reaching reforms, thereby imparting momentum to political Liberalism throughout Germany. There were hopes of a new Prussia, open to change, that would drive Germany towards unification. To this end, Liberals and Democrats even created the German National Association (*Deutscher Nationalverein*) in Frankfurt in 1859; the association re-embraced the 'Little Germany' strategy for Prussian-led national unification on a parliamentary basis that had been thwarted in 1849.

In practice, however, little changed. The *status quo* was reinforced by the appointment of Otto von Bismarck as Prime Minister of Prussia on 23 September 1862, marking the arrival on the Prussian and German political stage of a vigorous and resolute adversary of the liberal movement. Bismarck's appointment had been advocated in conservative circles close to King William, because the Liberal-dominated Prussian Chamber of Deputies was refusing to vote appropriations for army reforms, and he seemed to be the only man capable of overcoming the parliamentary resistance. And Bismarck lived up to his reputation. "Germany looks to Prussia not for its Liberalism but for its power", he told the Budget Commission of the House of Representatives on 30 September 1862, only a few days after his appointment, adding that "the great questions of our day cannot be solved by speeches and majority votes – that was the great mistake of 1848 and 1849 – but by iron and blood".

Bismarck thus snubbed Parliament and continued to govern, even without a budget, invoking a 'constitutional loophole' which, in his view, not only allowed the Government but actually compelled it, if Parliament did not approve the budget, to collect the taxes that fell due and incur any necessary expenditure in order to preserve the viability of the state.

In this way, Bismarck effectively set himself above the Constitution, but his gamble paid off. Although the conflict smouldered on and remained a major bone of contention between the Crown and Parliament until 1866, other events, such as the Polish uprising of 1863, the German-Danish War of 1864 and the conflict with Austria took centre stage, and when, following the Battle of Sadowa (Königgrätz) in July 1866, Prussia sealed its victory in the struggle for supremacy in Germany, the infringement of the Constitution paled into insignificance. On 3 September 1866, the Prussian Chamber of Deputies gave its retroactive approval to the budgets for the years from 1862 to 1865 and generously

This wood engraving shows Otto von Bismarck in the House of Representatives in 1863. Bismarck was a resolute opponent of liberalism, and this was one of the reasons why he had been appointed Minister-President in 1862 – conservative elements hoped that he would not bow to the Liberal-dominated Parliament in pursuit of his policies. And indeed he did govern against a majority of the House.

After Prussia and its allies had defeated the German Confederation, led by Austria, in the Seven Weeks' War, all of the individual German states north of the River Main formed the North German Confederation in 1866. The Constitution of 1 July 1867 turned what had begun as a military alliance into the first federal German state. The lithograph shows the constituent sitting of the North German Reichstag in the first Prussian House of Lords in Leipziger Strasse, Berlin, on 24 February 1867.

granted Bismarck an 'indemnity', exempting him from arraignment. This, however, had a lasting debilitating effect on parliamentarianism. Through his hard line and foreign-policy successes, Bismarck had subjugated Parliament and had induced the Prussian Chamber of Deputies to commit an 'original sin' from which parliamentarianism in Germany would not recover for a very long time.

The road to the Empire

After the victory over Austria and the German states that were allied with the Habsburg monarchy, the way was indeed clear for the *Kleindeutschland* solution to the German Question under Prussian leadership. The German Confederation was dissolved. In its place, as a first step towards a united Empire, the North German Confederation (*Norddeutscher Bund*) was created, comprising all the individual German states north of a line along the River Main, including the Hanseatic cities of Hamburg, Bremen and Lübeck. The states of southern Germany concluded defensive and offensive alliances with the North German Confederation.

The Constitution of the North German Confederation, which was promulgated on 17 April 1867 and entered into force on 1 July 1867, was based on a draft prepared by historian and politician Maximilian Duncker, who had belonged to the Frankfurt National Assembly in 1848/49 and then to the Prussian Chamber of Deputies before becoming a member of the constituent Reichstag of the North German Confederation in 1867, where he was one of the 'old Liberals'. Privy Councillor Duncker's text was revised several times by envoys and departmental civil servants and even by Bismarck himself until, on 15 December 1866, it was finally presented to the plenipotentiaries of the member governments of the North German Confederation as the 'Prussian draft'. Following the adoption of numerous amendments, the plenipotentiaries finally approved the new Constitution, which meant that it ultimately amounted to a joint proposal from the member states.

Next to the King of Prussia, who was to be the hereditary head of the Confederation, the Constitution established the Reichstag as its central organ. Its members were to be directly elected by equal, universal manhood suffrage and secret ballot. The political rights of Parliament, however, remained limited. The Federal Chancellor, Bismarck, was solely accountable to the King of Prussia, who presided over the Confederation, and not to Parliament, and this gave the Chancellor pivotal influence over the conduct of policy as long as he enjoyed the confidence of the monarch.

It was already clear to most contemporaries that the North German Confederation was not the culmination of the process of German unification but only a step on the way to the creation of a real nation state. The National Liberal deputy Johannes Miquel, for example, addressing the assembled North German Reichstag, said that the line along the River Main which formed the border between the North German Confederation and the states of southern Germany was "not the boundary between the spheres of influence of two great powers" but only "a stopping place for us, where we take in water and coal and draw breath, in order to pursue our journey shortly". And indeed the North German Confederation did not see out its first legislative term. In the heat of the Franco-Prussian War, on 10 December 1870, the 194 deputies present in the Reichstag voted by 188 to 6 that the North German Confederation be renamed the German Empire and that the title of German Emperor be bestowed on the King of Prussia. The proclamation of William I as German Emperor took place on 18 January 1871 in the Hall of Mirrors in the Palace of Versailles.

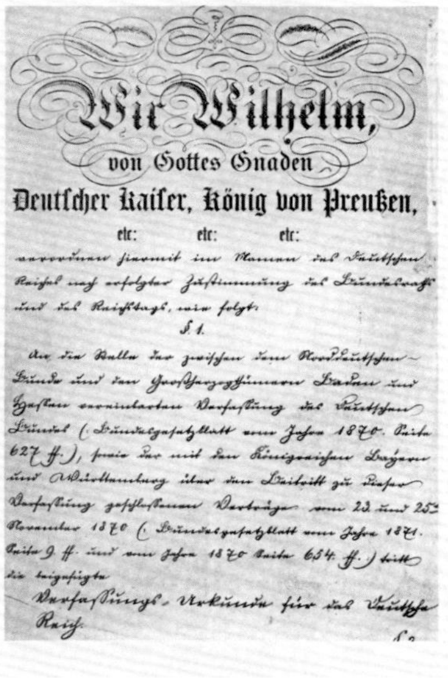
Wir Wilhelm,
von Gottes Gnaden
Deutscher Kaiser, König von Preußen,
etc: etc: etc:
verordnen hiermit im Namen des Deutschen Reichs nach erfolgter Zustimmung des Bundesraths und des Reichstags, was folgt:
§ 1.
An die Stelle der zwischen dem Norddeutschen Bunde und den Großherzogthümern Baden und Hessen vereinbarten Verfassung des Deutschen Bundes (Bundesgesetzblatt vom Jahre 1870. Seite 627 ff.), sowie der mit den Königreichen Bayern und Württemberg über den Beitritt zu dieser Verfassung geschlossenen Verträge vom 23. und 25. November 1870 (Bundesgesetzblatt vom Jahre 1871. Seite 9 ff. und vom Jahre 1870 Seite 654 ff.) tritt die beigefügte
Verfassungs-Urkunde für das Deutsche Reich.

On 1 January 1871, on the accession of the southern German states of Baden, Württemberg and Bavaria as well as the parts of Hesse-Darmstadt south of the Main to the North German Confederation and the entry into force of the new Constitution, the German Empire came into being. King William I of Prussia, however, was not proclaimed as German Emperor (*Kaiser*) until 18 January 1871, which is why the latter date was subsequently celebrated as the founding day of the Empire.

Parliamentarianism in the Empire

In 1871, the Constitution of the North German Confederation, with only a few amendments, was adopted as the Imperial Constitution. This meant that the Liberals' aim of achieving a voice in government for the people through a parliamentary system remained unfulfilled. Bismarck, however, did find himself compelled to take the will of the Reichstag into account in his calculations. In particular, the steady growth in the number of fields of government activity, and hence in the volume of imperial legislation, increased the importance of Parliament. Nevertheless, parliamentary deputies were not involved in the real exercise of governmental power until the First World War. The dualism between the parliament and government persisted and remained the greatest obstacle to democratic development in Germany.

Even today, historians differ over the question how, against this background, the role of the Reichstag as a parliamentary body is to be assessed – whether as a virtually inert institution wielding no great influence on the Emperor or on German policy or as a pioneering body working for parliamentary government 'by stealth' by progressively introducing constitutional checks to limit the power of the Emperor and gradually establishing a British-style parliamentary monarchy in Germany. There is evidence to support both points of view. Be that as it may, under the Constitution of 1871, all power lay with the Imperial Chancellor, who presided over the Federal Council (*Bundesrat*). The heads of the government departments were not independent government ministers but state secretaries, in other words civil servants under the authority of the Imperial Chancellor, who proposed them for appointment by the Emperor. The constitutionally enshrined 'accountability' of the Chancellor, on the other hand, was no more than an illusion, because the Constitution did not spell out its implications. For this reason, critics of the imperial procedures speak of an 'unfinished constitutional state', in which the main task of the Reichstag was to fight for a role within the Empire that it did not yet have, a role in which it could play an influential part in political decision-making.

The Constitution did give the Reichstag quite extensive powers, at least in the domains of legislation and approval of the budget. Over several decades, its power of the purse in particular proved increasingly effective as a means of exerting pressure on the Emperor and the Government. Hopes that parliamentary government might be introduced 'by stealth' were further encouraged when the Social Democratic Party of Germany (SPD) emerged from the general election of 1912 as the largest parliamentary group in the Reichstag. There seemed to be a real prospect of an increase in the powers of Parliament which would restrict the 'personal rule' of the Emperor and place constraints on the strong position of the Imperial Chancellor. This impression was reinforced by an amendment to the Rules of Procedure in that same year which made it possible to table a motion of censure against the Government. Although this, unlike a vote of no confidence in a parliamentary system, did not necessarily lead to the resignation of the Government, it did confirm the deputies, who had been granted the right to receive remuneration back in 1906, in their watchdog role *vis-à-vis* the Government.

The extent to which the hands of Parliament were still tied, however, was demonstrated by the so-called Zabern affair of 1913, which stemmed from the misconduct of an officer in the small garrison of Zabern (Saverne) in Alsace. Although the Reichstag adopted a motion of censure on 4 December 1913 and expressed its lack of confidence in the incumbent Imperial

Two of the Social Democrats' campaign posters for the 1912 Reichstag election. With 34.8 % of the vote, the SPD emerged as the clear winner, followed by the Centre Party, which secured fewer than half as many votes. This turned out to be the last parliamentary election in the German Empire.

The SPD, created in 1875 by a merger of the General German Workingmen's Association and the Social Democratic Workers' Party, was a driving force in the struggle to establish parliamentary democracy in the Empire in the early 20th century. This photograph shows the SPD party congress in Bremen in September 1904, which was attended by some 230 delegates.

Chancellor, Theobald von Bethmann Hollweg, who himself held liberal views, was close to the Progressive People's Party (*Fortschrittliche Volkspartei*) and tried to strike a balance between social democracy and conservatism, this initiative did not have serious consequences, because Bethmann Hollweg was able to ignore the vote of censure as long as he could rely on the backing of the Emperor, and in fact he remained in office until resigning for quite different reasons in 1917, when, during the Chancellor's clash with the Army High Command under Field Marshal Paul von Hindenburg and General Erich Ludendorff, known as the 'third Army High Command', the Emperor yielded to pressure from his senior military officers and withdrew his support.

The impotence of the Reichstag resulted not only from the powerful constitutional position of the Emperor and his Government but also from the weakness of Parliament itself, which, before the First World War, was a motley assortment of diverse political and special-interest groups. Some of these groups, especially in the Conservative camp, were still far removed from real party structures. Coalitions, a fact of political life in modern Germany, were largely unknown, and parliamentary majorities seldom remained intact for long. Accordingly, longer-term political strategies could scarcely be developed, let alone implemented.

This was compounded by the inveterate authoritarian structures of society in imperial Germany and the ubiquitous predominance of the military ethos, which affected the thinking of the Reichstag deputies too. Against this backdrop, the statement made in January 1910 by Free Conservative deputy Elard von Oldenburg-Januschau that "the King of Prussia and German Emperor must be able at any moment to tell a lieutenant to take a party of ten men and close down the Reichstag" was nothing exceptional. Opposition forces, such as the Social Democrats, were not infrequently referred to as 'enemies of the Reich' and were excluded from any political responsibility until the end of the monarchy in 1918. So the road to parliamentary democracy was never completed, and indeed the majority of deputies seemed quite happy with that.

The overthrow in 1918

After this, the outbreak of the First World War initially paralysed the moves towards the gradual introduction of parliamentary democracy that had been observable in the years before 1914. The Reichstag unanimously granted the Government's request for war credits, and even the deputies of the Social Democratic Party of Germany (SPD) set aside their convictions and voted for the motion rather than let themselves be branded 'traitors to the Fatherland'. Parliamentarians of all parties, meanwhile, remained devoid of any appreciable influence on the war itself. Neither during the crisis of July 1914 nor in the formulation of war policies over the next four years was the Government subject to parliamentary scrutiny to any significant degree. Even the civil authority of the Imperial Government was increasingly supplanted by the military authority of the Army High Command. Not until military defeat began to loom in the autumn of 1918 did major changes occur. The constitutional amendment adopted by the Reichstag on 22 October 1918 and signed by the Emperor on 28 October, whereby the Imperial Chancellor would henceforth require "the confidence of the Reichstag to discharge the duties of his office" came too late, however, to save the monarchy.

The collapse of the old regime, however, was not so much the result of revolutionary upheavals as a consequence of the course of the war, which forced the Army High Command to press for

Signing of the armistice in restaurant car No 2419 D in Compiègne on 11 November 1918; this painting, dating from about 1920, shows (left to right) Captain Ernst Vanselow, Count Alfred von Oberndorf, General Detlof von Winterfeldt, Captain Jack Marriott, Matthias Erzberger, Rear-Admiral George Hope, Admiral Sir Rosslyn Wemyss, Marshal Ferdinand Foch and General Maxime Weygand.

2. Extraausgabe. Sonnabend, den 9. November 1918.

Vorwärts

Berliner Volksblatt.

Zentralorgan der sozialdemokratischen Partei Deutschlands.

Der Kaiser hat abgedankt!

Der Reichskanzler hat folgenden Erlaß herausgegeben:

Seine Majestät der Kaiser und König haben sich entschlossen, dem Throne zu entsagen.

Der Reichskanzler bleibt noch so lange im Amte, bis die mit der Abdankung Seiner Majestät, dem Thronverzichte Seiner Kaiserlichen und Königlichen Hoheit des Kronprinzen des Deutschen Reichs und von Preußen und der Einsetzung der Regentschaft verbundenen Fragen geregelt sind. Er beabsichtigt, dem Regenten die Ernennung des Abgeordneten Ebert zum Reichskanzler und die Vorlage eines Gesetzentwurfs wegen der Ausschreibung allgemeiner Wahlen für eine verfassunggebende deutsche Nationalversammlung vorzuschlagen, der es obliegen würde, die künftige Staatsform des deutschen Volks einschließlich der Volksteile, die ihren Eintritt in die Reichsgrenzen wünschen sollten, endgültig festzustellen.

Berlin, den 9. November 1918. **Der Reichskanzler.**
Prinz Max von Baden.

Es wird nicht geschossen!

Der Reichskanzler hat angeordnet, daß seitens des Militärs von der Waffe kein Gebrauch gemacht werde.

Parteigenossen! Arbeiter! Soldaten!

Soeben sind das Alexanderregiment und die vierten Jäger geschlossen zum Volke übergegangen. Sozialdemokratische Reichstagsabgeordnete Wels u. a. haben zu den Truppen gesprochen. Offiziere haben sich den Soldaten angeschlossen.

Der sozialdemokratische Arbeiter- und Soldatenrat.

Gustav Noske, emissary of the Imperial Government, addresses the submarine crews in Kiel on 5 November 1918. Sailors from the German High Seas Fleet had previously refused to obey the order to put to sea for a 'final decisive battle' against the British Royal Navy and received support for their stance from the country's workers. This mutiny was the opening act of the November Revolution.

The signs of impending defeat forced the German High Command to press for a ceasefire in September 1918 and to urge Kaiser William II to introduce democracy by decree. They hoped that U.S. President Woodrow Wilson would adopt a more moderate negotiating line if dealing with a government formed by Parliament. Wilson, however, insisted on the abolition of the monarchy, and so the new Imperial Chancellor, Prince Max of Baden, proclaimed the abdication of the Emperor on 9 November 1918.

Immediately after the public announcement of his abdication, Kaiser William II fled into exile in the Netherlands. Frederick Ebert then asked Prince Max von Baden to hand over the office of Chancellor of the *Reich* to him, which Prince Max did. Philipp Scheidemann, Deputy Chairman of the SPD, in a bid to preempt the declaration of a socialist republic by the Spartacists, proclaimed the 'German Republic' from a balcony of the Reichstag building. The photograph depicting that scene, however, was a reconstruction after the event.

an immediate ceasefire on 29 September 1918. Given the likelihood of a military debacle, the Army High Command even urged Emperor William II to issue a decree introducing democracy and ordering a transition to a parliamentary system of government in Germany, the hope being that U.S. President Woodrow Wilson would be more inclined to support the German position if a government appointed by the Reichstag were to sue for peace.

The new Imperial Chancellor, Prince Max von Baden, who had included three members of the Centre Party and two Social Democrats in his government, wasted no time in expressing his support for a negotiated peace, but President Wilson made peace talks conditional on the overthrow of the monarchy. At the same time, a naval mutiny that had broken out in the imperial fleet at Wilhelmshaven and Kiel, where sailors, faced with the hopeless situation at the end of the First World War, refused to put to sea for one "final decisive battle" between the German High Seas Fleet and the British Royal Navy, was spreading to become a nationwide revolutionary movement. In many places spontaneously constituted workers' and soldiers' councils seized political and military control. Calls for the abdication of the Emperor grew ever louder.

On 9 November, Prince Max von Baden secured the abdication of William II and handed over his own office to Friedrich Ebert of the Social Democrats. On that same day, as the Emperor was already on his way to exile in the Netherlands, Ebert's party comrade Philipp Scheidemann proclaimed the 'German Republic' to the crowd gathered in front of the Reichstag building in Berlin. The monarchy had been abolished. If Ebert and Scheidemann were in any doubt about the enormity of the task confronting them, it became clear two hours later, when Karl Liebknecht, who led the Marxist Spartacus League along with Rosa Luxemburg, proclaimed the 'Free Socialist Republic' in the pleasance of the Royal Palace in Berlin and called for the establishment in Germany of a "new governmental order of the proletariat" on the model of Soviet Russia which would help to "complete the world revolution".

Revolution and Republic

Regardless of their ideological and political differences, the SPD and the Independent Social Democratic Party of Germany (USPD), which had been created in 1917 in protest against the policies of the majority SPD, met in Berlin on 10 November and formed a Council of People's Commissars, which was to function as a provisional government and prepare elections to a National Assembly. Once again it was Friedrich Ebert (SPD) who served as head of this provisional government. The alliance, however, lasted only a few weeks. With almost the entire *Reich* in the grip of unrest, which was brutally crushed in some instances, the USPD representatives – Hugo Haase, Wilhelm Dittmann and Emil Barth – resigned from the Council of People's Commissars on 29 December 1918 in protest at the heavy-handed action of the state authorities against the People's Naval Division (*Volksmarinedivision*); the Council now comprised only members of the majority SPD. At a national conference of the Spartacus League, held in Berlin from 30 December 1918 to 1 January 1919, parts of the USPD, together with other left-wing

During a demonstration against the dismissal of Chief Constable Emil Eichhorn of the USPD, some armed protesters occupied the Berlin press district; this photograph shows Spartacists behind barricades in front of the Rudolf Mosse newspaper offices in Schützenstrasse. The KPD and the USPD supported the occupation, and Karl Liebknecht even wanted to overthrow the Council of People's Commissars and so prevent the elections to the National Assembly. The uprising was crushed with the aid of *Freikorps* troops, and both Liebknecht and Rosa Luxemburg were murdered.

groups, founded the Communist Party of Germany (*Kommunistische Partei Deutschlands – KPD*) under the leadership of Rosa Luxemburg and Karl Liebknecht. Its attempts, sometimes involving horrific violence, to prevent the elections to the National Assembly on 19 January, however, were unsuccessful, and the elections took place as planned. The SPD, the Catholic Centre Party and the liberal German Democratic Party (*Deutsche Demokratische Partei – DDP*) emerged as the winners, amassing a clear majority; the German National People's Party (*Deutsch-Nationale Volkspartei – DNVP*) came a fairly distant fourth.

On 6 February 1919, the National Assembly gathered for its constituent sitting. For security reasons it had been moved to Weimar, in order to ensure that its deliberations would not be disrupted. On 11 February, it elected Friedrich Ebert President of the *Reich*, and two days later Philipp Scheidemann formed a Centre-Left government of SPD, DDP and Centre members that later came to be known as the 'Weimar Coalition'. A new wave of insurrections and strikes was suppressed or was crushed with the aid of a volunteer division under the command of Gustav Noske (SPD), the new Minister of Defence. The same applied to the Socialist-orientated Munich soviet republic which anarchist intellectuals and the Revolutionary Workers' Council had proclaimed on 6 and 7 April. This followed the assassination of the Bavarian Premier Kurt Eisner (USPD), who was shot on his way to the *Landtag* on 21 February.

On 31 July 1919, the new Constitution, the wording of which was largely taken from the text drafted by constitutional scholar Hugo Preuss, was adopted by the National Assembly in Weimar by 262 votes to 75. Closely modelled on the liberal and democratic legacy of 1848, it concentrated power in the hands of the institutions directly elected by the people, namely the Reichstag and, particularly at times of crisis, the President of the *Reich*, who, by virtue of Article 48, could even suspend fundamental rights in an emergency and take measures "to restore public safety and order". The Chancellor and ministers of the *Reich* depended on the confidence of the Reichstag to perform their duties and were required to resign if they lost its confidence. There was also scope for plebiscites. The Weimar Constitution thus created a great deal of scope for democratic development. When the Constitution was adopted on 31 July, Eduard David (SPD), Interior Minister of the *Reich*, even spoke of it as establishing the "most democratic democracy in the world".

At the same time, however, it soon became evident that this democracy was not sufficiently forearmed against abuse. The electoral system, based purely on proportional representation, was conducive to the fragmentation of parties in the Reichstag, and the very extensive powers vested in the President of the *Reich* could result, in extreme cases, in the head of state slipping into the role of a 'substitute emperor'. While the Constitution pointed the way to a democratic society with a stronger welfare state than the Empire had possessed, this could not resolve the contradictions that existed between the democratic Constitution

The Council of People's Commissars in November 1918. Left to right: Wilhelm Dittmann (USPD), Otto Landsberg (SPD), Hugo Haase (USPD), Friedrich Ebert (SPD), Emil Barth (USPD) and Philipp Scheidemann (SPD). After the Kaiser's abdication the Council served as an interim government and published a programme of government based on democracy and social welfare. By 29 December, however, the USPD members had already resigned from the government in protest at the action taken by Ebert during the Christmas unrest.

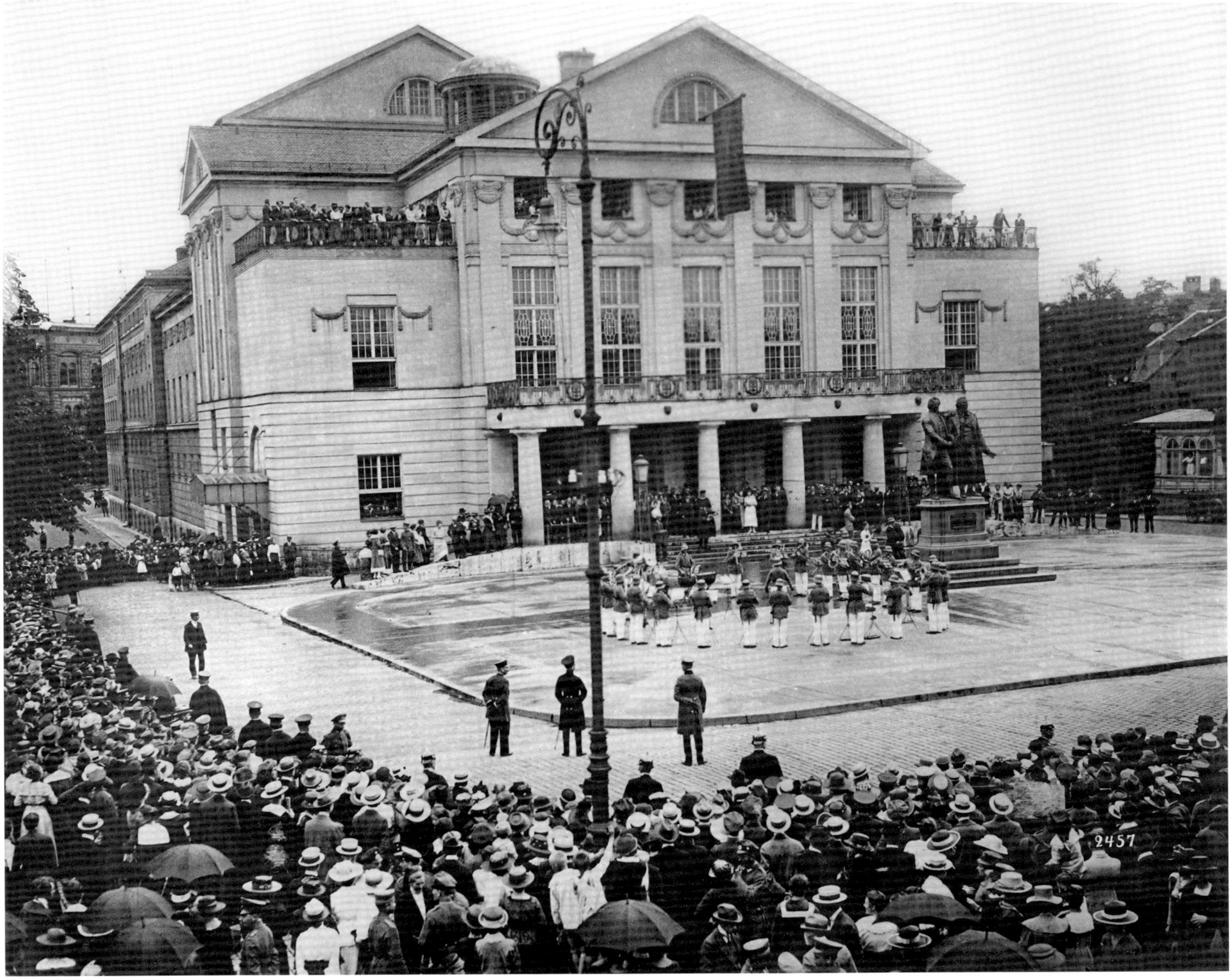

Following the elections of 19 January, the constituent sitting of the National Assembly took place in Weimar on 6 February 1919 (photo left). On 10 February, it adopted the Interim *Reich* Authority Act, and the following day it elected Friedrich Ebert as President *ad interim* of the *Reich*. His inauguration took place on the same day in front of the National Theatre in Weimar (photo above).

The Weimar Constitution was adopted in Weimar on 31 July 1919, signed by the President on 11 August and finally promulgated on 14 August. It was the first implemented democratic constitution of the German *Reich* and drew on the liberal and democratic tradition of the German Revolution of 1848/49. The photograph shows Josef Wirth (left) and President Friedrich Ebert reviewing a guard of honour on the avenue Unter den Linden in Berlin on 11 August 1921.

Die Verfassung
des Deutschen Reichs.
Vom 11. August 1919.

Das Deutsche Volk,
einig in seinen Stämmen und von dem Willen beseelt, sein Reich in Freiheit und Gerechtigkeit zu erneuen und zu festigen, dem inneren und dem äußeren Frieden zu dienen und den gesellschaftlichen Fortschritt zu fördern, hat sich diese Verfassung gegeben.

and social reality, which fell far short of the aims set by the Constitution and weighed heavily on the new Republic from the outset. Besides the internal unrest and rebellions, foremost among the liabilities that overshadowed the Republic, especially in its early years, were the war-guilt clause in the Treaty of Versailles and the demand for high reparation payments, which led to serious economic difficulties.

War guilt and reparations

The draft of the Treaty of Versailles was handed over to the German delegation, headed by Foreign Minister Count Ulrich von Brockdorff-Rantzau, in the Trianon Palace Hotel in Versailles on 7 May 1919. Article 231 of the Treaty bound Germany to accept "the responsibility of Germany and her allies for causing all the loss and damage to which the Allied and Associated Governments and their nationals have been subjected as a consequence of the war imposed upon them by the aggression of Germany and her allies". In addition to the reparation payments justified by this clause, Germany was to cede numerous territories and accept stringent arms limitations, including the reduction of the strength of the German armed forces to 100,000 men and the military occupation of the left bank of the Rhine and of a few bridgeheads on the right bank for a period of 15 years.

When the text of the Treaty, not undisputed among the Allies either, became known in Germany, it aroused indignation, which was by no means confined to right-wing and nationalist circles. The 'war-guilt clause' of Article 231, which served as the legal basis for all subsequent reparation demands, provoked the angriest reactions. "What hand would not wither that binds itself and us in these fetters? This treaty, in the view of the Government of the *Reich*, is unacceptable," declared Philipp Scheidemann before the National Assembly on 12 May and then resigned as head of government rather than sign the treaty. Ebert also considered resigning, but decided against it because, when all was said and done, "the entire nation cannot resign". Nevertheless, a large majority of the Reichstag deputies came out in favour of signing, to which there was no alternative. It would have been impossible to resume hostilities, as the general staff confirmed when they were consulted. On 28 June 1919, the Treaty was signed in the Hall of Mirrors of the Palace of Versailles – at the same spot where the German Empire was proclaimed in 1871. Following ratification, the Treaty entered into force on 10 January 1920 and promptly provoked further protests and attempted coups. Thereafter it provided right-wing forces in particular with a constant supply of ammunition for their arguments against the Republic and its representatives who were trying to fulfil the conditions of the Treaty.

No less onerous than the war-guilt clause were the reparation provisions of the Treaty of Versailles, under which the German *Reich* was to pay an initial instalment of 20 billion gold marks by May 1921. The final total set by the Reparations Commission in January 1921 was 226 billion gold marks, payable in 42 annual incremental instalments rising from two to six billion gold marks. Although the amount was soon revised to a lower figure, the burden of these payments still remained intolerable, not least in its psychological effects. The fact that the Government

The end of the First World War in international law came with the signing of the Treaty of Versailles on 28 June 1919. The German representatives, however, signed the treaty under protest, because it assigned sole responsibility for the outbreak of the war to Germany and its allies as well as imposing reparations, cessions of territory and arms limitations on the German Reich. On the title page of its edition of 25 May 1919, the Parisian daily newspaper *Le Petit Journal* displayed a colour print depicting the presentation of the Allied peace terms to the German delegation on 7 May 1919.

As a result of the reparation payments that the German *Reich* had to make, the German economy was hit by hyperinflation. The steep decline in the value of the mark could not be halted until the currency reform of 16 October 1923, which introduced the *rentenmark*, and an adjustment to the reparation payments. This image shows worthless banknotes being pulped in a waste-paper press.

The Government of the Weimar Republic felt compelled to accept and honour the Treaty of Versailles in order to avoid military action against Germany. Among the German public, who had hoped for a lenient peace settlement, the peace terms provoked anger and protests, such as this mass demonstration in the Berlin Pleasure Gardens. Revision of the Treaty became the stated aim of German foreign policy.

nevertheless tried to meet these demands as far as possible in order to stave off military action against Germany only earned it the hatred of the anti-democratic Right and the accusation of pursuing a 'fulfilment policy'. The first to fall victim to this hate campaign was Matthias Erzberger of the Centre Party, who had signed the armistice in 1918; Erzberger was murdered by two ex-officers – assassins belonging to the right-wing *Organisation Consul* terrorist force – in the Black Forest town of Bad Griesbach on 26 August 1921. Another consequence of the reparation payments was the spectacular collapse of the German currency, which not even further negotiations with the Allies could arrest. The latter even occupied the Ruhr area in January 1923 to lend more force to their demands. It took the currency reform of 16 October 1923 and the Dawes Plan of 16 April 1924, which adjusted the reparation payments in the light of the prevailing economic climate, to usher in a period of consolidation for the Republic, a period which lasted until the Great Depression of 1929.

The demise of the Republic

'Black Friday', 25 October 1929, when share values crashed on the New York stock exchange in Wall Street, triggering the Great Depression, also signalled the end of the 'Golden Twenties' in the Weimar Republic. In the course of the economic crisis, the radical political parties, especially the Communists (KPD) and the National Socialist German Workers' Party (*Nationalsozialistische Deutsche Arbeiterpartei – NSDAP*), gained ground at the expense of the moderate democratic parties. The cabinet of the Social Democratic Chancellor Hermann Müller, which had governed since 1928 on the basis of a Grand Coalition comprising the four strongest parties in the Reichstag – the SPD, the DNVP, the Centre and the German People's Party (*Deutsche Volkspartei – DVP*) – was forced to resign in 1930. Thereafter, there were only 'presidential cabinets', which essentially governed by means of emergency decrees enacted by the President of the *Reich* under Article 48 of the Weimar Constitution and were therefore entirely dependent on him.

The scene of the political and social conflicts that accompanied the depression and the spiralling unemployment, meanwhile, was shifting more and more from Parliament into the streets. The few parliamentary sittings that still took place were turbulent affairs, thanks to the unruly behaviour of the National Socialist and Communist deputies. It was extremely difficult for the President of the Reichstag, Paul Löbe, to ensure reasonably orderly proceedings.

The scope of the Reichstag to influence the composition of the Government or its policies was already limited in any case. Ordinary legislation was frequently superseded by the provisions of emergency decrees enacted by the President of the *Reich*. Dissolving the Reichstag was the stock response to stirrings of parliamentary opposition. And when the National Socialists emerged from the elections of 31 July 1932 as the largest parliamentary group, with 230 seats, and Hermann Göring was elected President of the Reichstag, the writing was on the wall for free parliamentary activity. The last election in the Weimar Republic took place a few months later, on 6 November 1932. It became necessary when President Hindenburg dismissed Franz von Papen's government after it had suffered a crushing defeat in

As the Weimar Republic neared its end, President Paul von Hindenburg increasingly governed the *Reich* with the aid of emergency orders. In the Reichstag elections of 31 July 1932, the anti-Republican NSDAP emerged as the strongest force with 230 seats, and Hermann Göring became President of the Reichstag. The photograph shows the newly elected Presidium of the Reichstag after the elections. Left to right: Walther Gräf (DNVP, Vice-President), Hermann Göring (NSDAP, President), Thomas Esser (Centre Party, Vice-President) and Hans Rauch (Bavarian People's Party, Vice-President).

Parliament. Although the NSDAP won only 196 seats this time, it remained by far the largest party. The anti-Republican parties, the NSDAP and the KPD, now had a total of 296 members in the Reichstag, which meant that they held more than half of the 585 parliamentary seats. The formation of a coalition government by the democratic parties thus remained impossible. In this situation, former infantry general Kurt von Schleicher, a close associate of Hindenburg who sat as an independent, was appointed Chancellor. He lasted only two months in office, however, and was replaced on 30 January 1933 by Adolf Hitler. The next election to the Reichstag, held on 5 March 1933, was conducted under the shadow of the National Socialist dictatorship.

The demise of the Weimar Republic, however, had its roots in a host of factors. Not least among these, along with the party-political fragmentation of the Reichstag, was that the parliamentary groups had no need to feel any more than a limited sense of responsibility for the formation and preservation of governments, because the business of government could proceed on the basis of Article 48 in any case, even without the backing of a parliamentary majority. Frequent changes of government, dissolutions of Parliament and minority cabinets had been the result. Not once did a legislative term run its full course. As a rule, governments had spent only a short time in office; their average lifespan had been eight months. In the 14-year existence of the Republic, no fewer than 20 governments had been in office. What is more, broad sections of the population and many of the elite in the administration, in education, the judiciary and the armed forces were indifferent or hostile towards the Republic. A democratic consensus in favour of saving the Republic at all costs, if it ever existed, did not survive the start of the Great Depression. It would therefore have taken a miracle to secure the survival of the Weimar Republic. Miracles, however, rarely happen anywhere – and the political world is no exception.

Gleichschaltung under National Socialist rule

When Hitler was appointed Chancellor on 30 January 1933, the National Socialists achieved their aim of seizing power in the *Reich*. The formation of the new government, however, took place entirely within the framework of the Constitution. Hitler initially headed a coalition government comprising representatives of the NSDAP and the DNVP as well as several conservative nationalist independents and Franz Seldte, co-founder and leader of the *Stahlhelm*, a 'league of front-line soldiers' that was founded in December 1918 as a paramilitary defence force of the Weimar Republic and was now regarded as the military wing of the DNVP. Only three of Hitler's ten ministers belonged to the NSDAP. Since the new government did not even command a majority in the Reichstag, it was dependent on the support of President Hindenburg and may therefore be numbered, at least initially, among the series of presidential cabinets. The stylised presentation of Hitler's accession to power as a 'seizure of power', in other words, is no more than a mystification of the truth by National Socialist propaganda.

Nor could there be any question, in those early days, of entirely abolishing the rule of law. On the other hand, the National Socialist leaders never left any doubt about their rejection of democracy as a form of government and their intention to amend existing laws and regulations in order to achieve their goal of wielding absolute power. The fire in the Reichstag building on the night of 27 to 28 February 1933 afforded them an early opportunity to enact an emergency order on 28 February 'for the protection of the nation and state', which suspended the fundamental rights of the German people and abolished freedom of the press and freedom of assembly. More and more opposition

After President Hindenburg had once more dissolved Parliament, the last elections in the Weimar Republic took place on 6 November 1932. The NSDAP was once again the largest party, though it won only 196 seats this time. Hindenburg appointed his close associate Kurt von Schleicher to serve as Chancellor of the *Reich* but replaced him with Adolf Hitler after only two months. Shown here is a torchlight procession of the 'national formations' – SA, SS and *Stahlhelm* forces – passing through the Brandenburg Gate.

In the night from 27 to 28 February 1933, most of the Reichstag building was destroyed in an arson attack. The NSDAP immediately used the fire as a pretext to enact, on 28 February, an emergency order 'for the protection of the nation and state', which suspended fundamental rights and abolished freedom of the press and freedom of assembly.

EM DEUTSCHEN VOLKE

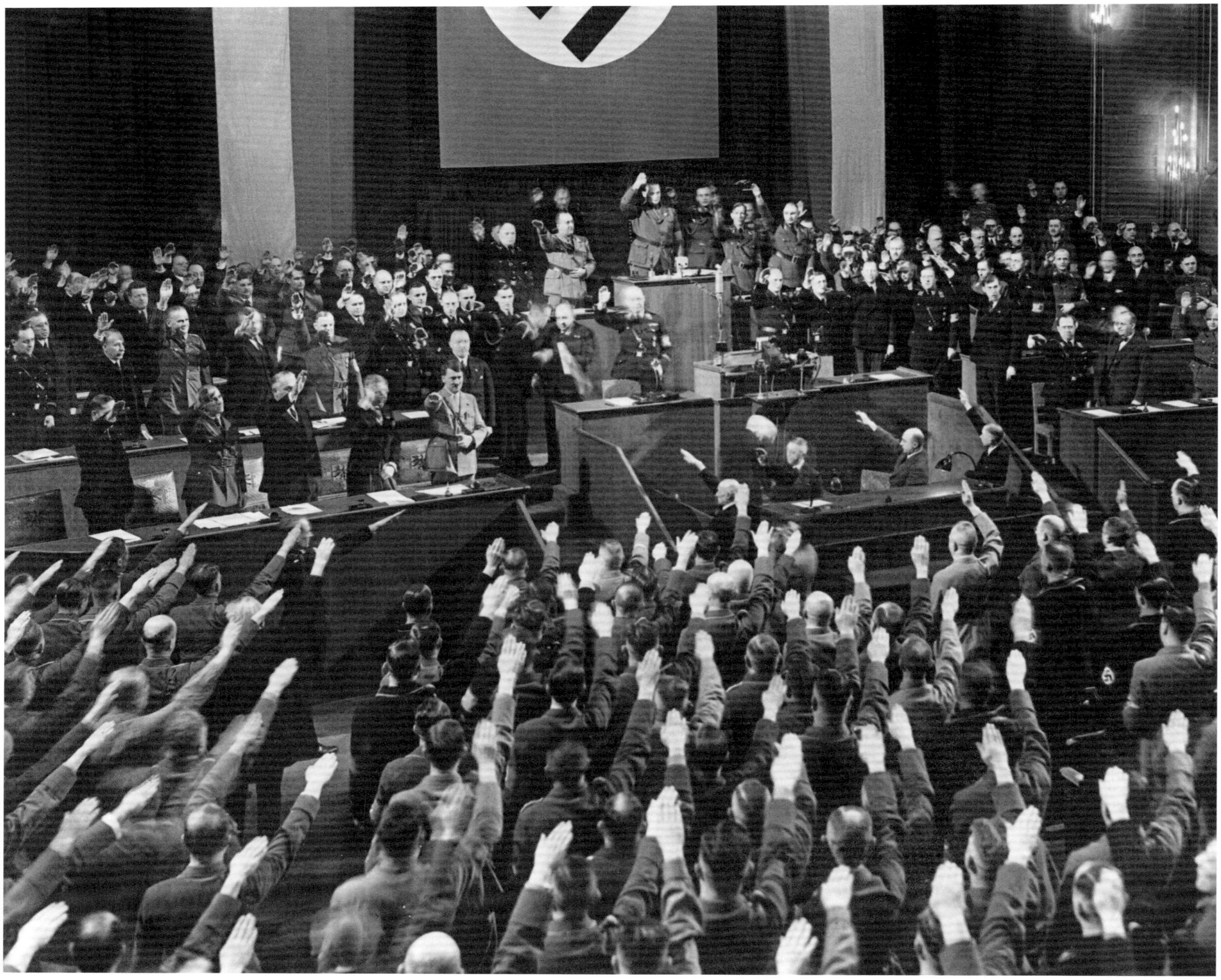

As a result of the Enabling Act, the NSDAP became the only lawful political party, and the process of bringing trade unions and other social organisations 'into line' (*Gleichschaltung*) was begun. All other parties dissolved themselves or were banned. The illustration shows Hitler's address to the Reichstag in January 1934, on the first anniversary of the 'seizure of power'. The participants in the sitting, held in the Kroll Opera House, are singing the *Deutschlandlied*, the German national anthem, with hands raised in the Nazis' 'German salute'.

supporters found themselves in prison or in unofficial concentration camps that were now being gradually established within the *Reich*. The first of these was created at a military training area on the Grosser Heuberg plain in the Swabian Jura, to which, according to newspaper reports, the first inmates from Württemberg and Hohenzollern were already being taken into 'protective custody' on 20 March 1933. Another camp was set up by the SA on a temporary basis on land belonging to a brewery in Oranienburg near Berlin. This was later developed into Sachsenhausen concentration camp.

There followed on 23 March the Law to Remedy the Distress of the People and the *Reich* (*Gesetz zur Behebung der Not von Volk und Reich*), more commonly known as the Enabling Act, which was adopted by the Reichstag itself, minus the Communist deputies, who had been arrested or forced to flee in the aftermath of the Reichstag fire. It suspended the rights of Parliament, practically excluded the Reichstag from the legislative process and empowered Hitler to govern the country as he saw fit. Not only the National Socialists but also the moderate conservative and liberal parties approved the Enabling Bill by a large majority in the Reichstag. Only the Social Democratic group under Otto Wels voted *en bloc* against it.

The Enabling Act marked the real beginning of National Socialist rule. The NSDAP progressively established itself as the only lawful political party, the 'official party'. The other parties, along with the trade unions and social organisations, were banned or 'brought into line' (the process of *Gleichschaltung*). Many deputies were arrested or forced to flee, and a considerable number of them were murdered in prisons and detention camps. The Reichstag was reduced to an assembly of loyal district governors who cheered Hitler's speeches and gave the dictatorship a veneer of apparent parliamentary legitimacy to which it could no longer lay even the remotest claim. The federal structure of the *Reich* that had been created under Bismarck was also dissolved. This meant the end of the *Länder* parliaments, the regional representative assemblies that had played a significant part in the democratic development of Germany in the period up to 1933. Following the death of President Paul von Hindenburg on 2 August 1934, moreover, Hitler became President of the *Reich* after that office had been merged with the chancellorship. Members of the German armed forces, the *Wehrmacht*, were henceforth required to swear an oath of personal allegiance to the *Führer*. The majority of the population responded to these developments with remarkable apathy, dutiful acquiescence or resignation. Victimisation and surveillance left them little choice. In addition, people were torn between patriotism and dislike of the regime. Nothing could alter the situation, not even the courageous resistance offered by trade unionists, Social Democrats, Communists and members of the churches and the armed forces as well as by numerous individuals. It took the military defeat in 1945 and the subsequent occupation regime established by the victors of the Second World War to create the conditions for the rebirth of democracy that the Germans themselves had no longer been able to achieve by their own efforts.

DEM DEUTSCHEN

Germany since 1945: establishment of democracy and unification

Everhard Holtmann

Introduction: paths from collapse to recovery

The military defeat of Germany in the Second World War led to total collapse of the political system. The National Socialist dictatorship, which had destroyed the constitutional basis of the Weimar Republic when Hitler came to power by pseudo-legal means in 1933, met its own end with the unconditional surrender of the German forces on 8 May 1945.

When the guns fell silent, the whole of Germany was plunged into a state of general paralysis, which persisted for several weeks and months. In many places, sometimes throughout entire areas, the infrastructure was no longer functioning. It took until the winter of 1946/47, which came to be known as the *Hungerwinter*, for the nation to feel the full impact of the shortages of the most fundamental necessities – food, housing and clothing. The destruction of these material foundations of human existence was a traumatic experience, in many cases leaving deep psychological scars. Another destabilising factor was the underground economy of the black marketeers, which conflicted at times with the social norms and law-abiding nature of an essentially moral civil society.

Given this precarious existence near the edge of the abyss, politics was viewed with a profound mistrust by many survivors of the war. The majority of those who had either willingly embraced the totalitarian rule of the Hitler regime, which encompassed every aspect of people's everyday existence, or passively adapted to it now turned their backs on public life or remained disaffected. By withdrawing into their own private world and playing no part in political life, many of them hoped to shake off the traces of their own involvement, be it deep or marginal, in the National Socialist system. In this way, the suppression of individual and collective guilt, rather than any attempt to come to terms with it, became one of the characteristic psychological

Trümmerfrauen ('rubble women') sifting through the ruins for reusable building material. After the war, women outnumbered men in Germany by about seven million, and an order issued by the Allied occupying powers required all women between the ages of 15 and 50 to report for rubble-clearing duty. To this end, some of the existing health and safety provisions relating to women were repealed.

As the capital of the German *Reich*, Berlin was a target for heavy Allied bombing raids. The first bombs were dropped on Berlin by British aircrews in the autumn of 1940, and from 1943 there was a huge increase in the number and scale of the air raids. The battle for Berlin in the final days of the war led to further destruction. By the end of the war almost half of all the city's buildings were destroyed; of the 226 bridges that had once stood in Berlin, only 98 were left. This aerial photograph shows the Zoo district with the Kaiser Wilhelm Memorial Church.

SCHWARZ WIRD WEISS oder MECHANISCHE ENTNAZIFIZIERUNG

M. Radler

Springt immer rein! Was kann euch schon passieren,
Ihr schwarzen Böcke aus dem braunen Haus!
Man wird euch schmerzlos rehabilitieren.
Als weiße Lämmer kommt ihr unten raus.

Wir wissen schon: Ihr seid es nie gewesen!
(Die andern sind ja immer schuld daran — —)
Wie schnell zum Guten wandeln sich die Bösen,
Man schwarz auf weiß im Bild hier sehen kann.

J. Menter

traits of German post-war society. It took the rebellious 'generation of 1968' to confront their fathers' generation publicly with the guilt issue, which they did with merciless severity and rigour, even to the point of being hurtful.

It may be inferred from the foregoing remarks that, while the break with dictatorship in 1945 was the deepest of incisions, there was no 'zero hour'. On the contrary, the route from collapse to recovery, besides being firmly staked out by the instructions and stipulations of the Allied occupying powers, designed – at least in the western occupation zones – to nurture democracy, was characterised by the continuing effects of a twofold German tradition: on the one hand, the politically untainted leaders who emerged, initially at the local level, to take the place of the ousted elite were able to draw on their own democratic beliefs and their experience dating from the period before the downfall of the Weimar Republic; on the other hand, an inherited susceptibility to authoritarian thinking was to prove extremely hardy among some sections of the population and persisted for many years.

Even in the early post-war years, divergent paths to political reconstruction were already being chosen in East and West Germany. While the democratic parties in the Soviet zone of occupation were confronted with an overpowering alliance of the military administration and KPD functionaries, engaged in a rapid drive to reshape the system into a Communist one-party regime, the west of Germany was embarking on the path of parliamentary democracy. The founding of the Federal Republic, however, did not wipe out the entire personal legacy of the Nazi regime. Among the senior functionaries in the new West German democratic state in the realms of public administration, higher education, business and the judiciary, people who had been tainted by National Socialist ideology continued to hold office until the 1970s. Allied plans for rigorous denazification were quickly stifled by the onset of the Cold War in 1946. In any case, the procedure adopted for this purpose had very soon proved to be a bureaucratic instrument of mass exoneration, a gigantic 'fellow-traveller factory', as historian Lutz Niethammer called it, the main purpose of which was the wholesale political whitewashing of most of those who were categorised as members of the National Socialist Party 'on paper only'.

Be that as it may, the inescapable destiny of the Weimar democracy, which was fated to be a 'republic without republicans', burdened by insufficient public approval because democratic attitudes had not developed among those very groups of people who played the leading roles in government, business and society, did not affect Germany after 1945. Part of the consensus forged in the early days of the Federal Republic of Germany by the political, industrial and social elites was a fundamental consent to the new democratic institutional order. The professional rehabilitation and social inclusion of fellow-travellers and even accomplices in National Socialist crimes was part of this tacit arrangement. This provoked indignation, and rightly so, especially among the victims of those crimes. In retrospect, however, it seems to be the political price that the fledgling Federal Republic had to pay for the consolidation of democracy within its borders.

The basic decision in favour of parliamentary democracy as the core of the post-1945 democratic order in West Germany

Rebuilding institutions from 1945 to 1949: 'bottom-up' democracy and the architecture of the Basic Law

At the beginning of August 1945, the Allied occupying powers were still sufficiently united to agree in the Potsdam Agreement on the elimination of Nazism and militarism, the immediate arrest and punishment of war criminals, the total disarmament of Germany and long-term control of the German industrial war

With the aid of Law No 104 of 5 March 1946 for Liberation from National Socialism and Militarism, German society in the western zones of occupation was to be freed from all National Socialist influences. In practice, however, the denazification procedure proved rather ineffective: of more than 2.5 million Germans who were required to answer to the tribunals, only 1.4% were categorised as 'Major Offenders' or 'Offenders'. More than a third of all cases were dropped. Many of those classified as 'followers' were subsequently able to pursue careers in the Federal Republic without let or hindrance. Max Radler (1904–1974) was already caricaturing that 'whitewashing' process in this cartoon from the satirical magazine *Der Simpl* in 1946.

At the Potsdam Conference, officially entitled the Berlin Conference, the three main World War II Allies met after the end of the war to discuss how to deal with defeated Germany. Along with President Harry S. Truman of the United States and Soviet *Generalissimus* Joseph Stalin, the photograph also shows British Prime Minister Winston Churchill, whose place at the negotiating table was taken by new Premier Clement Attlee following the electoral defeat of the Conservative Party.

Campaign posters for the first election to the *Land* Parliament in Hesse, held on 1 December 1946. *Länder* were re-established on the orders of the occupying powers, which began the re-establishment of political structures at the local level, then in the *Länder* and finally, in the western zones, at the federal level.

potential and the gradual restoration of political life on a democratic basis as the main post-war aims for occupied Germany. Even before the occupation regime was put in place, the experts on Germany from the U.S. and British general staffs who were planning for the post-war period had been discussing how the political system in the post-Hitler era could be designed to eradicate the authoritarian mentality they regarded as part of the German character and to enable the Germans to take their place in the concert of democratic nations.

The Americans and Britons drafted a programme of democratic re-education and reorientation. The French later pursued a similar approach, notwithstanding their intention of taking every possible step to prevent the re-emergence of a strong German nation state. The re-education programme – whose German title (*Umerziehung*) had unfortunate connotations – which was intended by the Allies to enable the Germans to acquire their own democratic political culture, was to be accompanied and supported by a rebuilding of political institutions from the bottom up. The vacuum created by the temporary disappearance of a central governmental authority in Germany was to be the climate in which the tender plant of democracy would grow from the grass-roots level to flourish in due season.

Local self-government

To this end, the first step was to restore local self-government, which had existed from the time of the 1808 reforms implemented by Freiherr vom Stein until the National Socialist *Gleichschaltung* and was the modern embodiment of an element of Prussian tradition. A confidential memorandum from the Foreign Office in London, for example, stated that local government should be founded on democratic principles throughout Germany. In particular, it said, there was a need to establish elected representative bodies. The newly elected municipal authorities should be accountable to the local electorate. The administration should be decentralised to give the elected councils full control over it. Public servants at all levels were to function henceforth as non-political executors of decisions made by the representative bodies.

These precepts were part of the new democratic institutional order, and even today they are still reflected in the spirit of local-government statutes in all of the German *Länder*. When Germany was reunited, they were adopted for the new institutional framework in eastern Germany too. The only principle that proved illusory back in the 1940s was the idea, modelled on the British civil service, of an apolitical local administrative authority, because, then as now, all practical experience showed that a starkly dualistic model in which powers were divided between an elected policymaking body and a purely executive administration ran counter to the dictates of effective political leadership. January and March 1946 saw the first free local elections to the municipal councils (*Gemeinderäte)* and the county councils (*Kreistage*) in the American zone; these were followed in the autumn by the same local elections in the British and French zones.

Creation of the *Länder*

At the same time, progress was being made towards the creation of constituent states (*Länder*). On 19 September 1945, the *Länder* of Hesse and Württemberg-Baden were founded within the U.S. zone of occupation. In the course of 1946, the new *Länder* of North Rhine-Westphalia and Schleswig-Holstein were established in the British zone. In October of that year, the old provinces of Hanover, Brunswick and Oldenburg were merged to form the new *Land* of Lower Saxony. In the area under French occupation, the *Länder* of Baden, Württemberg-Hohenzollern, Rhineland-Palatinate and the Saarland were created. Some of the 'hyphenated *Länder*' that were artificially constructed, partly as successors to the dismantled state of Prussia, subsequently developed into remarkably viable entities with a strong sense of identity. When the south-western states in the French and American zones were merged to form the new *Land* of Baden-Württemberg in 1952, after the Federal Republic had been founded, the new federal territorial structure was complete and would remain unaltered in the long term.

Establishment of the new political and parliamentary institutions

Parallel to the territorial restructuring of the *Länder*, their new political institutions were also established.

The process of forming these institutions took place in several stages and was also a gradual democratisation process. In the first stage, which began in Bavaria at the end of May 1945, state premiers ('Minister-Presidents') and state governments were appointed in the American and British zones. Their role was to execute the orders of the Allies. In October 1945 and February 1946 respectively, the heads of government in the U.S. zone formed the Council of the *Länder* (*Länderrat*) of the American Zone of Occupation, and those in the British zone formed the Zonal Advisory Council (*Zonenbeirat*). Decisions taken by these bodies had legal force unless they were vetoed by the military governments.

At this stage in the political and administrative life of the *Länder*, it would be premature to speak of genuine democratic scrutiny. Only gradually were the executive powers of the appointed premiers of the *Länder* reined in by the subsequent establishment of parliamentary democracy. In the early summer of 1946, elections to the constituent assemblies of the *Länder* took place. Most of the newly drafted state constitutions were put to the people of the respective *Länder* in referendums between 1946 and 1948. Whereas *Land* parliaments (*Landtage*) were initially appointed by the occupying powers, beginning in the summer of 1946, only a few months later the first *Land* elections were held, starting in the American zone in November and December 1946; all the *Land* parliaments in the British zone were elected on the same date in April 1947, and election day in the French zone was in May 1947. The newly constituted *Land* parliaments then elected state governments from the parliamentary groups of the parties that had secured an electoral majority. In March 1947, the U.S. military government had transferred legislative, executive and judicial regulatory powers to the *Länder* in the American zone. The inauguration of democratically elected state governments concluded the transitional phase during which governmental powers in the *Länder* had gradually been transferred into German hands and, at the same time, had been given democratic legitimacy.

Reorganisation of the administration in the Soviet zone of occupation

In the Soviet zone of occupation, the regional and zonal reorganisation of the administrative structures and democratic parties was effected more rapidly. Order No 2, issued by the Soviet military administration (SMAD) on 10 June 1945, authorised the creation of what were termed anti-Fascist political parties. In the course of the summer, provincial administrations were established. In July 1945, SMAD set up eleven German central administrations, which may be seen as the first step in the subsequent creation of a zonal government. In September 1946, local elections were held, and in October 1946, the five *Länder* of Brandenburg, Mecklenburg-Western Pomerania, Saxony, Saxony-Anhalt and Thuringia elected their state parliaments; in these state elections, the Socialist Unity Party (*Sozialistische Einheitspartei – SED*) obtained an average 47.5 % share of the vote.

The 'return to traditional administrative structures' demanded by SMAD and the level of centralism this entailed served to promote the 'anti-Fascist democratic transformation', which meant the primacy of the Communists and the SED. In the central

A symbolic handshake between Wilhelm Pieck (left) and Otto Grotewohl, the two co-chairmen of the newly created Socialist Unity Party (SED), in the Admiralspalast theatre, Berlin, on 22 April 1946. The SED was the product of a forced unification of the SPD and KPD and later became the state party of the GDR. On the right is Walter Ulbricht; on the right of the second row is Otto Buchwitz.

General Vasily I. Chuikov, head of the newly created Soviet Control Commission, successor body to the Soviet Military Administration, receives Minister-President Otto Grotewohl on 11 November 1949. One month earlier, on 10 October, the administrative powers of the SMA had been handed over to the Provisional Government of the GDR.

The Provisional People's Chamber, formerly the Second German People's Council, had enacted the Constitution of the GDR, which entered into force on 7 October 1949, thereby founding the German Democratic Republic. On 12 October 1949, at its second sitting, it announced the composition of the GDR Government and was presented with the government policy statement. Front row, left to right: Karl Steinhoff, Georg Dertinger, Walter Ulbricht, Otto Grotewohl, Hermann Kastner, Otto Nuschke and Luitpold Steidle. Back row, left to right: Herbert Hoffmann, Friedel Malter, Jonny Loehr, Hermann Matern, Johannes Dieckmann, Fritz Ebert, Elli Schmidt and Erich Geske.

administrative authorities which operated alongside the state parliaments and governments, they were over-represented, holding five out of the eleven top posts. Not even the municipal and state elections of 1946 can properly be called free elections, because they were preceded by the compulsory merger of the Communist Party of Germany (KPD) and the Social Democratic Party of Germany (SPD) to form the SED in April of that year, while the candidatures of members of the parties of the Centre-Right, the Christian Democratic Union (CDU) and the Liberal Democratic Party of Germany (LDPD) were often obstructed. The creation of the German Democratic Republic (GDR) on 7 October 1949 marked the completion of the division of Germany on the Eastern side.

Towards the Federal Republic – the Parliamentary Council and the creation of the Constitution

In the Western zones, the Council of the *Länder* and the Zonal Advisory Council foreshadowed, as it were, the exercise of governmental power by central institutions. Economic cooperation worked as a bonding agent, first within and then between zones. On 25 June 1947, the Economic Council of the Anglo-American Bizone, elected by the relevant *Land* parliaments, convened for the first time. The currency reform which entered into force for all three Western occupation zones on 20 June 1948 was the economic manifestation of Germany's widening division. On 1 August 1948, these three zones merged to form the Trizone. It was now plain to see that the creation of a partial state in western Germany in the form of the Federal Republic was also the political shape of things to come.

At this point the process of creating a constitution for the future democratic state in western Germany had already begun. In response to a proposal from the Western occupying powers, the Parliamentary Council was convened and began its deliberations on a constitution in Bonn on 1 September 1948. It had a total of 65 members, four of whom were women. The CDU and SPD had 27 representatives each, the Free Democratic Party (FDP) had five, and the Centre, the German Party (*Deutsche Partei – DP*) and the Communist KPD each provided two. There were also five non-voting deputies from Berlin. A good many members of the Parliamentary Council had belonged to the National Assembly of 1919 in Weimar and to the Reichstag of the first German Republic. The distribution of seats reflected the relative size of the *Länder* in terms of population and the party-political balance within the *Land* parliaments. Konrad Adenauer (CDU), who later became the first Chancellor of the Federal Republic, was elected chairman of the Council.

The mandate of the Parliamentary Council was to adopt a basic law for the new state; this instrument was to have the status of a provisional constitution. As one observer, the journalist Walter Henkels, noted, "The Germans were like people who had served a sentence and were now about to have their full civil rights restored". In a memorandum, the Western Allies set out their own ideas on the future governmental structure. Above all, they believed, the state should have strong federal features. The powers that should be vested in the future chamber of the *Länder* and the way in which fiscal sovereignty should be divided between the Federal Republic and its constituent states were the issues that provoked the longest-running conflicts between the Allied military governors and German politicians as well as among the German parties themselves.

From the Americans' point of view, the adoption of a constitution was the centrepiece of the controlled institutional change which, the specialised advisers of the U.S. armed forces firmly believed, was imperative if democratic thinking was to take root in post-war Germany. At advisers' meetings that had been taking place in the United States since the summer of 1944, the prevailing belief was that the German national character was capable of understanding human relationships only in terms of

The way in which the war effort had been financed had created a huge oversupply of money in the Third Reich. This glut continued to grow after 1945 and ultimately led to a monetary crisis. Barter increasingly took the place of payments in reichsmarks. Accordingly, to pave the way for the creation of a viable market economy, the deutschmark was introduced on 20 June 1948 and became the sole legal tender from the following day. Holders of old notes and coins were to pay them into reichsmark accounts and then apply for the conversion of their account.

On 23 May 1949, under a black, red and gold standard, the Basic Law for the Federal Republic of Germany is displayed on a table in the former assembly hall of the Academy of Education in Bonn. In the centre of the front row (left to right) are Paul Löbe, Theodor Heuss and Hans-Christoph Seebohm. The Parliamentary Council had gathered on that day for its final session at 4 p.m. The Basic Law was promulgated on 23 May and entered into force at midnight at the end of that day.

The four women on the Parliamentary Council who, along with the 61 male members, produced the Basic Law for the Federal Republic of Germany, are sometimes referred to as the 'Mothers of the Basic Law'. Left to right: Helene Wessel (Centre Party), Helene Weber (CDU), Friederike Nadig and Elisabeth Selbert (both SPD). Nadig and Selbert succeeded in having the principle of equality between men and women enshrined in the Basic Law.

The Basic Law for the Federal Republic of Germany laid the constitutional and political foundations of the Federal Republic. In the light of their experience of National Socialist dictatorship, the authors of the Basic Law enshrined a catalogue of directly enforceable fundamental rights in the new constitution.

‘dominance, submission and romantic revolt’. The only chance to alter this authoritarian character, they thought, was through a reconstruction of the German institutional architecture. “Institutional patterns”, as sociologist Talcott Parsons put it at the time, “are the backbone of the social system”.

The fact that the new institutions did actually have this effect of fostering democracy by force of habit is corroborated by knowledgeable contemporary witnesses. Dolf Sternberger, a political scientist and publicist who was lecturing at Heidelberg, wrote in the mid-fifties that the time of the Allied ‘educational experiment’ had demonstrated “that political institutions are able to educate the people who live with them and practise using them with far more lasting effect than any kind of direct teaching or propagation of ideology can achieve”. This is another reason why the Allied military governors kept trying to influence the constitutional deliberations of 1948/49. It would be wrong, however, to assume that the Basic Law was primarily the response to instructions given by the occupying powers to the members of the Parliamentary Council in the way that a company instructs its agents. On the contrary, the architecture of the Basic Law is the product of independent German thought. It is the result of specific reflection on concepts underlying the older German constitutions, which has led in some cases to the restoration of earlier constitutional traditions and in others to their deliberate rejection.

The Basic Law

The Basic Law *(Grundgesetz)* took shape as the fruit of a consensus, particularly between the two major political forces. Despite their sharply conflicting ideologies, the Christian Democratic Union/Christian Social Union (CDU/CSU) and the Social Democratic Party of Germany (SPD) proved sufficiently willing to make significant compromises. There was agreement on the creation of a state – a provisional state – in the territory of the Western zones. There was also agreement that the new constitutional instrument should enshrine a basic consensus on fundamental substantive and procedural principles, which would thus be declared inviolable and would no longer be open to negotiation between factions with conflicting interests. This was the breakthrough, in that it established solid foundations for the resolution of future conflicts by means of democratic rules. The main elements of this basic consensus that was reached in 1949 are the recognition of a catalogue of fundamental rights, the principle of majority decision-making by Parliament, provision for the protection of minorities, guaranteed primacy of the rule of law and the supply of basic public assets, underwritten by the welfare state.

The fact that it was recognisably rooted in values is one of the significant points that distinguish the Basic Law clearly from its predecessor, the Weimar Constitution of 1919. The latter had also been crafted as an essentially democratic instrument. The interpretation of some of its provisions, however, was to contribute to its own erosion, culminating in Hitler’s pseudo-legal assumption of power in 1933.

In the view of Michael Stolleis, a leading authority on constitutional law, the Basic Law largely adopted the fundamental rights enshrined in the Weimar Constitution but “made them clearer and more concrete and endowed them with directly binding force and safeguards”. The Basic Law introduced the first legal remedy to ‘activate’ the protection of fundamental rights in the form of the *Verfassungsbeschwerde*, or complaint of unconstitutionality. The fathers – and the few mothers – of the Basic Law of 1949 had learned other lessons too from the failure of the Weimar Constitution to withstand the challenge from anti-democratic and totalitarian forces. The principle of a constitution based on absolute values replaced the relativism of values in the Weimar Constitution. Besides the inviolability of the principles of the liberal democratic order, this also means that a core of

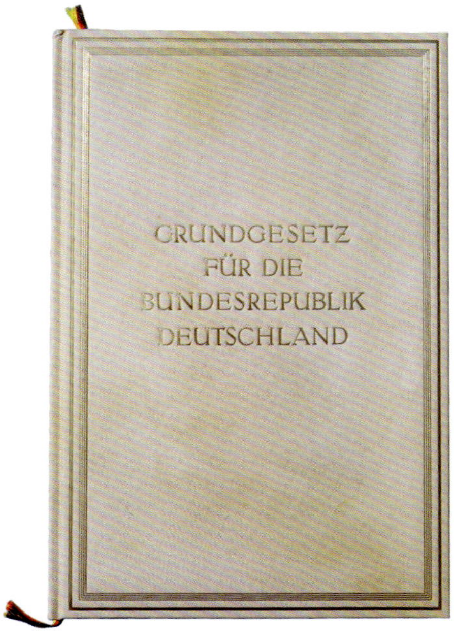

A facsimile of the original Constitution. The term *Grundgesetz* (Basic Law) was quite deliberately chosen by the Parliamentary Council as it was not intended as a permanent constitution. At that time it was still assumed that the division of Germany would not last long.

Konrad Adenauer, President of the Parliamentary Council and later Federal Chancellor, signs the Basic Law in Bonn on 23 May 1949 at 5 p.m. precisely. Having been ratified by all of the *Länder*, the Basic Law was signed by the President and Vice-Presidents at a ceremonial sitting of the Parliamentary Council and entered into force at midnight.

fundamental constitutional principles defined in Article 79(3) of the Basic Law – the so-called 'perpetuity clause' – is declared inalterable. The provisions specified by that clause, in other words, cannot be repealed or suspended, not even by the parliamentary majority normally required for constitutional amendments.

In addition, the Basic Law also proclaims the principle of militant democracy, i.e. a democratic constitutional order that is capable of defending itself. In the Weimar era, enemies of the democratic constitution were able to use its guarantees to undermine the constitutional order, and this is precisely what the Basic Law seeks to prevent. To protect the democratic order, provisions have been inserted which enable the Federal Constitutional Court, and it alone, to ban political parties (Article 21(2)) and to order the forfeiture of basic rights (Article 18) and which permit the prohibition of associations pursuing certain purposes or activities (Article 9(2)) and allow all Germans to resist attempts to abolish the constitutional order where no other remedy is possible (Article 20(4)). The decision not to invest the President of the Republic with any governmental powers but to make the government accountable to Parliament alone, the establishment of the Federal Constitutional Court as 'guardian of the Constitution' and the wider powers devolved to the federal states document the will of the Parliamentary Council to overcome the constitutional 'congenital defect' of the first German democracy.

Some of the 'lessons of Weimar' which were important to the architects of the Basic Law, still haunted by the fear that the experience of National Socialist dictatorship might repeat itself, may be assessed differently from a present-day perspective – one example being the Parliamentary Council's distinct aversion to the renewed enshrinement of instruments of direct democracy. The majority of the Council regarded referendums at that time as a 'gift to demagogues', in the oft-quoted words of Theodor Heuss.

On 8 May 1949, the Parliamentary Council adopted the constitutional draft by 53 votes to 12. It received its democratic legitimacy from the majority approval of ten *Land* parliaments – the parliaments of all the *Länder* except Bavaria, which wanted greater devolution of powers within the federal structure. On 23 May 1949, the Basic Law entered into force.

The new German party democracy

In the Parliamentary Council, the delegates from the *Länder* formed themselves into party-political groups from the outset. The constitutional model reflected in the Basic Law was therefore the product of conflicting views and mutual concessions by the political parties. To put it succinctly, the constitutional compromise embodied by the Basic Law bears the stamp of the new German party democracy. This derived not only from the political circumstances of the time, which effectively gave the democratic parties a key role in determining the new system of government. At the same time, people began to realise – the members of the elite groups more quickly, some sections of the population more hesitantly – that there was no truth in the preconception, still widely held during the Weimar era, that party politics was incompatible with good government; on the contrary, party politics is indispensable in a parliamentary system. Parties are needed to forge the link in the legislative process between the two arenas of federal policy – the Bundestag, with its competitive approach to democracy, and the Bundesrat, based on the consensus approach. Moreover, it is incumbent on political parties, which, in contrast to other, looser forms of involvement by civil society in the political process, embody an element of continuity in their aims and organisation, to mediate between the government and the governed. Parties are therefore part of the chain of democratic legitimisation in representative democracies. It was thus perfectly logical that party politics should have left its mark on the constituent process of 1948/49. From 1945, wrote Dolf Sternberger, "scarcely anyone from any side found it at all strange or remarkable that a state should be established or constructed on the basis of political parties".

Following the first elections to the Bundestag, held on 14 August 1949, the House convened for its constituent sitting on 7 September. President by age Paul Löbe, who had been President of the Reichstag from 1920 to 1932, chaired the sitting until the election of Erich Köhler as first President of the Bundestag. On 12 September Theodor Heuss was elected as the first President of the Federal Republic, and on 15 September Konrad Adenauer was elected to serve as the first Federal Chancellor.

On 23 October 1954, in the French Ministry of Foreign Affairs on the Quai d'Orsay, the Paris Agreements were signed. The accession of Germany and Italy to the modified Treaty of Brussels established the Western European Union (WEU), a military alliance dedicated to the preservation of peace in Europe. In addition, the agreements provided for German accession to NATO and the restoration of German sovereignty, although certain rights reserved by the Four Powers limited its exercise until the conclusion of the Two-Plus-Four Treaty.

Federal Chancellor Konrad Adenauer at the signing of the Final Act of the Nine-Power Conference in London on 28 September 1954. This Final Act recognised the Government of the Federal Republic of Germany as the only government entitled to speak for Germany in international affairs, opened the door for the accession of the Federal Republic to NATO and abolished the Occupation Statute. And so the London Conference largely laid the foundations of the Paris Agreements.

The Treaties of Rome of 25 March 1957 comprised the EEC Treaty and the Euratom Treaty, which founded the European Economic Community and the European Atomic Energy Community, as well as the Convention on certain institutions common to the European Communities. These agreements marked the start of a development that ultimately brought forth the European Union (EU).

The Basic Law reconciles differing ideological positions

In many respects, the constitutional compromise that was sealed in the Basic Law in 1948/49 represents the lowest common denominator between the ideological positions of democratic Socialism, Catholic social doctrine and business-friendly Liberalism. It was undisputed that, in addition to the directly elected Parliament, an assembly representing the *Länder* should be established. There was, however, disagreement about whether it should be a federal council, comprising delegates from the state parliaments, or an elected senate and about its powers (equal rights or a federal council with a right of veto). The two main parliamentary groups finally agreed on the federal council (*Bundesrat*) concept.

There was agreement in principle on the inclusion of fundamental rights. What was at issue, however, was whether these fundamental rights should remain confined to the canon of classic civil rights, guaranteeing individual freedom, equality before the law and the inviolability of property, or whether the catalogue should be extended to include guaranteed economic, social and cultural rights. In the end, business-friendly positions and conservative values, as held by the parties of the Centre-Right, tended to prevail, one example being the inclusion of parental rights and the special protection of the state for marriage and the family in Article 6 of the Basic Law. By comparison, the nationalisation clause (Article 15) was left relatively non-prescriptive, explicitly stating that means of production could only be nationalised on the basis of a law.

Similarly, the parties of the Left were unable to secure the inclusion of fundamental social rights, which would have given individuals the right to social protection and extensive participation in society. Thereafter, however, the proponents of the concept of socially committed government by democratic majority did register a very significant success by having the postulates of the 'social state' enshrined in Articles 20 and 28 of the Basic Law and in combining this principle with those of democracy and the rule of law. In this way they created a democracy founded on social justice and the rule of law. The idea of a democracy bound by the principles of social justice is clearly reflected in an early ruling of the Federal Constitutional Court, dating from 1954. The legislature, in the view of the Court, was certainly entitled to create federal laws "which intervene in economic life to provide order and guidance". The image of human beings that underlies the Basic Law, said the Court, was "not that of an isolated sovereign individual". On the contrary, the Basic Law had sought to resolve the tension between the individual and the community "by stressing the association and the identification of the person with the community". This, however, meant that "the individual must consent to the limits which the legislature imposes on his freedom of action in order to maintain and promote the communal life of society within the bounds of general acceptability [...]".

Principles of the parliamentary system of government

One of the key decisions taken by the Parliamentary Council was the choice of an unrestricted parliamentary system of government. The Basic Law thus confirmed for the Federal Republic as a whole what had already been common practice in the *Länder* of the Trizone for years, as mentioned above. The form of parliamentary democracy that has existed since then in the Federal Republic of Germany combines the principles of sovereignty of the people (Article 20 of the Basic Law) and responsibility of the government to Parliament (Articles 63 and 68) with the representation principle. Respect for the will of the people translates into the primacy of Parliament, which means that governmental activity is always subject to the formative will and the scrutiny of Parliament. The primacy of Parliament is exemplified by the rule that armed deployments of the federal armed forces (Bundeswehr) abroad require the consent of the

Bundestag. On the other hand, there is a reserved core area of Federal Government activity which is the sole responsibility of the executive. The Federal Constitutional Court recently ruled, for example, that the Government is under no obligation to give the Bundestag prior notice of the approval of arms exports.

Only in two places, Articles 29 and 118, does the Basic Law contain a plebiscitary element. The Federal Government's power to initiate legislation is shared with the Bundestag and Bundesrat. The appointment (investiture) of the Federal Government takes place through the adoption of a formal vote of confidence by the Bundestag. Thereafter, the government remains dependent on the confidence of the parliamentary majority. In the event of a constructive vote of no confidence under Article 67 of the Basic Law, the election of a new Federal Chancellor brings about a change of government. The Federal Government, however, can only exercise the right to dissolve Parliament indirectly, using the instrument of a motion for a vote of confidence (Art. 68), which only the Chancellor may table. In such cases, which have occurred in 1972, 1982 and 2005, it is at the discretion of the President of the Federal Republic whether to order fresh parliamentary elections or to leave a minority government in office. Such reserved presidential powers are restricted in the Basic Law to a very few exceptional situations of this kind, in contrast to the arrangement whereby the President and Chancellor of the *Reich* formed a dual executive in the Weimar Republic.

The continuation in office of the Federal Government depends on its majority in the Bundestag, as the authors of the Basic Law intended. The two opposite political poles are not the Federal Government and Parliament itself but rather the government majority and the opposition in Parliament. If this parliamentary interaction is to be effective, a loyal opposition, committed to the established system of government, is certainly essential. Indeed, it is only the existence of political parties that enables the government majority and the opposition to interact effectively in the parliamentary framework. It is the parties in Parliament, or rather the *parliamentary groups* formed by them, which provide the government with a stable majority on the one hand and lend the opposition the necessary firepower on the other. In addition, the compatibility of the tenure of a parliamentary seat with ministerial office serves to reinforce the link between the executive and legislative elements of the government majority. The political system of the Federal Republic as set out on the constitutional drawing board is therefore very close to a pure parliamentary democracy.

The Basic Law as a living constitution: the dynamics of parliamentarianism and government from the 1950s to the second decade of the 21st century

Like any institution, the parliamentary democracy created by virtue of the Constitution of 1949 simply prescribed a formal framework and did not entirely constrict the freedom of action of the various players operating within that framework. The interaction of political institutions and politicians was therefore able to generate its own particular momentum in the course of the following years and decades. The elected politicians tested the new institutions, probing the scope and the limits of the institutional structure and developing their own 'made-to-measure' strategies within that structure. Conversely, the institutions revealed their own potential for development and improvement. In the politicians' practical dealings with 'their'

Federal Chancellor Helmut Schmidt, seen here with Egon Franke, Federal Minister for Intra-German Relations (left) during the debate on the constructive motion of no confidence tabled against him by the CDU/CSU and FDP. After the Social Democratic-Liberal coalition fell victim to internal conflicts, Schmidt initially continued to lead a minority government while the FDP began coalition talks with the CDU/CSU. On 1 October 1982, the second constructive motion of no confidence in the history of the Federal Republic was put to the House. Schmidt lost the vote, and therefore the chancellorship, to Helmut Kohl.

political institutions, it became clear which features of these institutions were obstacles to action and which of them offered scope for more action. Within the framework of these institutions, the course taken by internal German politics after the establishment of the Federal Republic remained, to some extent, mapped out in advance. Nevertheless, the holders of political office and parliamentary mandates who trod this institutionally pre-ordained path had opportunities to alter it along the way and certainly did take those opportunities.

The 'route map' which the constitutionally enshrined institutions provided for political players as well as the freedom of action accorded them by the political system are reflected in the style of government, in the intertwining of federal and state politics and in the working methods of the German Bundestag. The 1950s certainly saw the development of dynamic parliamentarianism, encompassing not only the Bundestag but also the Federal Government and the political parties as well as the departmental civil service and what is known as the corporate sector, comprising the associations with close links to politics and quasi-governmental organisations.

The dominant role of the head of government

Compared with the authors of the Weimar Constitution, the drafters of the Basic Law, as we have seen, made the government more heavily dependent on majority support in Parliament. However, notwithstanding the sharp focus on the need for parliamentary consent in the cases referred to above, an effective and responsible government is also a fundamental requirement of the democratic order in the Federal Republic. Accordingly, as the judges of the Constitutional Court ruled back in 1959, the Federal Government must retain the powers "which it requires to perform governing functions independently and on its own responsibility on behalf of the people and Parliament".

In Germany, responsible government is subject to three overarching precepts of political leadership. The first is the fact that, under Article 65 of the Basic Law, the Federal Chancellor elected by the Bundestag determines the general policy guidelines; it is also in response to the Chancellor's proposals that the Federal President appoints and dismisses government ministers. The second is that the Bundestag is not empowered to force the dismissal of a minister by means of a vote of no confidence. The third is that individual ministers are not directly responsible to Parliament. These three precepts form the *Kanzlerprinzip* or 'chancellorship principle' and underline the prominent position of the head of government in the German constitutional system.

Within the policy guidelines laid down by the Chancellor, the ministers do, however, run their own departments independently and on their own responsibility (the *Ressortprinzip*, or departmental principle). If differences of opinion arise between ministers, the Federal Government, as a collegial body, settles such differences by a majority decision; this is known as the cabinet principle (*Kabinettsprinzip*). The departmental and cabinet principles quite significantly restrict the Chancellor's freedom to take decisions at will. In addition, coalition agreements occasionally act as a straitjacket, forcing the Chancellor to let the coalition partner have its say on personnel and policy decisions.

Nevertheless, beginning in the Adenauer era, there developed in the Federal Republic a form of governmental leadership to which the name *Kanzlerdemokratie* ('chancellor democracy') is applied – a democratic system in which a dominant role is played by the head of government. This term does not in any way refer to a particular style or method of government by power projection. On the contrary, it means that the incumbent Federal Chancellor's personal leadership qualities interact effectively with the structural guarantees that enable him or her to exercise these qualities in the main governing party, in the government majority in Parliament and in the public domain.

From 13 August 1961 to 9 November 1989, the four sectors of the city that were a legacy of the Second World War were split by the Berlin Wall, which divided the Soviet-controlled eastern sector from the other three sectors overseen by the Western Allied Powers. The purpose of the Wall was to make the intra-German border an insurmountable barrier.

Federal Chancellor Konrad Adenauer and President Charles De Gaulle after the signing of the Élysée Treaty in the *Salon Murat* of the Élysée Palace in Paris on 22 January 1963. In that Treaty, the two states undertook to consult each other on all important matters of foreign, security, youth and cultural policy and to hold regular intergovernmental meetings. The agreement marked a clear turning point in relations between the two countries after they had long been sworn enemies and had clashed in numerous conflicts.

At the end of his trip to Germany, John F. Kennedy _ became the first U.S. President to visit West Berlin, where he arrived on 26 June 1963 to commemorate the 15th anniversary of the Berlin Airlift. The people there acclaimed him as the guarantor of the city's freedom. The image shows President Kennedy leaving Tegel Airport in Berlin; on his right in the car are Willy Brandt, Governing Mayor of Berlin, and Federal Chancellor Konrad Adenauer.

Another characteristic of this model of political leadership is that parliamentary elections become a kind of referendum in which the people elect a chancellor, because the contest between the parties generally develops into a personal duel between two prospective chancellors.

Political scientists have identified five prerequisites for the successful exercise of this form of political leadership:

– The chancellor's position must be unchallenged within the cabinet; with the aid of ample media publicity, he or she must also be held in high regard by the population.

– He or she must be able to count on the solid backing of his or her own party; in order to guarantee this level of support, the chancellor should generally be the chairperson of the main governing party too.

– Within the cabinet, among the parliamentary groups of the governing coalition and in the eyes of special-interest groups, the chancellor must be perceived as someone who can assert his or her authority.

– The chancellor must also have the political skills to be able to facilitate the decision-making process by enlisting the support of the majority of the Bundesrat, where the *Länder* are represented and which, in a federally structured country, is often dominated by a different party from the majority party in the Bundestag.

– The final prerequisite is that the chancellor, to establish a high profile as the dominant figure in a *Kanzlerdemokratie*, must engage personally in the field of foreign affairs.

The Bundestag: both 'debating parliament' and 'working parliament'

Even the strongest Chancellor of the Federal Republic needs constant parliamentary support. A chancellor's visible authority actually derives from the adversarial relationship between the government and opposition camps. The Bundestag is rather like the foundation stone of the German system of *Kanzlerdemokratie*. In research into parliamentary systems and practice, a distinction is made between two absolutes – the pure 'debating parliament' and the pure 'working parliament'. In this bipolar model, the debating parliament is characterised by open political cross-fire between the government and opposition benches in the plenary chamber. An emphatically competitive political struggle, waged in the parliamentary arena but addressed to the public at large, dominates in this type of assembly. The competition principle prevails, its outward manifestation being the disciplined concerted action of each parliamentary group. In the working parliament, by contrast, the real political activity takes place in committee. The division of responsibilities among the permanent committees of the Bundestag reflects the desire and the duty of parliamentarians to be involved in the detailed work on legislative proposals. In this form of 'parliamentary co-governing', rhetorical skills are less important, and no conscious attempt is made to reduce every issue to black and white. On the contrary, the Member of Parliament operates in committee as one of a 'team of specialists' comprising politicians and departmental civil servants who meet behind closed doors and cooperate closely with the departmental experts who attend their meetings. It is therefore unrealistic to conclude from a rather empty debating chamber that Members of Parliament are somehow failing in their duty.

Konrad Adenauer leaving the podium after his farewell speech to the Bundestag in Bonn on 15 October 1963. After fourteen years at the helm, during which time he had led five federal governments, the first Chancellor of the Federal Republic resigned from office. Eugen Gerstenmaier, President of the Bundestag, paid tribute to Adenauer for his achievements and took leave of him with the words, "Konrad Adenauer has earned the gratitude of the Fatherland".

On the basis of this stereotyped division, the German Bundestag may be categorised as a hybrid, combining elements of the debating and the working parliament. In other words, it is far from being a mere appendage to a government dominated by a powerful chancellor, a debating forum portraying a stylised tableau of confrontation between the governing majority and the opposition, but, in its legislative role, has long since developed a new working style of its own and shaped its own contribution. The fact that the Bundestag has incorporated elements of both parliamentary types is also largely due to the constitutional system of cooperative federalism and, deriving from this system, a relatively high degree of decentralisation of power within the German political parties as well as to the fact that, in practice, the content of the great majority of legislative initiatives is assembled by the departmental civil service. All of these factors strengthen the element of democracy based on bargaining processes in the parliamentarianism of the Federal Republic, thereby reinforcing the impression of a parliament working outside the public spotlight.

On the other hand, the political confrontation between the government majority and the opposition minority is a defining feature of everyday life in Parliament.

This asymmetrical balance of forces is at least partially counteracted in the Rules of Procedure of the German Bundestag by means of appropriate procedural guarantees and parliamentary rights of scrutiny, of which the opposition is always more likely to avail itself. It is the opposition groups which make most use, or even exclusive use, of parliamentary rights of initiative with a high public impact, such as question time or debates on matters of topical interest. In previous electoral terms, the opposition groups have accounted for the majority, sometimes 95 to 100 %, of all recourse to the instruments of major and minor interpellations, questions submitted by individual Members, summonses to members of the Federal Government to address Parliament and answer questions and motions of censure against cabinet ministers or motions calling for their dismissal. But the work of the opposition is not confined to the public forum of the debating chamber. The opposition groups in the Bundestag also focus their efforts on the parliamentary committees, trying to exert their influence on legislation through deep involvement in the specialised work of the committees. This sort of cooperative opposition, which has been the norm in the Bundestag to date, is sometimes none too far removed from indirect participation in government.

Opportunities for a 'co-governing opposition' also arise when opposition groups in the Bundestag try to influence votes in the Bundesrat through *Land* governments in which their respective parties are represented.

The 'free mandate' and parliamentary-group discipline – irreconcilable opposites?

Article 38 of the Basic Law lays down that the Members of the Bundestag "shall be representatives of the whole people, not bound by orders and instructions, and responsible only to their conscience". This independence of the elected representatives of the people, which is denoted by the term 'free mandate', is the core of the classical liberal concept of political representation.

Even in a state constituted as a modern party democracy, the essentially protective function of the free mandate has not lost its significance. The desire to protect each individual Member of the Bundestag from the exertion of external pressure by interest groups and from the imposition of sanctions by party and parliamentary-group executive committees is a logical extension of the democratic ideal. On the other hand, it is firmly established today that the representation of special interests in Parliament is legitimate. Moreover, the notion that parliamentarians are

individuals who take their own 'autonomous' decisions runs counter to the thrust of modern parliamentarianism. Both Parliament as a whole and the individual elected representatives, in fact, derive their political potency from the fact that they form parliamentary groups "on account of similar political aims", to quote Rule 10 of the Rules of Procedure of the German Bundestag. A collective parliamentary will, or several bodies with concurrent common wills – and hence the formation of viable majorities – cannot materialise until similar convictions have been pooled in this way. The individual Member of Parliament also benefits from the division of responsibilities within the parliamentary groups, for no individual is able to become equally conversant with every single area of political activity. Accordingly, each Member relies on those colleagues who have specialised knowledge of particular matters; conversely, each can establish a reputation within the group by bringing his or her own expertise to bear.

Be that as it may, it remains impossible to eliminate all tension between the free exercise of a mandate and parliamentary-group discipline, and this tension is one of the characteristics of the dynamic parliamentarianism that has evolved in the Federal Republic of Germany. Particularly when the government has a slender majority in the Bundestag, a conflict between a few 'dissenters' and the majority of a parliamentary group can have serious political implications, because in certain circumstances it may deprive the government of a majority within the governing coalition on important votes or even permanently endanger the government majority. In the first coalition under Willy Brandt and Walter Scheel, for instance, the SPD/FDP majority crumbled when members of the coalition groups defected to the CDU/CSU or decided not to vote with the government, triggering an early general election in 1972. To cite another example, in September 2001 the SPD-Green coalition failed to muster a majority when 19 Members on the government side voted against the deployment of German troops in Macedonia.

Whenever it is a matter of securing a majority within the government's own ranks, the conflict of loyalties between individual Members and their parliamentary groups logically assumes another dimension and becomes a 'three-way pull' involving dissenters, group executive committees and government leaders. During the Macedonia controversy of 2001, Chancellor Gerhard Schröder emphatically reminded his SPD parliamentary group of its responsibility "not to let misguided actions endanger the government's viability". On the same occasion, Franz Müntefering, Chairman of the SPD group in the Bundestag, threatened dissidents that their actions would have consequences for their political careers. Places on the lists of candidates for the next general election, he said, were decided by the regional party congresses, and their delegates would "naturally be aware of the conduct of individual Members of Parliament".

Members who are subjected to such pressure 'from above' can generally count on public sympathy. They appear to be victims of 'blackmail' driven by power politics or to be unfairly exposed to the scourge of the 'party whip' within their parliamentary groups. Against this one-sided defence of the free mandate, it must be said that a parliamentary group has every reason to exert a certain degree of pressure to bring its dissenting members into line with the group's political platform. The limits of such pressure are reached when matters of conscience are at stake in a parliamentary vote. Conflicts of conscience, however, seldom lend themselves to unequivocal legal definition; life-or-death decisions, for example, such as those concerning the law relating to the termination of pregnancies, or decisions on the period of prescription for violent crimes committed by the National

The first spontaneous debate on a matter of topical interest, which took place in the Bundestag on 10 February 1965. The parliamentary groups had tabled a joint motion for an addition to the Rules of Procedure providing for such debates, and the motion was adopted on 27 January 1965. The purpose of introducing a spontaneous short debate was to make plenary sittings more relevant and interesting again. More than 100 of these topical debates are now held in every parliamentary term.

Socialist regime, are undoubtedly a matter of conscience. According to scholars of constitutional law, questions of conscience are confined to a relatively small number of borderline issues. Even though it is impossible to compile an exhaustive catalogue of the issues in question, Members of Parliament cannot legitimately invoke freedom of conscience every time they dissent from the position of their parliamentary group.

It should ultimately be remembered that it is not only the parliamentary group which exerts pressure on individual dissenters but also the dissenters who put the majority of the group under pressure by announcing their intention to cast a dissenting vote, particularly in cases where the survival of the government hangs on a few votes. At the end of the day, no Member of the Bundestag can be compelled by his or her parliamentary group to toe the party line in a vote. In other words, the safeguards enshrined in Article 38 of the Basic Law guarantee the personal freedom of Members of Parliament to vote as they see fit. This serves to prevent certain extreme impositions which could result from the party system.

The Federation and the *Länder* – development towards unitary federalism

In the autumn of 2002, the Bundestag and Bundesrat appointed a joint Commission on Federalism. This marked a new stage in the discussion which had been taking place in the Federal Republic for some considerable time on a fundamental reshaping of the relationship between the national and regional tiers of government. Under the microscope were two complex manifestations of policy interlocking, namely joint financing and the disentanglement of the legislative powers of the Federation from those of the *Länder*. A position paper for the Conference of Minister-Presidents of the *Länder* listed the main arguments for constitutional reform:

– Firstly, as a result of the progressive development of federal legislation, the division of powers between the federal and regional levels had 'become skewed'. There was therefore a need to recover from the Federation powers that belonged to the *Länder* and in particular to their parliaments.

– Secondly, the existing federal legislative process repeatedly created 'stalemates' between the Bundestag and the Bundesrat. Such immobilisation of the decision-making machinery had to be curbed.

– Thirdly, because of the interlocking spheres of competence of the Federation and the *Länder*, decision-making procedures were becoming cumbersome, and it was no longer plain to see where responsibility for decisions lay. A clear apportionment of political responsibilities was therefore a necessity.

– Fourthly, the addition of the European tier made decision-making processes even more complex and cumbersome. It was therefore essential to develop simpler and less time-consuming procedures for the transposition of Community legislation into German law.

Reform of the federal system in three steps

On 1 September 2006 the first stage of the extensive reform of the federal system entered into force. Until then, the Basic Law had listed relatively few areas in which regulatory powers were vested entirely in the hands of the federal legislature or of the state legislatures. Since 2006 federal framework legislation has been abolished, and other subjects from the realm of concurrent legislation have been unequivocally assigned to the federal sphere of competence, as in the cases of nuclear energy and counter-terrorism, or to the responsibility of the *Länder*, as in the cases of prison administration and public-service law. The bulk of legislative activity remains subject to concurrent legislative powers. This category includes criminal law, labour law and matters relating to economic, transport, housing and

The federal system has twice been reformed, redefining relations between the Federation and the *Länder*. The first reform package, enacted in 2006, considerably disentangled concurrent lawmaking powers and assigned more legislative competence to the *Länder*. In 2009, the second reform package focused on the federal system of financial management and introduced a public-borrowing cap. The image shows the *Europasaal* of the Federal Chancellery in Berlin at the start of a meeting of the Minister-Presidents with Federal Chancellor Gerhard Schröder (back row, centre) and Federal Government representatives on 16 December 2004.

environmental policy. In these areas, Article 72 of the Basic Law largely assigns legislative power to the *Länder* as long as, and to the extent that, the Federation does not exercise its right to legislate, which it may do in cases where regulation by federal legislation would benefit the country as a whole, for example by maintaining "equivalence of living conditions" or "legal or economic unity".

In the minds of the authors of the Basic Law, concurrent legislative powers meant that regulation by the *Länder* would normally be assumed unless otherwise provided. In practice, however, prior to the reforms of 2006, the Federation made copious use of the right to avail itself of these powers, thereby subjecting the *Länder* to federal legislation in almost all policy areas other than those involving primary state legislation, such as local government and schools. Citing the need to find the most uniform solution possible to political problems, the Federation assumed more and more governmental responsibilities. As a result, the powers of the *Länder* were eroded. This process is described as 'unitarisation'. The development, over the course of several decades, towards unitary federalism had its constitutional origins in Article 72 of the Basic Law and was subsequently reinforced by other legal instruments and legally binding agreements between the Federation and the *Länder*. One area where this development took place was in the co-regulation of administrative procedures: Article 84 of the Basic Law states that the Federal Government may be authorised by a federal law to issue instructions regarding administrative procedures, in other words to prescribe the form, manner and method in which the law is to be executed by the *Länder*, which are normally fully responsible for the execution of federal laws. In practice, the Federation had been making ample use of this power of authorisation and was consequently accused by the *Länder* of undermining their administrative competence.

The reforms are an attempt to halt this trend towards unitarism. Since 2006, the *Länder* have been empowered to amend implementing regulations for federal laws by means of divergent state legislation. As part of the 2006 reform of the federal system, concurrent legislation was unravelled to a great extent, and only for a third of all areas of public policy was the Federation still required to prove that federal legislation was 'necessary'. The *Länder*, for their part, were given the right to enact their own laws on a wide range of subjects, such as spatial planning and nature conservation.

The Federation continues to influence the policies of the *Länder* through the instrument of joint tasks *(Gemeinschaftsaufgaben)*, although these are now fewer in number as a result of the reform package of 2006. As part of the major fiscal and administrative reforms of 1969, the Federation and the *Länder* agreed that the following would be regarded as joint tasks: the promotion of regional economic structures, the expansion and construction of institutions of higher education (no longer a joint task since 2006), the improvement of regional economic structures and the improvement of the agrarian structure and measures of coastal protection (Article 91a of the Basic Law) as well as educational planning (also removed from the list in 2006) and research (Article 91b). At least half of the expenditure on the relevant projects is still to be met from the federal budget. Planning is to be undertaken jointly by the Federation and the *Länder*.

Matters relating to the financial framework of the federal system had not been addressed by the reforms of September 2006. A revision of this framework, however, became an urgent requirement, particularly since the Federal Consolidation Pact is due to expire in 2019, and the transfer payments made to eastern Germany under the Pact are already being phased out, while the *Länder* of eastern Germany also lost their status as Objective 1 development areas as a result of the eastward and southward enlargement of the EU. This second stage in the reform of the federal system, which was a far more complex undertaking in

view of the fundamental political differences between supporters of 'fiscal federalism' and those of redistributive federalism, was initiated at the end of May 2009 and comprised a minimalist solution. At the heart of this round of reforms is a mechanism known as the 'debt brake', whereby the federal states are prohibited from running a structural deficit with effect from 2020.

From 2016, new federal debt must not exceed 0.35 % of gross domestic product (GDP). As a means of consolidating the finances of the five poorer *Länder*, the latter receive an annual total of 800 million euros over a ten-year period, half of which comes from the federal treasury.

The Federal Government has set itself the ambitious political target of ensuring the completion of negotiations between the federal and state authorities on the third stage of reform of the federal system by 2017. The core element of this third stage is to be the reframing of the constitutional rules governing public finances, particularly the reallocation of tax receipts and reform of the system of revenue equalisation between 'donor' and 'recipient' *Länder*. Another objective of this round of reforms is to find ways to reduce the debt burden of the poorer *Länder* that are running high structural deficits. The negotiations are expected to revisit the question of the distribution of tasks within the federal system, since that is the key to creating scope for the provision of sufficient funding for the local authorities to meet their obligations.

Cooperative federalism in a 'joint-decision trap'?

In contrast to unitary systems of government, in which the will of the state is formed centrally, the German constitutional order does not endow Parliament with unrestricted sovereignty but limits it through the right of the *Länder* to participate in federal legislation. This cooperation between the Federation and the constituent states is the reason why German federalism has reached an advanced stage of political interdependence. This interdependence is even reflected in the vertical division of responsibilities between the federal level and the *Länder* which is enshrined in the Basic Law itself. The relevant provisions, contained in Articles 83 and 84, essentially describe a model of functional separation, in that the *Länder* are charged to execute federal laws "as matters of their own concern". This means that most of the power to execute federal legislation is devolved to the *Länder* in the multi-tiered German system of government. The Federation itself has scarcely any administrative infrastructure and therefore largely avails itself of the state administrations. The Federation and the *Länder*, as well as the *Länder* amongst themselves, are thus dependent on cooperation. The term 'cooperative federalism' has gained currency as a description of this phenomenon.

This borderline between federal and state powers also serves to illustrate how cooperative federalism in Germany generated such dynamism in the past that joint decision-making increasingly blurred the original clear distinction between the functions of the top two tiers of government. From the outset, the *Länder* were empowered by Article 50 of the Basic Law to participate through the Bundesrat in federal legislation and administration. This meant that federal laws which amended the Constitution, affected the fiscal revenue of the *Länder* or encroached on the administrative sovereignty of the *Länder* were subject to the consent of the Bundesrat, the chamber of the federal states.

The administrative competence of the *Länder* is affected whenever they are required by statute to execute a federal law, as prescribed by Articles 83 and 84 of the Basic Law. In such cases, before the latest reform of the federal system, a federal law automatically required the consent of the Bundesrat. Indeed, the Constitutional Court had ruled that every law which affected the administrative sovereignty of the *Länder*, were it only in one single point, required consent in its entirety. Thanks to this broad interpretation by the constitutional judges, the *Länder* possessed powerful leverage, in cases where the political colours of the Bundestag and Bundesrat differed and the Bundestag had adopted a controversial law, to influence the substantive provisions of that law in accordance with the wishes of the majority of the Bundesrat.

In the public debate and in academic circles, the undesirable consequences of this interlocking federalism were long the target of criticism, being regarded as a self-imposed paralysis of the political system. And, indeed, the high proportion of bills requiring the consent of the Bundesrat, varying between some 43 % in the first electoral term of the Bundestag (1949–1953) and about 60 % in the 13th term, enables the opposition parties – provided they hold a majority in the Bundesrat – to frustrate the political will of the majority in the Bundestag. If the Bundesrat rejects a law, the next step may be a mediation process in which both chambers negotiate a compromise, sometimes after quite laborious deliberations. Recourse to the mediation committee set up for this purpose by the Bundesrat and Bundestag has often enabled anti-government majorities in the Bundesrat to wrest substantial concessions from the majority in the Bundestag.

The critics of this prescribed mediation procedure bemoan the fact that it operates in practice like an embargo on reforms, because the marathon negotiations following referral to the mediation committee are time-consuming, and the ultimate solution can only represent the lowest common denominator, with the result that the decisions which the committee is required to take often fall far short of the ideal outcome. The federal system of government is thus caught in a twofold trap, because it is too inflexible to deal effectively with problems on the one hand and also because it is neither able nor willing to cast off the shackles of rigid interlocking, since the participants in the system are either engaged in the pursuit of short-term interests or anxious to preserve their power of veto.

Nevertheless, the assumption that this sort of 'joint-decision trap' operates is not borne out by statistics, which show that remarkably few bills requiring its consent are ultimately vetoed by the Bundesrat. There is evidently a great deal of willingness on the part of political adversaries in the Bundestag and Bundesrat to reach agreement. The strength to escape from the 'joint-decision trap', in other words, is certainly not lacking. It is undoubtedly true, however, that the Bundestag has become dependent on the Bundesrat, at least in cases where legislation requires the consent of the latter. This shift in the balance towards legislative power-sharing by the Bundestag and Bundesrat was not foreseen, let alone intended, by the authors of the Basic Law.

The Minister-Presidents of the *Länder*, however, do not in any way see themselves as the extended arm of their respective federal parties. The political conflicts in which they become involved are often waged between the federal and state authorities, and in such cases the *Länder* close ranks in cross-party solidarity against central government, for example when it comes to the distribution of tax revenues or of the financial burden of German unification. The opposition leaders at the federal level therefore have limited scope to use the Bundesrat, through their 'own' state governments, as a 'party-political counterweight' to the Federal Government.

Not least among the objectives of the 2006 reform of the federal system was the creation of an escape route out of the 'joint-decision trap'. The amended version of Article 84 of the Basic Law allows the Federation to establish authorities and administrative procedure in the *Länder* without the consent of the latter. In return, the *Länder*, as mentioned above, have been empowered to enact divergent legislative provisions of their own. This means that a large number of federal bills will no longer require the consent of the Bundesrat in future, which is generally considered to have been the main cause of legislative stalemates in the past. According to estimates made before the reforms took effect, the proportion of bills requiring consent would fall from about 60 % to between 35 % and 40 %. Initial assessments suggest, however, that the reduction could be more modest.

A diminishing role for Parliament?

In its noblest and most important function, that of the national legislature, there is a widespread view that the Bundestag has lost some of its authority. In this diagnosis, the 'diminishing role' or 'impotence' of Parliament is seen as the corollary of increased powers of control in the hands of the government and administration.

The following reasons are given for this perceived shift in the balance of power away from Parliament:

– firstly, the majority of bills are introduced on the initiative of the Federal Government;

– then there is the fact that statutory instruments, which are drawn up by the administration on the basis of legal authorisations and are essentially intended only to release the parliamentary legislators from the need to deal with every detail, have developed into a grey area offering scope for parallel extraparliamentary legislative activity;

– there is also the German practice described as 'executive federalism', whereby the negotiation of substantive legal provisions, which must be harmonised not only among the *Länder* but also between the Federal Government and the constituent states, has long since been entrusted to the departmental civil service;

– critics condemn the fact that the 'negotiating government' which strikes bargains with interest groups in various areas of government policy is usurping the legislative primacy of Parliament; package deals made in this context between associations and the government, they say, are presented to the Bundestag as a *fait accompli*;

– the decline in the role of Parliament within the political system of the Federal Republic is accelerated by the increasingly common practice of the Federal Government of relocating the debate on complex and politically sensitive issues to meetings of commissions of experts, which then effectively assume responsibility for work on the preparation of legislation;

– there is also the unmistakable overlaying of national legislative powers of the Bundestag with the matrix of European Community law; in the realm of federal transport legislation, for example, some 65 % of all provisions stem from Community law;

– lastly, the stability mechanisms that have been adopted by virtue of EU legislation, such as the financial aid for Greece and the euro rescue package, for the purpose of alleviating the debt crisis in the euro area raise the question whether such measures prejudice the participation and information rights of the Bundestag and Bundesrat and, in particular, the overall budgetary responsibility of the Bundestag.

If these seven arguments regarding Parliament's diminishing role are subjected to critical examination, it emerges that they vary in their impact on the Bundestag.

Introduction of bills

Statistics show that, of the 9,273 bills introduced in the Bundestag from 1949 to 2002, some 57 % were tabled by the government, 35 % were the result of parliamentary initiatives, about one in five being tabled by the opposition, and 8 % derived from initiatives taken by the Bundesrat. If we examine the 6,022 bills which were adopted as laws, we find that the proportion of government initiatives rises to 75 % and, conversely, that the share of direct parliamentary initiatives shrinks to 18 %. Considering that government bills are often formally introduced by the parliamentary groups in the governing coalition as a means of accelerating the procedure, it is obvious that the government does play a preponderant role in the production of legislation.

This basic pattern has remained unchanged ever since. In the current 18th electoral term, 94 of the bills that were introduced in the Bundestag and Bundesrat up to the beginning of October 2014 stemmed from government proposals, 37 were presented in motions tabled by *Länder*, and 31 were the product of initiatives from within the Bundestag, ten of them being introduced by groups belonging to the governing coalition. Mere statistical number games, however, do not provide unequivocal proof that the executive controls the legislature. The fact that the percentage of adopted bills introduced by Parliament is dwindling is due to the parliamentary roles played by the governing majority and the opposition, which ensure that bills tabled by the latter seldom have any chance of adoption by the Bundestag. In particular, moreover, a statistical breakdown alone provides no indication of the degree of informal parliamentary involvement in the legislative process.

This informal involvement occurs when those concerned – specialised politicians from the parliamentary groups, specialists from the departmental civil servants and, in some cases, external interested parties and advisers – exchange arguments, examine alternative proposals and gauge the prospects for an agreement.

These activities begin before the formal introduction of a bill. Indeed, it is standard practice at the operational level of the federal ministry charged with the preparation of a bill to engage in confidential consultations with specialised party politicians or spokespersons of the parliamentary groups on Bundestag committees even before the first departmental working paper or position paper has been compiled in order to assess whether the planned legislation is likely to be adopted and where potential pitfalls lie. Although Parliament as a whole is not involved in this process, selected parliamentarians do play an informal part in the departmental preparation of draft legislation.

In addition, during the deliberations in committee, the Bundestag retrieves some more of the influence it has allegedly lost. At this stage, parliamentarians, departmental civil servants, Bundesrat delegates representing the *Länder*, enlisted interest groups and – performing a coordinating role – the management of the parliamentary groups all work closely together. Although the parliamentary majority does not normally fail to do the bidding of the government, there are certainly opportunities for Members of Parliament, including those from the ranks of the opposition, to table amendments.

The practice of 'executive federalism'

Even in those other informal decision-making circles whose existence is frequently cited as evidence of parliamentary 'powerlessness', the Bundestag is not excluded – at least not entirely. This also applies to the power structure in the system of 'executive federalism'. There can be no doubt that administratively driven horizontal coordination among the *Länder*, whose ministers conclude agreements with each other on matters such as the reciprocal recognition of educational qualifications, undermines the decision-making sovereignty of the state parliaments. The only option for parliamentarians in the *Länder* is to give their retroactive approval to such agreements, which are concluded at the conferences of state premiers or departmental ministers, because anything else would jeopardise what is often a hard-won consensus among the *Länder*. It goes without saying, however, that this concerns the parliaments of the *Länder*, not the Bundestag.

The negotiating government

In cases where agreements are made between the Federation and the *Länder*, these contacts are also a matter for the departmental administrations in both tiers of government. But policy specialists from the majority groups in the Bundestag are regularly invited to the meetings between individual federal ministers and their state counterparts. At this pre-decision stage, then, selected representatives of the national parliament actually play a part. It would therefore be incorrect to make a sweeping statement to the effect that a 'negotiating government' is incompatible with parliamentary democracy. Extraparliamentary agreements need not always devalue Parliament and parliamentary procedures – not, at any rate, when the state negotiates 'in-house', as in the case of agreements between the Federation and the *Länder*. In the view of political scientist Arthur Benz, "Although negotiation and cooperation improve the effectiveness of government activity, they entail inequality of participatory opportunities, infringe the principle of open government and devalue democratic controls".

Government by expert commissions

"Commissions flourish as Parliament withers" ran the headline of an article by the journalist Robert Leicht in November 2001. This headline puts into words a sense of uneasiness which repeatedly surfaces in the public debate in Germany, a sense that the policymaking role of Parliament is being eclipsed and that political decisions are now being reached elsewhere: by commissions and councils which are set up by the Chancellor and which are known by resonant titles such as the National Ethics Council or by the name of their chairmen – Hartz, Rürup, etc. The tone there is set, says Leich, by the invited representatives of powerful interest groups who have no democratic legitimacy. It is only to be expected, he adds, that the negotiated consensus will take no account of the common good.

Yet even in the realm of 'government by commissions', the thesis of the disempowered Parliament rests on shaky foundations. It is true that the parliamentary groups in the Bundestag are not necessarily involved in the work of government-appointed commissions. This means that information, which is naturally an important resource for political decision-making, is liable to be unevenly distributed within the system of government. On the other hand, the Bundestag can appoint its own study commissions, which it has done time and again. Accordingly, there is no reason to deny governments the right to obtain specific information with the aid of commissions of experts.

In any event, this is by no means a new practice for the Federal Government. In 2003, Sven Siefken, a political scientist, produced figures showing that the number of specialised bodies commissioned by the Federal Government peaked in 1978, when more than 350 were active, that there were fewer than 200 in the early 1990s and that this figure fell to below 150, where it remained from the mid-nineties through the early years of the new century. This roughly corresponds to the level of such activity in the mid-1960s. On the other hand, wrote Siefken, the number of reports in German newspapers on these commissions of experts more than trebled in the period from 1995 to 2002. The alleged 'commissionitis' epidemic is thus revealed to be largely an artificial creation of the media. Moreover, all the practical cases which have been examined prove the point that the findings of commissions merely express recommendations, which are never translated lock, stock and barrel into statutory provisions but actually require a political decision in each case. Ultimately, the formal right of the Bundestag to take the final decision is not affected.

Statutory instruments and the EU as limitations on legislative competence

The two remaining factors do, however, demonstrably and tangibly limit the legislative competence of the Bundestag. One of these is the impact of the aforementioned statutory instruments

The Minister-Presidents of the *Länder* gather in the Federal Chancellery on 24 September 2015 for a Federal Government/*Länder* conference on the subject of asylum and refugee policy, which was chaired by Federal Chancellor Angela Merkel. The Heads of Government of the *Länder* had already deliberated on the subject at a Minister-Presidents' conference in June of that year. The first such gathering took place in early June 1947; the purpose of these conferences is to discuss issues specific to the *Länder* and to formulate common positions of the *Länder* governments.

Bundestag President Norbert Lammert, CDU/CSU (left), welcomes the members of the German Ethics Council on 28 April 2016. The Ethics Council is both a forum for dialogue and an advisory body and performs its duties on the basis of the Ethics Council Act of 1 August 2007. Half of its 26 members are proposed by the Federal Government and the other half by the Bundestag, all members being appointed by the President of the Federal Republic. To guarantee their independence, prospective members must not belong either to a legislative body of the Federal Republic or a *Land* or to the Federal Government or a *Land* government.

generated by the administration. The other is the steadily rising tide of EU laws and regulations. In the case of statutory instruments, these are legal instruments which are subordinate in status to Acts of Parliament and through which the limited delegated legislative powers of government ministries are exercised. The way in which the will of the legislature is implemented in individual cases and the discretionary powers at the disposal of the executive authorities are therefore largely determined by the executive itself.

Under Article 80 of the Basic Law, the delegation of the power to enact statutory instruments requires authorisation by law. This means that the empowering act must specify the content, purpose and scope of the statutory instrument to be issued. This constitutional safeguard, however, is evidently ineffective in many cases. Back in 1976, the study commission on constitutional reform appointed by the Bundestag strongly criticised this state of affairs. The volume of statutory instruments issued by the Federation alone doubled from 877 to 1,753 between the first and the thirteenth electoral terms of the Bundestag. The extent of these quasi-legislative powers which the administration has unceremoniously appropriated is therefore considerable. Thereafter, however, the number of these instruments plummeted, with a total of only 80 being enacted over the next five electoral terms as of October 2014.

The European Union also uses legislation as an instrument of control. The period since the 1960s has seen rapid growth in the body of European law. In the period from 1998 to 2004 alone, almost 19,000 European regulations and directives were adopted. The number of submissions from the European institutions that the Bundestag dealt with in its first 15 electoral terms, from 1949 to 2005, amounted to more than 21,000. In the 16th and 17th terms (2005–2013), there were another 8,208, of which 6,504 were Council proposals and 1,280 were European Parliament resolutions. Between the 1990–94 electoral term and the 2009–13 term, the number of these submissions doubled.

The figures reflect the unremitting process of legislative powers being transferred from the Member States to the supranational institutions. The national parliaments have seen their primary legislative competence diminish accordingly. In the case of directives, which are addressed to national parliaments and administrations for transposition into national law, the Bundestag does have a certain degree of discretion to implement the prescribed Community instrument within a timescale and in a form that accord with Germany's own legal tradition. By establishing a liaison office in Brussels in 2007 and its own in-house European Affairs Directorate, the Bundestag has also been trying to involve itself informally in the political processes of the EU at an earlier stage.

The rescue packages that are assembled within the EU to aid the recovery of financially weakened Member States present a new and formidable challenge, not only because of the sheer volumes of money involved but also because of the accompanying danger that they will curtail the budgetary control rights of national parliaments. In response to a series of actions brought by political parties and individual Members of Parliament, the Federal Constitutional Court has consistently ruled that the constant influence of the Bundestag must be preserved whenever Germany gives any guarantees in the framework of rescue programmes. Even in the decision-making system of the EU, which is characterised by intergovernmental decision-making procedures, the Court has ruled that the Bundestag must retain the right of oversight with regard to fundamental budgetary decisions and that its approval is required for each major federal measure of financial aid.

With Gunther Krichbaum (CDU/CSU), chairman of the Bundestag Committee on the Affairs of the European Union, presiding and with Federal Chancellor Angela Merkel (CDU/SCU) in attendance, a joint meeting takes place with the EU Affairs Committee of the National Assembly of the French Republic on 2 December 2015.

Sifted down to a small field and moderately polarised: political parties in the German Bundestag from 1949 to 1990

It was taken for granted by the victorious Allied powers in the watershed year of 1945 and by German politicians in the post-war years that political parties had a key mediating role to play between civil society and the newly emerging democratic state. The only point on which they differed was the pace at which the establishment of the democratic party system should proceed. The three Western occupying powers, with their authority to license political parties, wanted to confine the organisational development of parties to the municipal and county levels in the initial stages, in accordance with their strategy of controlled 'bottom-up' democratisation from the grass-roots level. Consequently, they did not permit the organisation of parties throughout their zones of occupation until the turn of the year (1945/46). Leading German politicians, however, such as Kurt Schumacher of the SPD and Konrad Adenauer, Jakob Kaiser and Ernst Lemmer, all from the CDU, systematically pre-empted this authorisation by taking informal action without delay, regardless of the Allies' phased plans, to hasten the establishment of regional and supraregional networks and coordination offices for their parties. In October 1945, the Bavarian offshoot of the Christian Democrats, the Christian Social Union (CSU), was founded in Würzburg.

By the time of the elections to the first German Bundestag, an effective party system had developed at the local, county and state levels in the three western zones. On 14 August 1949, representatives of eleven parties or other bodies and three independents took their seats in the Bundestag. The CDU/CSU won 31 % of the vote and 139 seats, the SPD 29.2 % (131), the FDP 11.9 % (52), the KPD 5.7 % (17), the Bavaria Party 4.2 % (17), the German Party (DP) 4 % (17), the Centre 3.1 % (10), the Union for Economic Reconstruction (*Wirtschaftliche Aufbau-Vereinigung – WAV*) 2.9 % (12), the German Right Party (*Deutsche Rechtspartei*) 1.8 % (5) and the Southern Schleswig Voters' Association 0.3 % of the vote and three seats. The Berlin House of Representatives sent eight of its members with purely consultative powers – five from the SPD, two from the CDU and one from the FDP.

In this multiplicity of political parties in the *Bundeshaus*, the federal parliament building in Bonn, concerned observers saw the spectre of Weimar, where the fragmentation of the party landscape had hindered stable government. In actual fact, their fears proved to be unfounded, because even that first election result of 1949 revealed the contours of the moderate bipolar party system which remained characteristic of the political landscape in the Federal Republic of Germany until 2005. Within the customary left-right spectrum of party-political affiliations, the areas to the left and right of the centre point are each occupied by a mass party. In 1949, the CDU/CSU and SPD together amassed more than 60 % of valid second votes cast. This concentration of votes on the two main parties became more marked in subsequent elections, varying between 75 % and more than 90 %. In the general election of 2005 their cumulative share dropped to 69.4 % – the first time after 1949 that it had fallen below the 70 % threshold. In the 2009 election, the cumulative vote of the CDU/CSU and SPD came to only 56.8 %, the lowest figure in any election to date. Four years later, however, in 2013, the two mass parties managed to pull out of this electoral nosedive, increasing their cumulative share of the vote by more than ten percentage points to 67.2 %.

The integrative power of the mass political parties

The initial wide diversity of parties represented in Parliament subsequently turned out to be a short-lived side effect of the transformation from dictatorship to democracy in 1945. At the time of the first general election in 1949, the German electorate

Photo call in the Bundestag for the first Federal Government immediately after being sworn in on 20 September 1949. First row, left to right: Anton Storch (CDU, Labour), Ludwig Erhard (CDU, Economics), Federal Chancellor and Minister for Foreign Affairs Konrad Adenauer (CDU), Franz Blücher (FDP, Marshall Plan Affairs), Jakob Kaiser (CDU, All-German Affairs), Hans Lukaschek (CDU, Expellees and Refugees). Second row, left to right: Wilhelm Niklas (CSU, Food), Eberhard Wildermuth (FDP, Housing Construction), Thomas Dehler (FDP, Justice). Third row, left to right: Heinrich Hellwege (DP, Bundesrat), Hans Schuberth (CSU, Post and Telecommunications), Gustav Heinemann (CDU, Interior), Fritz Schäffer (CSU, Finance) und Hans-Christoph Seebohm (DP, Transport).

had evidently not yet completed its adjustment to the new party-political constellation. Regional parties such as the German Party in Hanover or the arch-federalist Bavaria Party, as well as populist single-issue parties like the Union for Economic Reconstruction and right-wing conservative organisations like the German Right Party (renamed German *Reich* Party in 1950), initially experienced a wave of support that helped them to win seats in the Bundestag, although this was partly due to the less stringent limitation clause that applied in that first election. Alongside the CDU and CSU, the Centre also remained extant for a time, trying to maintain its tradition as a mass confessional party rallying the political support of the Catholic population. To the left of the SPD, the KPD continued to muster a hard core of voters on the Communist Left.

This diversity of parties had effectively come to an end by the time of the 1957 general election, when the CDU and CSU won an absolute majority of the vote (50.2 %) and of seats in the Bundestag (270); apart from the SPD, which had made slight gains and now had 31.8 % of the vote and 169 seats, the only other parties left in Parliament were the FDP with 41 and the German Party (DP) with 17 seats. The DP, in fact, only qualified for entry into the Bundestag by virtue of an electoral pact with the CDU, which enabled it to win the necessary number of safe constituency seats. By the time of the second election to the Bundestag, held in 1953, the small parties had already been decimated, with the Bavaria Party, the Centre, the Union for Economic Reconstruction, the Communists, the German *Reich* Party and the South Schleswig Voters' Association all failing to muster sufficient support to remain in Parliament. Only one new parliamentary group, the Pan-German Bloc of Expellees and Disempowered Persons (*Gesamtdeutscher Block der Heimatvertriebenen und Entrechteten – BHE*) won a place in the Bundestag in 1953. The integrative power of the two major parties, particularly the ecumenical rallying strategy of the CDU/CSU, designed to bring political Catholicism and committed Protestants under the umbrella of a single party, had already begun to bear fruit. Ten years had elapsed after the adoption of this strategy before the SPD undertook a comparable modernisation drive of its own in the form of its Godesberg Programme of 1959, which enshrined the party's endorsement of Western integration and the social market economy and enabled the Social Democrats to break the '30 % barrier' in elections and to start transforming themselves from a working-class party to a mass party in terms of both policy and voter acceptance.

Bans on political parties and the five-per-cent clause

As well as the centrifugal force of the mass political parties, which was fed by the lengthy period of unbroken economic growth in the Federal Republic that began in the early 1950s and continued until the mid-1960s, institutional factors such as changes to electoral law and the use of the power to ban unconstitutional political parties as defined by Article 21 of the Basic Law also contributed to a narrowing of the party-political spectrum. From the 1953 election, the five-per-cent clause applied throughout the Federal Republic in elections to the Bundestag. In that year, the BHE, the expellees' party, managed to secure election to the Bundestag with 5.9 % of the vote and 27 seats, but for the next three decades no new party succeeded in gaining entry to the Bundestag under its own steam by winning at least five per cent of the valid votes cast throughout the Federal Republic in a general election. The Centre managed to enter Parliament for one last time in 1953 on the coat-tails of the CDU, which stood aside in a safe constituency seat. Similar deals ensured that the DP would again be represented in the Bundestag by virtue of the 15 constituency seats it won in Lower Saxony, the CDU having waived the right to put up its own candidates

in eight constituencies. The right-wing extremist NPD failed in its attempt to enter Parliament in 1969, winning only 4.3 % of the vote. On the application of the Federal Government, the Federal Constitutional Court banned the right-wing extremist Socialist *Reich* Party (SRP) in 1952 and the Communist Party of Germany (KPD) in 1956 as unconstitutional parties. These bans helped to ensure that the membership of extremist parties on the far right and left of the German political spectrum dwindled to statistically insignificant levels, at which they remained for several decades.

Development of voter bases

Although the fragmentation of the party system in the Weimar Republic did not continue in the Federal Republic, there are numerous instances of Weimar traditions being carried forward into Bonn. Thirty-two of the 402 Members of the first Bundestag had belonged to the Reichstag before 1933 and some had even been deputies in the National Assembly of 1919. Likewise, voting patterns in the first parliamentary election in 1949 already showed signs of both continuity and change. Indeed, if we compare the 1949 election with the Reichstag elections of 1932, the CDU/CSU and the SPD registered above-average results in 1949 in the constituencies that had been their strongholds, or those of their political predecessors, in the Weimar period. This demonstrates that, even in that first post-war general election, both of the mass political parties in the Federal Republic succeeded in harnessing the electoral support of their traditional socio-economic constituencies – the Catholic voter base of the once-dominant Centre Party and the trade unionists and industrial workers who had voted for the older workers' parties. From this core of political allegiance were formed in the subsequent decades those stable 'social coalitions' which guaranteed the CDU/CSU and the SPD a reliable voter base that endured into the 1980s.

At an extraordinary SPD party congress in Bad Godesberg civic centre on 15 November 1959, the delegates adopted the new party policy programme, known as the Godesberg Programme, by a large majority. It transformed the SPD from a socialist labour party to a people's party and remained in force as the party programme until 1989; key elements of the programme still apply today.

Although social changes since then have been dissolving entrenched social structures and beliefs in inherited values and the binding power of social background has long since been eroded, the old alliances between each of the major parties and certain 'sympathising groups' within society are still recognisable in the voting patterns of the German electorate. In the general election of 2013, 39 % of trade-union members were still voting SPD. On the other side, the CDU and CSU remained predominant in their own ideological heartland, winning the votes of 72 % of Catholics with strong church links. Nevertheless, the parties' traditional voter bases are steadily dwindling. Conversely, the percentage of floating voters has been rocketing.

Clear majorities: governing coalitions and opposition in the Bundestag, 1949 to 1990

The relatively high degree of common political ground, particularly between the two mass parties, which is down to the existence of a broad middle class, has laid the parliamentary foundations for a stable system of government by coalition. This assertion does not overlook the fact that the history of the Federal Republic has also seen periods of sharp and uncompromising polarisation. The early pursuit of integration into the West, of the social market economy and of rearmament, aims which were achieved in the period from 1949 to 1957, was bitterly contested and created deep divisions between the positions of the governing majority and the opposition, as did the later conflict between advocates and opponents of the new *Ostpolitik*. The deep mutual distrust underlying the political atmosphere that developed during the first electoral term of the Bundestag is reflected in the genuine fears expressed by members of the SPD Executive after the 1953 election that the CDU would use its overwhelming electoral victory to remould West Germany's parliamentary democracy into an authoritarian regime. In the wider historical context, however, that sense of alarm was no more than a brief episode. What had a more lasting political impact was the fact that many of the great reforms enacted in the realm of social policy in the 1950s, such as the programme for the construction of publicly subsidised low-rent housing, the imposition of a levy for the equalisation of burdens arising from the National Socialist regime and the introduction of index-linked pensions, were adopted with the support of both the CDU/CSU and the Social Democrats.

The reduction of the political landscape to a small field of competing parties soon after the founding of the Federal Republic and the duopoly of the two major parties to the right and left of centre which existed from the outset in the Bundestag and encompassed the bulk of the electorate, coupled with the continuing weakness of parties on the far right and left of the political spectrum, permitted the formation of stable coalition governments from the very start. Even the first government under Konrad Adenauer, despite having the slimmest possible majority of one seat, was able to act without jeopardising its parliamentary position because it faced a fragmented opposition comprising a total of seven parliamentary groups or groupings. During the period from 1949 to 1965, the CDU, forming a united parliamentary group with its Bavarian sister party, the CSU, provided the Federal Chancellor in five successive coalition governments with various junior coalition partners. Although the CDU and CSU secured an absolute majority of votes and seats in the 1957 election, Konrad Adenauer decided that the German Party would continue to be represented in his cabinet.

After the 1961 election, in which the CDU/CSU won less than 50 % of the vote, Adenauer turned to the FDP this time to help him form his fourth government. Since the FDP, in its election campaign, had expressly opposed Adenauer's continuation in office, this U-turn saw it lampooned by its adversaries for many years as the 'doormat party'. In 1963, Ludwig Erhard, who had served for many years as Minister of Economic Affairs, replaced Adenauer as Federal Chancellor. Although he enjoyed great popularity as the 'father of the economic miracle', Erhard's spell as Federal Chancellor was dogged by political misfortune and lasted only three years. On 1 December 1966, in the course of the sixth electoral term, the CDU/CSU and SPD formed a grand coalition, led by Kurt Georg Kiesinger of the CDU.

The Grand Coalition of 1966

The three years of the first federal government to be formed by a grand coalition feature prominently in the historical sequence of German governments for two reasons. First of all, it provided the large parliamentary majority that was required for the implementation of major domestic reforms, some of which were fiercely contested. The Stability and Growth Act (*Stabilitäts- und Wachstumsgesetz*) of 1967 paved the way for an anti-cyclical budgetary policy and created macroeconomic control mechanisms that helped the government to overcome the Federal Republic's first appreciable economic recession, which occurred in 1966/67. The major fiscal reforms of 1969 extended the system of cooperative federalism by providing the aforementioned scope for joint federal and state funding, which is coming under increasing fire today as a manifestation of policy interlocking and was rolled back to some extent in 2006.

The emergency laws of 1967, which gave the Federal Government certain emergency powers in a state of tension, were condemned by some sections of the population, particularly the critical student generation, as a dangerous encroachment on fundamental rights and attacked as a prelude to 'government repression'. Another reason why the creation of the Grand Coalition encouraged the development of an extraparliamentary opposition was that the new coalition seemed to confirm a theory, derived from neo-Marxist ideology, that the Federal Republic was evolving into a one-party state.

Left: The departing Federal Chancellor Konrad Adenauer (right) in conversation with his successor, Ludwig Erhard (left) during a formal farewell banquet for Adenauer's cabinet in Palais Schaumburg, Bonn, on 11 October 1963. Adenauer's resignation cleared the way for the election of Erhard, who had served under him as Minister of Economics and, since 1957, as Vice-Chancellor. Adenauer did not believe that Erhard was chancellor material but did not manage to prevent his succession.

Opposite page, bottom left: On 30 November 1966, the CDU nominee for the chancellorship, Kurt Georg Kiesinger, and SPD chairman Willy Brandt announce the decision to form a Grand Coalition.

Opposite page, bottom right: Federal Chancellor Kurt Georg Kiesinger speaking in the Bundestag debate on emergency laws that were intended to permit restrictions on the exercise of fundamental rights. After a third reading, the bills were adopted with the votes of the CDU/CSU Members and a majority of the SPD Members. Because of their experiences from the Weimar period, the authors of the Basic Law had initially refrained from including emergency provisions for times of crisis.

Above: The Democracy in Crisis group (*Kuratorium 'Notstand der Demokratie'*) and the Campaign for Democracy and Disarmament organised marches converging on Bonn on 11 May 1968 to protest against the Grand Coalition's emergency legislation.

The period of the first CDU/CSU and SPD coalition is also of far-reaching importance because it laid the foundations for the first change in the main party of government in the Federal Republic. A fateful step was taken in this direction in 1967, when CDU politicians began to campaign for electoral reform with the aim of replacing the current additional-member system of proportional representation with a first-past-the-post system. This would inevitably have meant the end of FDP representation in Parliament. The fact that this move to amend the electoral law was thwarted by SPD opposition was no doubt instrumental in the decision of the FDP leadership to make an electoral pact with Willy Brandt on the evening of the general election of 1969.

The Social Democratic-Liberal governments

The early years of the SPD-FDP coalition, under the chancellorship of Willy Brandt, are associated with the new policy towards the countries of Eastern Europe (*Ostpolitik*) and with the programme of domestic reforms in the fields of justice, education and social policy. Both of these political projects, incidentally, helped to reconcile the representatives of the critical young generation to a great extent with the parliamentary system of government. Brandt himself personified a morally convincing desire to come to terms with Germany's National Socialist past. This, along with the oft-quoted slogan from his first government policy statement – "Let us risk more democracy" – built robust bridges to the extraparliamentary opposition. As a result of the reconciliation of younger people with the party system of government, the social profile of the SPD underwent quite dramatic change over a short period of time. The percentage of its membership under the age of 35 rose continuously from 55 % in 1969 to almost 66 % in 1971. The change of government in 1969 also indirectly accelerated the process of structural change in the CDU. The new and unaccustomed role in opposition compelled the CDU, as its leader, Kurt Georg Kiesinger, said at the time, "to act at long last on the intention we have been proclaiming for years of becoming a membership party too".

The guiding precepts of the second period of the Social Democratic-Liberal coalition, under the chancellorship of Helmut Schmidt, were continuity and concentration. The foreign and security policies introduced under Willy Brandt were continued. The signing of the Final Act of the Helsinki Conference on Security and Co-operation in Europe (CSCE) by both German States brought further progress in the 'normalisation' of their mutual relations. Internal security became more of a major political priority in the wake of terrorist acts perpetrated by the Red Army Faction. As in the first term of the SPD-FDP coalition government, its final days were marked by a gradual but irreversible erosion of its majority support, which is in striking contrast to the manifestly high degree of stability of all the other federal governments. Significantly, the only two constructive motions of no confidence that have ever been tabled in the history of the Bundestag both date from the period of the Centre-Left coalition. While Willy Brandt narrowly survived the first of these on 27 April 1972, the motion of 1 October 1982 to replace Helmut Schmidt as Chancellor with Helmut Kohl of the CDU was more successful. By deciding to change coalition partners, the FDP engineered the return to power of the CDU/CSU.

The subsequent Kohl era, which lasted for some 16 years, will go down in history on account of one event that eclipsed all others in his long period in office, namely the achievement of German unification. Before the window of reunification opened unexpectedly in the momentous year of 1989, much of Helmut Kohl's attention in the field of foreign policy had been focused on the aim of completing the project of European union, and indeed he achieved demonstrable successes in pursuit of that goal. The government's record in the field of domestic policy during his long chancellorship was less distinguished. Towards the end of the Kohl era, from about 1997, there was much public talk of a 'reform logjam'.

German student leader Rudi Dutschke (centre) and his wife Gretchen (left) at a demonstration. The protest movement against the emergency legislation spawned the Extraparliamentary Opposition (APO), which is often equated with the student movement. The main force behind the student APO, also known as the 1968 Movement, was the Socialist German Student League (SDS).

During his visit to the Polish capital on 7 December 1970, after laying a wreath at the memorial to those who lost their lives during the Warsaw Ghetto uprising, Federal Chancellor Willy Brandt kneels in their memory, a gesture that came to be known as the Warsaw Genuflexion. There followed the signing of the Treaty of Warsaw, which was part of the new *Ostpolitik* of the Social Democratic-Liberal coalition led by Brandt.

Top: Federal Chancellor Helmut Schmidt, Chairman of the GDR State Council Erich Honecker, U.S. President Gerald Ford and Austrian Federal Chancellor Bruno Kreisky at the Conference on Security and Co-operation in Europe (CSCE).The signing of the Final Act in Helsinki on 1 August 1975 also led to 'normalisation' of relations between the two German states.

Bottom left: Helmut Schmidt is sworn in as Federal Chancellor on 15 May 1974. He took over the office from Willy Brandt, who had resigned after one of his close aides had been exposed as a GDR agent. While in office, Schmidt had to deal with the economic recession and oil crises of the 1970s and the terrorist acts of the Red Army Faction.

Bottom right: Following the successful motion of no confidence tabled by the CDU/CSU and the FDP, Helmut Schmidt congratulates his successor, Helmut Kohl. In his 16 years in office, Chancellor Kohl guided the Federal Republic through the process of reunification and won praise for his contribution to the completion of European union.

Opposite page, left: Following negotiations with the foreign ministers of the Soviet Union, the GDR and Czechoslovakia on the margins of the UN General Assembly in New York, Federal Foreign Minister Hans-Dietrich Genscher arrived in the German Embassy in Prague on 30 September 1989. There was great jubilation when, at 6.58 p.m., he announced to the refugees gathered there that they had permission, with immediate effect, to leave the country and enter the Federal Republic.

Opposite page, right: In response to the mass demonstrations and the continuing 'desertion of the Republic', the SED government drafted a new Travel Act, which was to allow citizens of the GDR direct exit to the Federal Republic. At a press conference on the evening of 9 November 1989, Günter Schabowski, a member of the Politburo of the SED Central Committee and First Secretary of the Berlin District Executive of the SED, announced the immediate opening of the borders even before the border personnel had been informed. The fall of the Wall marked the start of the process of reunifying the divided country.

Towards the 'Third Republic' – German unification and its impact on the parliamentary system of government

In exceptional political situations, the executive normally takes centre stage. This is precisely what happened in the course of the historic events that culminated in German unification on 3 October 1990. As these events unfolded, the Governments of the Federal Republic and of the GDR, along with their senior officials, were cast in the leading roles. It was the heads of government, the ministers and the departmental specialists who prepared and conducted the negotiations with their counterparts in the other German Government and with the former occupying powers, which were still responsible in international law for 'Germany as a whole'.

There can therefore be no doubt that the government was in control of the unification process in 1989/90. None the less, the German Bundestag did not in any way content itself with a mere walk-on part. The fact is that, in a parliamentary system of government, it is the government majority in Parliament which empowers the Government to act and guarantees its freedom of action. Moreover, it is the sovereign Parliament that formally ratifies international agreements. It is not surprising, then, that the parliamentary groups of the governing coalition at that time, the CDU/CSU and FDP, were actively involved in planning the structure of the negotiations and contractual instruments which would establish a united Germany. In so far as the consent of the Bundesrat was required, the SPD, which was in the majority there, was also able to exert influence, even though it was in opposition in the Bundestag.

In September 1989, when signs of a crumbling East German state multiplied in the wake of the occupation of the West German embassies in Budapest, Prague and Warsaw by thousands of GDR citizens, the role of the Bundestag as a debating parliament also acquired greater prominence. Time and again, the parliamentary groups delivered statements on the German Question, which were intended less for internal consumption than for the public in both German States. Speakers from every group interpreted the mass flights to the embassy buildings of the Federal Republic as a verdict on the unwillingness of the East German leaders to contemplate reforms. On the evening of 9 November, a somewhat impromptu remark made by Günter Schabowski, a member of the SED Politburo, at a press conference resulted in the opening of the GDR's borders with the Federal Republic and of the Berlin Wall. In the Bundestag, where a law for the promotion of registered associations was being debated, the news triggered a spontaneous change of subject. Hans-Jochen Vogel (SPD), leader of the opposition, appealed to all parties in the Bundestag to "forget their disagreements and pull together" with a view to helping the people of the GDR to bring about change in their own country.

On 13 November, the People's Chamber, voting by secret ballot for the first time, elected a new President of the Chamber and then elected Hans Modrow (SED) as the new Chairman of the Council of Ministers. During the budget debate in the Bundestag on 28 November 1989, Chancellor Helmut Kohl presented his ten-point programme, in which he proposed a phased plan for the unification of Germany. In point 5, he stated that the Federal Government was prepared "to develop confederative structures between the two states in Germany with a view to creating a federation, that is to say a federal state structure, in Germany." Helmut Kohl formulated the strategic vision more explicitly in point 10: "Reunification – that is regaining national unity – remains the political goal of the Federal Government".

MANDATSENTZUG
DDR-MILITÄR
ASTERIX ins Politbüro!
98,8
ABBAU DER
NEUES DENKEN
FREIHEIT
Viele Worte
Abschaffung der Privilegien
Neues Wahlgesetz
Reisefreiheit für Alle
LEGALISIEREN STATT KRIMINALISIEREN!
Die Regierung kann man ändern
MACHT MONOPOL
Neid!
I. LANGE
M. MÜLLER
LORENZ

Left: A kaleidoscope of banners on Alexanderplatz in Berlin on 4 November 1989. This was the largest demonstration since the birth of the GDR, attended by more than half a million GDR citizens. They called for more democracy and reforms. The first of the 'Monday demonstrations' had taken place in Leipzig on 4 September 1989, but during that autumn people took to the streets in many other GDR cities and on other days of the week too, chanting *Wir sind das Volk* ('We are the people').

Cross-border traffic at the Invalidenstrasse crossing on 10 November 1989, the day after the borders were opened. The previous evening, following the announcement of the new Travel Act, thousands of people had clamoured for immediate opening of the borders, even before the border personnel had been informed. The first GDR citizens to cross the border were Annemarie Reffert and her 16-year-old daughter, who were cleared to drive across from Marienborn to Helmstedt on showing their identity cards at 9.15 p.m.

The SPD parliamentary group expressed approval of Kohl's programme. The Greens, on the other hand, reaffirmed their commitment to a strict policy of preserving two States. There was, they said, "no sound reason" for reunification. After Helmut Kohl's visit to Moscow on 10 February 1990, during which the Soviet President and General Secretary Mikhail Gorbachev had given the green light for unification, SPD group chairman Hans-Jochen Vogel, speaking in the Bundestag, called on the Federal Government to cooperate more closely with Parliament in all matters relating to German unification. He proposed the establishment of a joint committee of the Bundestag and Bundesrat to deliberate on any impending decisions.

On the following day, a committee on German unity was indeed established, albeit a cabinet committee to assist the Government. Its various working parties were to deal with the imminent establishment of an economic and monetary union. There were heated exchanges in the Bundestag debate of 15 February on the German Question as several state premiers from the SPD intervened in the debate to assert the right of the *Länder* to participate in any decision on the creation of an enlarged federally structured Germany including the territory of the GDR. Chancellor Kohl denied the *Länder* their wish to be involved in the negotiations on the proposed economic and monetary union but did agree that preparations for the negotiations with the GDR should be made jointly with the heads of government of the *Länder*.

On 18 March, free elections to the People's Chamber were held in the GDR. The result was a clear victory for the CDU and the small parties with which it had formed the Alliance for Germany. The Social Democrats and Liberals were also represented in the new government in East Berlin. On 12 April, Lothar de Maizière (CDU) was elected premier by 265 to 108 votes; the Party of Democratic Socialism (PDS), Alliance 90/The Greens and the Democratic Farmers' Party and Democratic Women's Federation of Germany voted against de Maizière.

On 21 June, the Bundestag and the People's Chamber ratified the Treaty establishing a Monetary, Economic and Social Union and simultaneously approved identical resolutions on the German-Polish frontier, in which assurances were given that the existing border between Poland and Germany was regarded as the definitive frontier and that Germany would not assert any territorial claims against Poland. In the Bundestag, 60 Members of Parliament from the ranks of the Greens and the SPD voted against the Treaty establishing a Monetary, Economic and Social Union, while 15 Members from the CDU/CSU parliamentary group refused to approve the resolution on the German-Polish frontier.

Accession of the GDR to the area of application of the Basic Law

On 23 August 1990, the new freely elected People's Chamber decided by a large majority of 294 to 62, with seven abstentions, that the GDR would accede to the area of application of the Basic Law. On the following day, the party leaders in Bonn set up five working parties to discuss outstanding issues such as the restitution of private property in the GDR and the possibility that a new constitution would have to be drafted. On 20 September, at its last sitting prior to unification, the Bundestag ratified the Unification Treaty by an overwhelming majority of 442 to 47, with three abstentions. On the same day, the People's Chamber approved the Treaty by 299 to 80 votes, with one abstention.

On 28 November 1989, during a debate at second reading of the Budget Bill for 1990 in the temporary seat of Parliament in the former Bonn Waterworks, Federal Chancellor Helmut Kohl presented his ten-point programme to overcome the division of Germany and of Europe. This programme provided for 'confederal structures' linking the two German states during a transitional stage, which would culminate in the establishment of a "federation, a federal system of government".

Federal Chancellor Helmut Kohl with Mikhail Gorbachev, General Secretary of the Soviet Communist Party, at their Moscow talks of 10 February 1990. During these talks, Gorbachev still opposed NATO membership for a reunited Germany, seeking to prevent any weakening of the Warsaw Pact. The Western Powers, however, regarded NATO membership as an imperative requirement. The Soviet Union ultimately ceded to their wish.

Constituent sitting on 5 April 1990 of the first People's Chamber to be elected freely by secret ballot in the GDR. Sabine Bergmann-Pohl (CDU), who was elected President of the Chamber, is the central figure in the foreground.

GDR Minister-President Lothar de Maizière, Federal Chancellor Helmut Kohl, GDR Finance Minister Walter Romberg and Federal Finance Minister Theo Waigel (right) toast the signing of the State Treaty between the Federal Republic of Germany and the German Democratic Republic establishing a Monetary, Economic and Social Union. The Treaty was signed in Bonn on 18 May 1990 and entered into force on 1 July 1990.

The Members of the Bundestag and of the GDR People's Chamber met in the Reichstag building in Berlin on 4 October 1990 to set their seal on German unification, which had taken formal effect the previous evening. The photograph shows former Federal Chancellor Willy Brandt addressing the Parliament of the whole of Germany. Among those on the government bench are Helmut Kohl, Hans-Dietrich Genscher, Wolfgang Schäuble, Theo Waigel and Norbert Blüm.

für gepflegte Wäsche
Perwoll
Lenor

Wir gestalten für Sie
am 2.7.1990
öffnen wir
bereits um 9⁰⁰

On 1 July 1990, the State Treaty between the Federal Republic of Germany and the German Democratic Republic establishing a Monetary, Economic and Social Union entered into force, which was a decisive step towards reunification of the two German states. From that time on, the deutschmark was the sole legal tender in the GDR, and GDR marks could be exchanged for the new currency. There followed a veritable stampede for the coveted western money; in the first few hours of monetary union, it is estimated that a total of more than 2.6 billion deutschmarks was paid out to citizens of the GDR.

schaften oder gemäß entsprechenden Rechtsakten der Europäischen Gemeinschaften durch Rechtsverordnung die Anwendung und Durchführung des Europäischen Gemeinschaftsrechts oder des auf Grund dieses Rechts ergangenen Bundesrechts in dem in Artikel 3 des Vertrages genannten Gebiet teilweise aufzuschieben, zu erleichtern und die betroffenen Rechtsvorschriften anzupassen; dies gilt insbesondere für die von den Europäischen Gemeinschaften getroffenen Regelungen des Umwelt-, Verkehrs-, Agrar- und Arbeitsschutzrechts und für die zur Verwirklichung des Binnenmarktes geltenden Rechtsakte der Europäischen Gemeinschaften im Warenverkehr und bei der Dienstleistungs- und Niederlassungsfreiheit. Verordnungsermächtigungen in anderen Vorschriften bleiben unberührt.

Artikel 5

Rückkehr zum einheitlichen Verordnungsrang, Aufhebung und Änderung von Verwaltungsvorschriften

(1) Die auf der Anlage I zu Artikel 8 des Vertrages beruhenden Teile der dort geänderten Rechtsverordnungen sowie die Maßgaben zu Rechtsverordnungen können auf Grund und im Rahmen der jeweils einschlägigen Ermächtigungen durch Rechtsverordnung geändert werden. Das auf Grund von Artikel 9 Abs. 2 bis 4 in Verbindung mit Anlage II zu dem Vertrag im Range einer Rechtsverordnung fortbestehende Bundesrecht sowie die Maßgaben dazu können durch Rechtsverordnung geändert oder aufgehoben werden.

(2) Soweit Verwaltungsvorschriften der Deutschen Demokratischen Republik nach Artikel 9 Abs. 2 in Verbindung mit Anlage II zu dem Vertrag fortbestehen, können sie durch Verwaltungsvorschrift geändert oder aufgehoben werden.

Artikel 6

Neufassung der durch den Vertrag geänderten Gesetze

Der jeweils zuständige Bundesminister kann den Wortlaut eines durch den Vertrag geänderten Gesetzes in der am Tage nach der Verkündung dieses Gesetzes oder der am Tage des Inkrafttretens der Änderung geltenden Fassung im Bundesgesetzblatt bekanntmachen.

Artikel 7

Berlin-Klausel

Dieses Gesetz gilt auch im Land Berlin, sofern das Land Berlin die Anwendung dieses Gesetzes feststellt. Rechtsverordnungen, die auf Grund dieses Gesetzes erlassen werden, gelten im Land Berlin nach § 14 des Dritten Überleitungsgesetzes.

Artikel 8

Inkrafttreten

(1) Dieses Gesetz tritt am Tage nach seiner Verkündung in Kraft.

(2) Der Tag, an dem der Vertrag einschließlich der in Artikel 1 Satz 1 aufgeführten weiteren Urkunden nach Artikel 45 des Vertrages zwischen der Bundesrepublik Deutschland und der Deutschen Demokratischen Republik über die Herstellung der Einheit Deutschlands in Kraft tritt, ist im Bundesgesetzblatt bekanntzugeben.

Das vorstehende Gesetz wird hiermit ausgefertigt und wird im Bundesgesetzblatt verkündet.

Bonn, den 23. September 1990

Der Bundespräsident

Der Bundeskanzler

Der Bundesminister des Innern

2

Der Bundesminister des Auswärtigen

Der Bundesminister der Finanzen

Der Bundesminister für Ernährung, Landwirtschaft und Forsten

Der Bundesminister für Arbeit und Sozialordnung

Der Bundesminister für Jugend, Familie, Frauen und Gesundheit

Der Bundesminister für Umwelt, Naturschutz und Reaktorsicherheit

Der Bundesminister für Raumordnung, Bauwesen und Städtebau

Der Bundesminister für Bildung und Wissenschaft

Der Bundesminister der Justiz

Der Bundesminister für Wirtschaft

Der Bundesminister für innerdeutsche Beziehungen

Der Bundesminister der Verteidigung

Für den Bundesminister für Verkehr
Der Bundesminister für Post und Telekommunikation

Der Bundesminister für Post und Telekommunikation

Der Bundesminister für Forschung und Technologie

Der Bundesminister für wirtschaftliche Zusammenarbeit

After the first State Treaty, that is to say the Treaty of 18 May 1990 establishing a Monetary, Economic and Social Union, had established social and monetary unity between the two German states, political unity was established by the Unification Treaty of 31 August. The Treaty dissolved the German Democratic Republic by virtue of the latter's accession to the Federal Republic of Germany and so unified Germany. The Treaty entered into force on 29 September 1990.

When unification took effect on 3 October 1990, the territory covered by the constitutional and political institutions of the Federal Republic of Germany was extended to eastern Germany. The term *Institutionentransfer* ('institutional transfer') was coined to describe the process, which had begun before 3 October, of dismantling, restructuring and rebuilding the long-established public institutions and bodies of the GDR and introducing West German institutions and rules to replace those of the East. This transfer involved not only Federal German constitutional and statute law but also the institutional powers and regulatory mechanisms of parliamentary democracy, such as the federal structure, local government, the quasi-governmental system of welfare provision supported by independent agencies and the party system. On 3 October, the districts into which the territory of the GDR had been divided for administrative purposes were dissolved and replaced by the restoration within their old boundaries of the five East German *Länder* of Brandenburg, Mecklenburg-Western Pomerania, Saxony, Saxony-Anhalt and Thuringia.

Convergence problems

The overnight switch to unfamiliar institutions, such as laws based on the West German legal tradition, the principle of the rule of law and parliamentary procedures in a pluralist democracy, demanded enormous adaptation efforts on the part of the East German people, some of whom found the experience painful and unjust. The process of adapting mentally to the new situation was made all the more difficult by the abandonment of the existing economic system that followed the economic and political collapse of the GDR. Nevertheless, a great deal of progress was achieved in modernising outdated East German industrial plants, in merging the systems of social security into a single German system and in renovating the failing infrastructure under the 'Solidarity Pact' by means of regular transfers of financial resources from the federal treasury and the western *Länder*. Economists have calculated that the net transfer from east to west in the period from 1990 to 2013 amounted to almost two trillion euros. Although this special form of financial redistribution within Germany is far from having covered the entire social costs arising from the legacy of the GDR, it has certainly cushioned their impact.

West Germans and East Germans, then, have been equally involved, albeit in different ways, in this continuous process of gradual convergence between the two worlds and the divided cultures in which they used to live. The fact that this process has nevertheless been remarkably peaceable cannot be ascribed solely to the constant flow of financial assistance. On the contrary, the growth of a sense of community is also due to the fact that unification has certainly not been a one-sided process of adaptation by the East to the West German model. Where West German institutions have been transferred and adopted, researchers largely agree that distinct East German paths to development have been mapped out and followed. This was the case with the restructuring of labour markets and corporate production, with the development of democratic awareness, with the application of West German statute law, with the parliamentary style adopted by East German Members of the Bundestag and with the founding and development of regional associations of the national political parties. Moreover, western institutions have also adapted to eastern practices. For example, the stronger elements of direct democracy embedded in the new constitutions of the East German *Länder* resulted in the subsequent reform of the constitutions of the old *Länder* to bring them into line.

The foreign ministers of the two German states and of the four victorious powers of the Second World War met on 5 May 1990 in Bonn for an initial round of 'Two-Plus-Four' talks. The negotiations focused on the external aspects of German unification. The photograph shows the foreign ministers' press conference in the Maritim Hotel, Bonn. Left to right: Eduard Shevardnadze (USSR), Roland Dumas (France), Markus Meckel (GDR), Hans-Dietrich Genscher (Federal Republic of Germany), Douglas Hurd (United Kingdom) and James A. Baker (United States).

At the constituent meeting of the first Bundestag of united Germany in the Reichstag building, Berlin, on 20 December 1990, 77-year-old Willy Brandt, Honorary Chairman of the SPD and President by age of the Bundestag, delivered the opening speech. In the elections of 2 December 1990, the CDU/CSU and the FDP together had obtained a sufficient majority to govern, and so the coalition under Helmut Kohl formed the Federal Government once again.

The quintessentially East German features of the political transformation of 1989/90 – the role of the mass demonstrations as a driving force of the peaceful revolution, the key political role played by the citizens' action movements and the status of the 'Round Tables' as universally recognised steering bodies with self-endowed general political and executive powers – were crucial to the successful conversion from Communist dictatorship to parliamentary democracy; from the historical perspective, however, they were ultimately transitional in character. Only some of the leading ideologists of the opposition movement remained politically active in the newly formed parties and elected assemblies. The Round Tables could not be a permanent substitute for democratically legitimised parliaments either. They had served their purpose once free parliamentary elections marked the end of the transitional stage of tentative democracy. Most of all, the spontaneity of the mass demonstrations could not possibly be sustained.

Be that as it may, the 'East German path to development' was not simply abandoned once German unity became an everyday fact of life, nor did it remain a transitory phenomenon. As mentioned above, this is observable in the way in which federal institutions were subject to alterations and special arrangements when they began to operate in eastern Germany; some of these institutions, in fact, also underwent nationwide change as a result of unification. For example, although the 'refederalisation of the GDR' through the restoration of the five eastern *Länder* was already prefigured in the Basic Law, the fact that the parliaments of those *Länder* chose not only to strengthen the direct legislative powers of the people in their constitutions but also to limit the powers of state governments by granting more extensive rights to the opposition and the state parliaments has lent the politics of the East German *Länder* its own distinctive profile.

Relatively little, on the other hand, came out of the Joint Commission of the Bundestag and Bundesrat on the Constitution, which, acting on a mandate contained in Article 5 of the Unification Treaty, examined the Basic Law with a view to assessing the need for reforms. Of the amendments proposed on 28 October 1993, only a few proved capable of obtaining the requisite majority in the Bundestag. Protection of the environment was incorporated into the Basic Law as a state goal (Article 20a). Article 72(2), the clause defining the reasons which would warrant regulation by federal legislation, was watered down, the criterion of imperative need giving way to that of necessity. One reason for this was the need to ensure that the state could continue to play an effective part in forging a common identity among the people of Germany. Since then, federal legislation has been warranted if it serves to maintain equivalent rather than equal living conditions. The proposed inclusion of a provision in the Basic Law for popular initiatives, public petitions for a referendum and referendums at the national level was not supported by the requisite two-thirds majority of the Joint Commission on the Constitution.

Direct democracy is held in conspicuously high regard by leaders in eastern Germany as well as by the population there. In 1990, Germans were asked in a survey what they regarded as the essential elements of democracy. While no fewer than 55 % of West Germans opted for "public participation in many decisions", the same response was chosen by 68 % of East Germans. "Referendums on important issues" were favoured by 75 % of East German respondents, compared with 52 % of the West Germans. In other respects, there was already a remarkably high degree of consensus in both parts of Germany, even in 1990, the year of unification, on basic democratic principles such as fundamental rights, elections by secret ballot, the multiparty system and the primacy of the rule of law.

The party system after unification

The party landscape in West and East Germany is largely uniform, following the expansion of the field of activity of West German parties into the new *Länder*. This trend is emphasised by the observable nationwide consolidation in recent years of a left-wing party that was previously confined to East Germany, namely The Left Party/PDS. In more recent times, newly created parties such as the Pirates and Alternative for Germany (AfD) have operated nationwide from the outset.

The transfer of the West German party system as a result of unification was prefigured in the results of the election to the People's Chamber on 18 March 1990, when the CDU surprisingly emerged as the clear victor with 40.8 % of the vote. The German Social Union (*Deutsche Soziale Union*), its partner in the Alliance for Germany, polled 6.3 %. The SPD obtained 21.9 % of the vote and the PDS, the successor party to the SED, 16.4 %. The Liberals (Free Democratic Federation – DFP, LDP and FDP) polled 5.3 %. The aggregate share of the vote won by Alliance 90 and The Greens, still campaigning separately at this stage, came to 4.9 %.

The party-political constellation that developed in East Germany in the wake of these elections may be described as tripolar, with the CDU and the SPD being joined by the PDS, which later became The Left Party, as a thirdmajor political party. The PDS took on the role of a party representing regional interests, focusing chiefly on eastern Germany. The FDP (except in Saxony and Saxony-Anhalt) and Alliance 90/The Greens were no more than small marginalised parties, particularly in elections to the state parliaments. Other characteristics of the East German party landscape that are still recognisable to this day are a relatively low degree of party affiliation, a smaller membership base, a sparser network of branches and the lack of historically rooted recruitment patterns in elections. Since the traditional links between the working class and the Social Democrats were severed during the GDR era and since Catholics account for a tiny minority – about three per cent – of the East German population, the SPD and CDU have been unable to tap into traditional voter bases linked to either party by history, trade unionism or religious affiliations. In general, the political parties in eastern Germany are even more male-dominated than in the west, they are more secular, and – with the exception of the Left Party – their membership is younger.

The consolidation of The Left Party as an eastern party is the only phenomenon that may be interpreted as a coalition formed between a political party and certain groups in society united by common interests and values. The fact that The Left Party has managed to retain the electoral support of many of the "psychological losers of unification" – in other words, higher-ranking officials who, though not necessarily unemployed now, have been deprived of their career prospects and their privileged social status – is a form of integration that has undoubtedly helped to consolidate the democratic political system in eastern Germany.

On 20 June 1991, the Bundestag adopted the decision on the seat of parliament and government, as a result of which the Bundestag moved to the capital city, Berlin. The photograph shows the debate leading up to this decision in the plenary chamber in the old Bonn waterworks. The formalities of the removal were later regulated by the Act Implementing the German Bundestag Decision of 20 June 1991 on Completion of the Unification of Germany, known for short as the Bonn-Berlin Act, which was adopted on 26 April 1994.

Impact on the Bundestag

Next to the Bundesrat, the German Bundestag is the constitutional organ that has undergone the most extensive institutional change as a result of unification. The first outward sign of this change was the presence in the Bundestag on Unification Day of 144 East German Members appointed by the People's Chamber. Further changes came with the amendment of the Federal Electoral Act before the elections to the Bundestag on 12 December 1990 for its twelfth electoral term, its first as the Parliament of a united Germany. The number of seats was increased from 518 to 656, excluding overhang mandates; this new total, however, was reduced to 598 in 2002. Seventy-two new constituencies were created in the new federal states. On account of 24 overhang mandates, all of which without exception were won by the CDU/CSU, the total number of Members rose again in 2009 from the regular figure of 598 to 622. As the result of an amendment to the electoral law, the 18th Bundestag, elected in 2013, contains 631 Members, including four with overhang mandates and 29 with balancing mandates.

The original intention of the legislature that the conventional limitation clause which required parties to obtain 5 % of the total vote to qualify for entry into Parliament should continue to apply throughout the Federal Republic in 1990 was overruled by the Federal Constitutional Court on the grounds that it would unfairly restrict competition between the political parties. There was only a three-month period, said the judges, between the creation of the national electoral territory and the date of the first national elections. This, they objected, "deprives a number of parties of an adequate opportunity to extend their area of operation to electoral territory which is new to them and to put their case and campaign for votes in that territory with any prospect of success".

The amended Electoral Act provided for a separate 5 % barrier in East and West Germany. If a party achieved 5 % of the vote in only one of the two parts of Germany, its regional lists of candidates were taken into account in the distribution of parliamentary seats in the other part too. In the Bundestag election of 1990, the PDS and Alliance 90/The Greens benefited from this provision. The PDS polled 11.1 % of second votes in the eastern *Länder* but only 0.3 % in the West; this represented a 2.4 % share of the national vote. The West German Greens, with 4.8 % of the second vote, would have fallen below the cut-off point under the old limitation clause, but they obtained entry to the 12th German Bundestag by virtue of the fact that the East German Alliance 90 movement, which was running with the Greens on a united party list, won 6 % of the eastern vote. There are clear parallels with the situation in the early history of the Federal Republic from 1949 to 1957. At that time too, the provisions of electoral law, acting as an institutional filter, influenced the development of the party system, albeit in the opposite direction. Whereas the Electoral Act curbed the fragmentation of the party landscape in those days, in 1990 it created the conditions for a larger number of parties to operate at the national level.

The early general election of 18 September 2005 altered this party constellation quite significantly, both in eastern Germany and in the Federal Republic as a whole. The PDS, which had won more than three constituency seats in 1994 and 5.1 % of the second vote in 1998, thereby avoiding elimination under the limitation clause, but had then seen its share of the vote fall to 4 % in 2002, leaving it with only two constituency seats in the Bundestag, secured 8.7 % of the second vote in its new Left Party/PDS constellation, which made it a larger parliamentary group than that of the Greens. In eastern Germany, The Left Party made substantial gains, increasing the PDS vote by 8.5 percentage points, and the 4.9 % it polled in the west was within touching distance of the five-per-cent threshold. The new alliance of the Left formed by the PDS and WASG had thus established itself as a fifth national force in the Federal German party system, which was confirmed by subsequent state election results in three western *Länder* – Bremen, Lower Saxony and Hamburg.

The Greens (8.1 % – down 0.5 of a percentage point) and the FDP (9.8 % – up 2.4 points) changed places in 2005. The stalemate between the two major parliamentary groups persisted, with a slight shift in the balance – the CDU/CSU polling 35.2 % of the vote, while the SPD obtained 34.3 %. Since The Left Party was not regarded by the other parties – or even by its own leaders – as a potential member of a governing coalition and other coalition formats (a 'black and yellow' alliance of CDU/CSU and FDP or a 'red and green' pact between the SPD and the Greens) could not muster a parliamentary majority, the only option left was the formation of a grand coalition.

The Bundestag elections of 2009 significantly shifted the political balance once again. As the electoral researchers of Infratest Dimap observed, that election "confirmed the five-party system established at the time of reunification but shifted the balance clearly in favour of the small parties in the Bundestag". While the CDU/CSU more or less held their ground, slipping by only 1.4 percentage points to 33.8 %, SPD losses went into double figures, at 11.2 percentage points, leaving the Social Democrats with 23 % of the vote. The FDP secured 14.6 % of the vote, an increase of 4.7 percentage points, The Left Party increased its share of the vote by 3.2 percentage points to 11.9 %, and The Greens obtained 10.7 %, 2.6 percentage points more than in 2005. With 322 seats, the new Federal Government, a coalition of CDU/CSU and FDP, had a stable parliamentary majority.

In the 2013 general election, the CDU/CSU consolidated their position as the largest parliamentary group with 41.5 % of the vote. The SPD recovered some of its lost ground with a 25.7 % share. The Left Party (8.6 %) and The Greens (8.4 %) both suffered losses. The FDP vote slumped by a hefty 9.8 percentage points to only 4.8 %, which meant that no FDP members were returned to Parliament. The Alternative for Germany (AfD) party, newcomers to the party system, obtained 4.7 % of the vote and

The transfer of the seat of parliament and government from Bonn to Berlin was largely effected in the summer of 1999. The Federal Government and the legislature, however, retained some second seats in Bonn, which has resulted in the Federal Republic having a 'split' seat of government today. Left: items bound for Berlin await removal in front of the Bundestag Building in Bonn. Right: furniture removers bring packing cases into the Reichstag building through the east entrance.

The Treaty of Lisbon, initially known as the Reform Treaty or as the Basic Treaty of the European Union, was signed on 13 December 2007 under the Portuguese presidency of the Council and entered into force on 1 December 2009. It reformed the EU Treaty and the EC Treaty. The image shows Hans-Gert Poettering, President of the European Parliament, delivering a speech during the signing ceremony in Lisbon.

so likewise fell victim to the 5 % limitation clause. The new Grand Coalition of CDU/CSU and SPD amassed a combined total of 504 seats, giving it an overwhelming majority over the opposition parties, which had a total of 127 seats.

From mass party to cartel party? Transformation of the party system

According to the spirit of the Basic Law, the political parties are non-governmental bodies and are not therefore directly affected by plans to reform the system of government. Nevertheless, the parties are, of necessity, involved in the reform project – on the one hand, because they are supposed to rally public support for the reform policy and, on the other hand, because the key functions of the parties do not become dispensable in a leaner and more efficiently organised state. Even in a reformed and possibly more competitive federal system, the key role of party politicians in forging links between the various tiers and arenas of political activity will remain a vital factor.

The parties themselves, moreover, have long been profoundly affected by the reform debate. Especially in the period since the major parties began to experience falling, and at times plummeting, membership figures, they have had to consider how long they can continue, with a shrinking organisational structure, to perform their traditional functions of articulating the needs of society, recruiting political staff and providing channels of communication between the government and those it governs. The model of a 'cartel party', which enjoys a degree of currency in party literature, is not a desirable option in a party democracy. A party of this type, run professionally by an elite cartel of full-time political managers who are remote from the party's grass roots and transformed into a 'government agency', is no substitute for a mass political party, which, though it may often be maligned for trying to be all things to all people, remains dependent on a committed membership. The fact that the current German party system is far from conducive to the triumphant ascent of the cartel party augurs well for the future.

Can the Bundestag remain 'EU-compatible'?

For a long time, many political observers took it as read that the Bundestag, like the parliaments of other EU Member States, could be regarded as one of the losers of the European integration process because its powers of legislation and oversight were diminished whenever decision-making competence on matters of national importance was conferred on the EU. There seemed to be no doubt that the direction in which the multi-tiered European system was developing would result in national parliaments no longer overseeing the executive in their own countries and in governments, which were the decision-making bodies in the EU framework, effectively controlling the parliaments of their respective countries. This reversal of the primacy of Parliament was cemented in the wake of the European financial crisis, because the Bundestag, like its European sister parliaments, assumed a share of political responsibility for rescue packages worth billions of euros without any direct right of oversight over the Head of Government who was helping to reach decisions on these matters in the Council of the EU.

The Treaty of Lisbon concluded by the EU Member States and subsequent judgments of the Federal Constitutional Court, however, have gone some way to redressing the skewed division of powers in the multi-tiered European system in favour of the Bundestag. The Treaty of Lisbon vested national and subnational parliaments within the EU with the right to conduct what are known as subsidiarity checks. The basis for these checks is prior information from the EU institutions about their projects. The Bundestag is one of the participants in this 'early-warning system'. Moreover, in its 2009 judgment on the Act Approving the Treaty of Lisbon, the Federal Constitutional Court found that the Bundestag had a wide-ranging general responsibility in matters of budgetary policy. This means that Parliament must be involved whenever powers to take decisions with budgetary implications are conferred on a supranational organisation. In this way the traditional budgetary sovereignty of Parliament, that is to say the right to determine the type and volume of government revenue and expenditure, is to be preserved.

Institutional adjustments of this kind, by their very nature, cannot entirely offset the asymmetry of information that characterises the multi-tiered European system. Recent research by political scientists, however, has established that parliamentary players operating 'between Berlin and Brussels' have long since developed strategies of their own to narrow the information gap experienced by national – in this case German – politicians regarding EU policies in their respective specialised fields. Coordination between the European Parliament, the Bundestag, the *Länder* parliaments and parliamentarians of other member countries has now become the norm within political parties as well as within specialised policy areas. By establishing its own European Affairs Directorate within its administrative structure, the Bundestag has increased its capacity to process information. This, admittedly, has not established parity between the information at the disposal of the EU executive and that which is available to the Bundestag, for the flood of rules that emanates steadily from the EU makes it difficult for the Bundestag to digest all new developments, if only because of their sheer quantity. There is no doubt scope for further improvement in information management and for closer scrutiny. Nevertheless, the present set-up enables the Bundestag to display a considerable degree of 'EU-compatibility'.

This photograph, taken on 2 July 2014, shows the inside of the plenary chamber of the European Parliament. The Treaty of Lisbon considerably widened the powers of the European Parliament. Together with the Council of the European Union, it is now responsible for both legislation and approval of the budget.

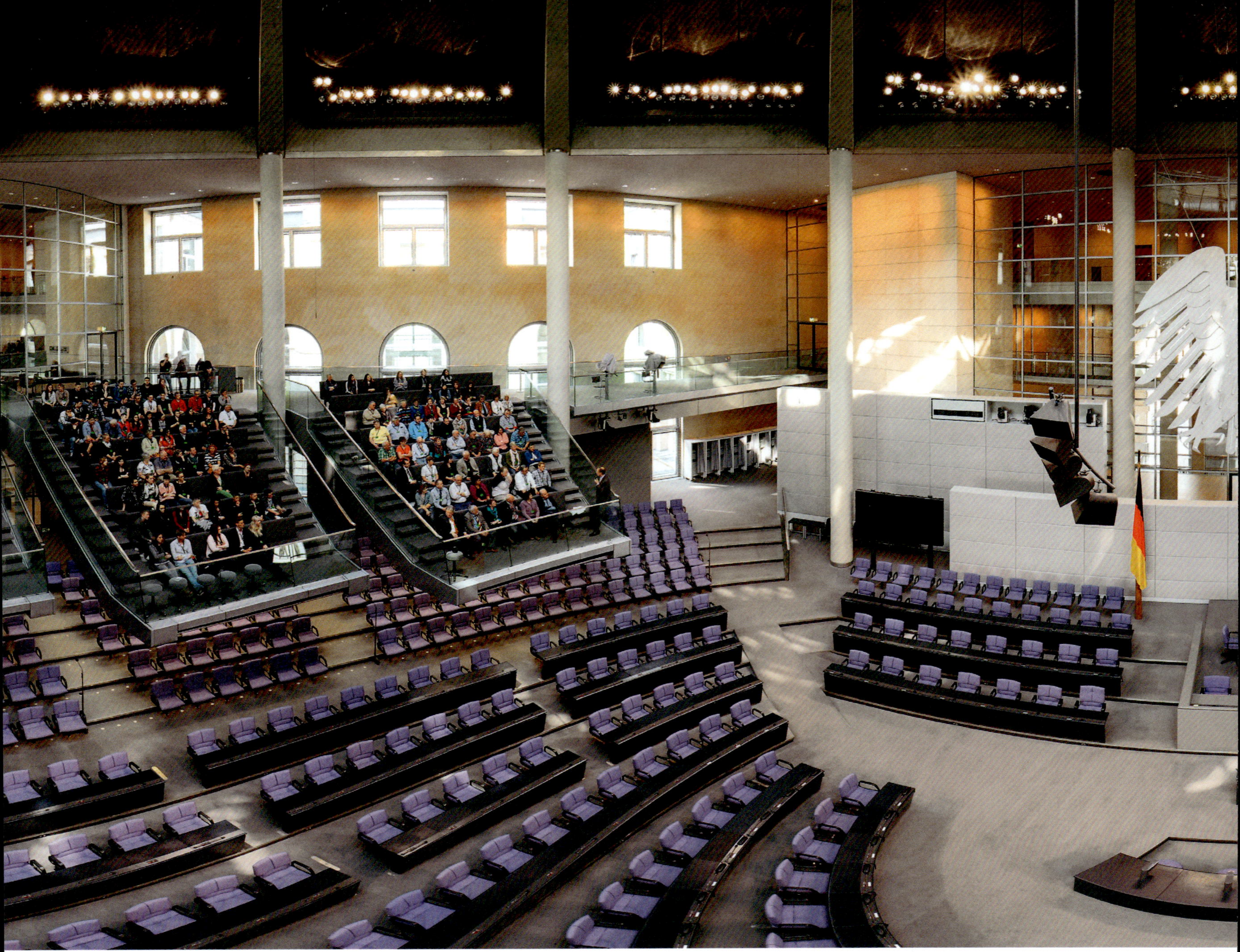

Functions, organisation and decision-making processes of the German Bundestag

Wolfgang Ismayr

Introduction

The German Bundestag was a cornerstone of the constitutional system of the 'old' Federal Republic and has remained so since the unification of Germany on 3 October 1990. This continues to apply despite manifold processes of social, technological and political change, culminating in the European integration process, which have increased the demands placed on the Parliament and Government in their work. Moreover, governments are now expected to be more open to public scrutiny in their political decision-making and to maintain a flow of communication to grass-roots party organisations and the general public. Since moving from Bonn to Berlin, the new federal capital, in 1999, the Members of the Bundestag have been operating in a new environment.

The plenary chamber, shown here during the 20th sitting of the Bundestag on 13 March 2014, is the largest place of assembly in the Reichstag building. Besides the Bundestag, the Federal Convention also meets here. The chamber is entirely surrounded by glazing, though which it can be viewed from outside at any time and which symbolises the transparency of parliamentary business.

Parliamentary democracy

The Parliamentary Council, comprising representatives of the regional parliaments, in fulfilling its mandate to draft a provisional constitution in 1948/49, emphasised the pivotal role of the Bundestag in the parliamentary system of government of the Federal Republic of Germany. As the only central organ of the constitution which is directly elected by the people, the Bundestag enjoys a particularly high degree of democratic legitimacy and bears special responsibility. In contrast to most other parliamentary democracies, Germany has a head of government (the Federal Chancellor) who is formally elected by Parliament. The Bundestag can even elect a different person from the one proposed by the Head of State (the President of the Federal Republic), whose right of proposal is limited to the first round of voting. In addition, the position of the head of government in relation to the head of state is considerably stronger now than it was in the constitution of the Weimar Republic. The President of the Federal Republic only possesses indirect democratic legitimacy, and the presidential role is largely confined to ceremonial duties. By contrast with the Weimar Republic and with numerous Western democracies, in the Federal Republic a binding vote of no confidence can only target the head of government, not individual ministers. A Federal Chancellor, and hence the government too, cannot be unseated in this way unless the Bundestag, in passing its vote of no confidence by an absolute majority, also elects a new Chancellor (constructive vote of no confidence).

Furthermore, unlike the constitutions of the federal states (*Länder*) that were adopted before it, the Basic Law (*Grundgesetz*) makes no provision for any form of direct democracy other than that prescribed by Article 29 in the event of any proposed reorganisation of the federal territory. Another defining feature of the constitutional order is the explicit recognition of political parties in the constitution and the provision in Article 21 for a Political Parties Act (the *Parteiengesetz*) regulating details of the democratic principles to which the internal organisation of political parties must conform. There is also the possibility of having the Federal Constitutional Court review legislation for conformity with the Basic Law.

The aforementioned provisions regarding the right of the Bundestag, directly elected by the people, to vote the head of government into and out of office laid the constitutional foundations for a parliamentary democratic system of government. In this system, the government is dependent for its survival on the confidence of a parliamentary majority. In a multi-party democracy, the political consequence of this fundamental constitutional decision is a close link between the government and the parliamentary majority on whose support it depends. The role of the opposition groups in this case is to scrutinise the actions of the government publicly, to criticise it and to formulate alternatives to the policies of the governing majority. In a departure from the 'classic' dualism of parliament and government that characterises constitutional monarchies and presidential systems of government, this 'new dualism' of governing majority and opposition groups has taken root to a certain extent in the Federal Republic of Germany as in other countries. This development has been fostered on the one hand by the fact that government ministers are generally Members of the Bundestag and attend the internal meetings of their respective parliamentary groups, but a more significant factor in promoting this development has been the emergence in practice of a bipolar system comprising three to five parties represented in the Bundestag.

It would be wrong, however, to superimpose onto the German political system the premises underlying the British two-party system of democracy. The reasons for this lie in the fact that coalition governments are the norm in Germany, in the very prominent role of the Federal Constitutional Court, in the federal system and, increasingly, in the transfer of powers to the European Union. These factors give rise to a wide range of negotiation processes which, to some extent, lessen the impact of competition between the parties.

Federalism and the role of the Bundesrat

The process of formulating political aims and arriving at decisions in the Federal Republic of Germany is strongly influenced by the federal structure of the country and the specific role of the Bundesrat. While legislative powers lie primarily with the Federation, the constituent states (*Länder*) and local authorities are largely responsible for applying the law. The Bundesrat, comprising members of the state governments, is unique in the world as far as its composition and working methods are concerned. It was not designed by the Parliamentary Council to rank alongside the Bundestag as the second chamber of a single legislative entity, nor, in constitutional terms, has it been allotted such a role today. With its right to initiate legislation, to veto any of a large number of laws that require its assent and to lodge an objection to any other federal laws, however, the Bundesrat is akin to a parliamentary body in functional terms. It also possesses significant executive powers.

As its political clout has increased, party politics and the formation of blocs have come to play a far greater part in the workings of the Bundesrat since 1969. The progressive transfer of legislative powers to the Federation, with the Bundesrat participating in the legislative process, has weakened the parliaments of the *Länder* on the one hand, but on the other hand it has meant closer involvement in federal lawmaking for members of the state governments represented in the Bundesrat and their senior civil servants. The same applies to the Federal Government's statutory instruments. Power does not truly change hands at the national level unless a change of government, based on a majority for a party or alliance of parties in the Bundestag, is reinforced by a pro-government majority in the Bundesrat. The consequence of this is that the parliamentary elections in the 16 federal states have increasingly been dominated by national politics. Fluctuations between more confrontational and more cooperative phases of the democratic process, depending on the party-political composition of the Bundesrat, are a particular feature of parliamentary life in the Federal Republic of Germany. The aim of the numerous constitutional amendments enacted in connection with the first stage of reform of the federal system in 2006 was to enhance the effectiveness of both the Bundestag and the *Land* parliaments and to improve the quality of legislation. This aim was to be achieved by means of provisions reducing the number of laws that require the consent of the Bundesrat as well as by transferring legislative powers and assigning them more clearly. Even after these reforms, the Bundesrat has remained a key player in the German system of government.

The Members of Parliament

Party allegiance and increasing professionalism

The Bundestag is characterised by a strongly party-political orientation and a marked division of responsibilities, both of these features having become more distinctive with the passage of time. The political parties have a *de facto* monopoly when it comes to determining who sits in Parliament. Since the second parliamentary election, held in 1953, all Members of the Bundestag have been elected as the constituency candidate of a political party or as one of the candidates on a party list; almost all of them have also been party members. Not least among the reasons for this is the electoral system itself. Since the start of the 15th electoral term in 2002, by which time a decision had been taken to reduce the number of Members for the sake of greater efficiency, the Bundestag has comprised at least 598 Members. On German reunification in 1990, the number of constituencies had been increased from 248 to 328.

In Article 38, the Basic Law merely establishes the principle of general, direct, free, equal and secret elections. The electoral system, on the other hand – the additional-member system of proportional representation – is laid down in the Federal Electoral Act (*Bundeswahlgesetz*). Under the additional-member system, the electorate uses its first vote to return a candidate from each of the single-member constituencies, which have numbered 299 since the general election of 2002. The same number of parliamentary seats is distributed on the sole basis of the second vote, which is cast for a *Land* party list. Where a

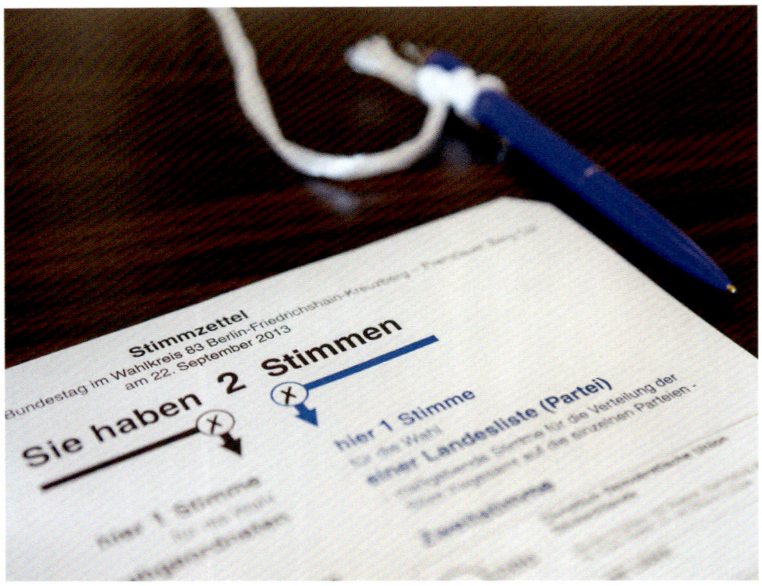

Ballot paper for the election of the 18th Bundestag. In Bundestag elections as well as in elections to many of the *Land* parliaments, voters cast their first vote for a candidate standing in their constituency. The candidate with the largest number of votes wins the constituency seat in the Bundestag.

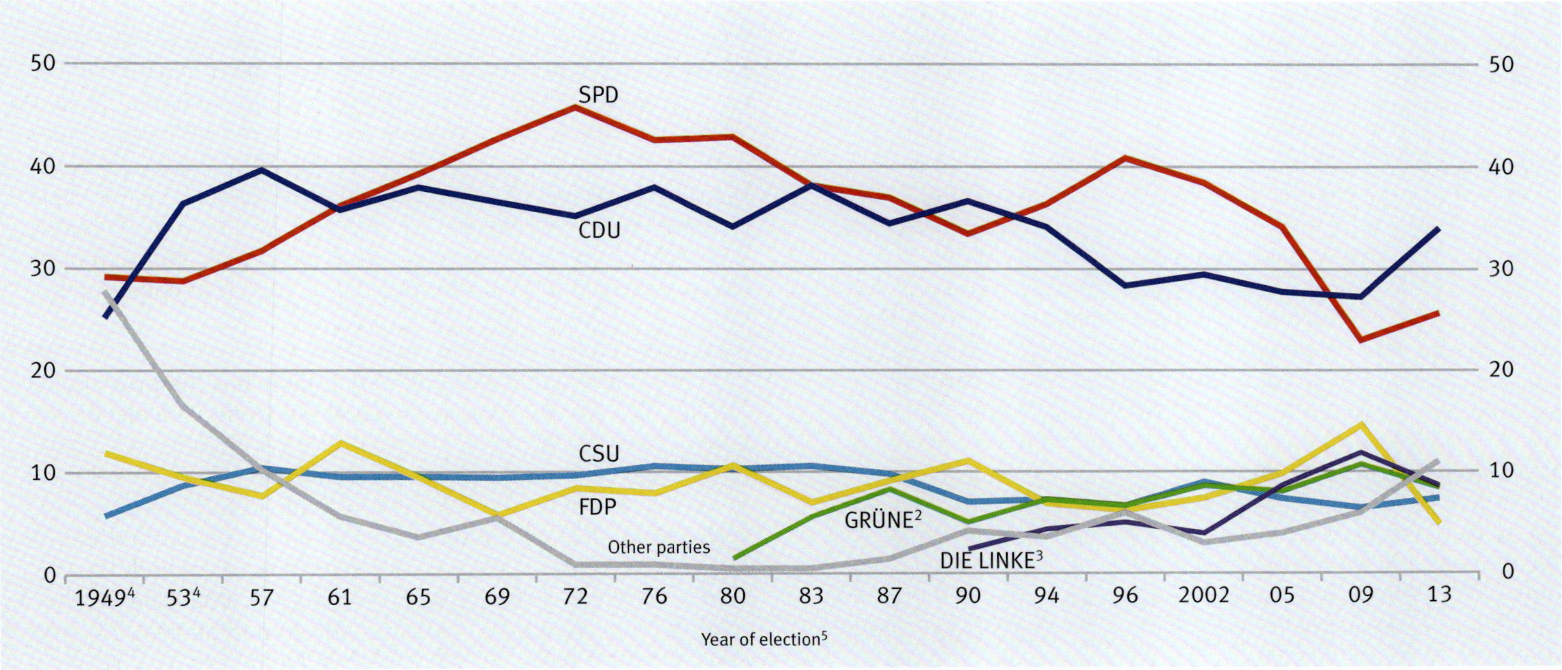

Percentages of the valid second votes since 1949:
Voters cast their second vote for a party and so determine the distribution of seats in the Bundestag. If a party wins more constituency seats in a *Land* by virtue of first votes than its percentage of the second votes would merit, extra parliamentary seats – 'overhang mandates' – are created, which also influence the distribution of seats in Parliament.

1 Second votes since 1953
2 The Greens (since 1990: Alliance 90/The Greens)
3 The Left Party (PDS until 17 July 2005)
4 Without Saarland
5 Elections from 1990 onwards cover the territory that has belonged to the Federal Republic since 3 October 1990.

party has more of its constituency candidates elected to the Bundestag from a particular *Land* than it would be entitled to on the basis of its share of second votes in that *Land*, this results in additional seats, called 'overhang mandates'. Since 2013, the law governing elections to the Bundestag has fully offset overhang mandates with balancing mandates for the other parties. Because of these overhang and balancing mandates, the 18th Bundestag, which was elected in September 2013, comprises 631 Members.

One significant curtailment of the principle of proportional representation, introduced for the sake of governability, is the clause under which the seats filled from party lists are distributed among the parties that obtain at least five per cent of the second votes cast throughout the Federal Republic or, as in the case of the PDS in 1994, win at least three constituency seats. People who vote for smaller parties in particular often tend to cast their first and second votes for different parties, and in this way they can express, for example, their preference for a particular coalition. As a result of the close collaboration between the government and the groups forming the parliamentary majority, not only the Federal Chancellor but also the federal ministers are generally prominent representatives of their respective parties. As in most Western European systems, they need not be Members of Parliament, but the Constitution provides for that possibility. This has been conducive to the formation of governments on the basis of party politics.

Holding office in local and regional party organisations is an important and indeed almost indispensable stage in the career of any politician who aspires to a seat in the Bundestag. A further successful apprenticeship in parliamentary-group and party posts is regarded as the normal road to ministerial office. Even after being elected to the Bundestag, more than half of all Members of Parliament remain office-bearers in their local or regional party organisations, while about a quarter keep their electoral mandates in local government, often for a long period of time. In addition, most Members of Parliament hold posts on the district, regional and national executive committees and specialised commissions of political parties and associations. Members of Parliament attach top priority to their work in specialised party bodies, in particular. The career profile and duties of a Member of Parliament favour candidates from occupations close to the world of politics, such as lawyers, teachers and lecturers, white-collar employees in the private sector and the staff of political parties and associations.

With an estimated working week of 60 to 70 hours, the Members of the Bundestag are, with few exceptions, full-time parliamentarians. This workload is generally maintained even in weeks when the House is not sitting. In their constituencies, Members of Parliament are expected to maintain a frequent presence and to have a ready ear for the interests of the region and the concerns of individuals and plead their case in the federal capital.

Under Article 48 of the Basic Law, "Members shall be entitled to remuneration adequate to ensure their independence". The Federal Constitutional Court also takes the view, expressed in its landmark 1975 judgement on Members' remuneration, that what was once a form of voluntary service has become a full-time profession. Since then, the level of Members' remuneration has gradually been adapted to reflect this. At the present time, Members of Parliament receive euros 9,082 per month. This is supplemented, under the heading of Members' allowances, by a tax-free, flat-rate expenses allowance of about euros 4,300. Under the terms of a judgment delivered by the Federal Constitutional Court, the Members of Parliament themselves must regularly determine the amount of their remuneration. In so doing, they use as their reference framework the monthly remuneration of a judge at a supreme federal court. Besides their pay and allowances, Members of the Bundestag receive a generous pension on reaching retirement age. Under the rules that have been in force since 2008, superannuation benefits amount to 2.5 % of Members' remuneration for one full year of service and are increased by another 2.5 % for each additional year of membership. The maximum pension amounts to 67.5 % of the Members' remuneration rate and is payable only after 27 years' service.

Since 1969, resources have been available to each Member of the Bundestag for the employment of personal staff, and this allocation was increased in 2015 to euros 16,019 per month (gross). The Bundestag Administration directly pays the staff employed by Members, excluding the Member's spouse, relatives and in-laws. Of the 4,400 or so members of staff who currently work for Members of Parliament, mainly on a part-time basis, slightly more than half are employed in constituency offices. Members and their staff can also make use of the non-partisan Research Service of the Bundestag Administration, which were founded in 1970/71 with approximately 60 research analysts, although it should also be said that the capacity of the services has scarcely been expanded since its creation. It is part of the Directorate-General for Research and External Relations, which comprises the Directorates for Research Services, International Relations and Petitions and Submissions. Other directorates-general in the Bundestag administration, which is staffed by about 2,900 people, are the Directorate-General for Parliament and Members, which includes the Parliamentary Services and Services for Members Directorates, the Directorate-General for Information and Documentation and the Directorate-General for Central Services. The offices of the Members, the parliamentary groups and the Bundestag administration are equipped with all the appropriate information and communication technology.

The federal budget also funds the support services for the parliamentary groups, which employ some 900 personnel. Their subject specialists, however, primarily assist the group leadership and the chairs of working groups. Opposition groups, which receive a supplementary opposition allowance, rely more heavily on these support services than groups in governing coalitions, which have far more ready access to the assistance of the departmental civil service.

On the day after her election as Germany's first woman chancellor on 22 November 2005, a photograph of Angela Merkel is hung in the Berlin restaurant *KanzlerEck* alongside portraits of the previous federal chancellors. Top row, from left: Konrad Adenauer (CDU), Ludwig Erhard (CDU), Kurt Georg Kiesinger (CDU) and Willy Brandt (SPD); bottom row, from left: Helmut Schmidt (SPD), Helmut Kohl (CDU) and Gerhard Schröder (SPD).

Professional and interest profiles

Some 90 % of Members of Parliament have university degrees. About a third of all Members have been recruited from the public sector, approximately one in three of them from teaching professions. Private-sector employees, self-employed persons and members of the liberal professions account for almost two fifths of the Members of the Bundestag, but their representation is considerably higher in the CDU/CSU and – until its exit from the Bundestag in 2013 – the FDP than in the other parliamentary groups. This difference is greatest in the category of self-employed persons in industry, trade and the crafts sector as well as in agriculture. Only a very few manual workers and housewives have seats in the Bundestag.

The data on occupational structure and activity in associations indicate marked differences in interest profiles within the parliamentary groups and committees. It may be assumed that membership of associations will shape Members' responses to particular issues and give certain associations a greater chance of influencing parliamentary decision-making. Trade-union officials are to be found primarily in the ranks of the SPD parliamentary group, while members of bodies representing entrepreneurs, owners of small and medium-sized businesses and the liberal professions are found chiefly in the CDU/CSU parliamentary group.

Since the 1980s the percentage of women in Parliament has steadily risen and amounted to 36.8 % in March 2016. Not least among the reasons for this are quota arrangements governing the selection of candidates for election to the Bundestag. Women also hold about a third of the executive offices in Parliament, although this figure varies widely between the individual bodies and parliamentary groups.

The scope for individual Members to influence political decisions

When the Bundestag is first constituted after a general election, the Members of Parliament belonging to a given party form a parliamentary group. Under the Bundestag Rules of Procedure, it takes at least five per cent of the Members of the Bundestag to form a parliamentary group; at the time of writing, this means 31 Members. These Members must belong to the same party or – to quote the additional wording inserted in 1969 for the sake of the CDU and CSU – to parties which, on account of similar political aims, do not compete with each other in any *Land*. Since then, the CDU and the CSU have been able to form a joint group for each electoral term, which they had done ever since 1949, without having to seek the approval of the House.

Members cannot normally exercise their rights effectively unless they belong to such a group. The Federal Constitutional Court has recognised the practical importance of parliamentary groups in a multiparty democracy, emphasising that they are "determinant factors in the political opinion-forming process". The Court, however, saw no need for enshrinement of their legal status. Likewise, the new Parliamentary Groups Act (*Fraktionsgesetz*), which entered into force in 1995 as an integral component of the Members of the Bundestag Act (*Abgeordnetengesetz*), confines itself to laying down the main rights and responsibilities of parliamentary groups.

For many years, beginning with the fourth electoral term (1961–1965), there were only three political groups, two of which would form the governing coalition. After the Green Party first entered the Bundestag in 1983, the Opposition comprised two parliamentary groups – except in the 12th electoral term from 1990 to 1994 – which competed with each other as well as challenging the government of the day. This constellation has influenced the nature and intensity of the processes by which aims

In the 1983 parliamentary elections, The Greens won their first seats in the Bundestag. The new Members were conspicuous by their unorthodox clothing – trainers, jeans and sweaters – and by their frequent outdoor meetings and the introduction of an official bicycle. In May 1993 they merged with the GDR civil-rights movement *Bündnis 90* (Alliance 90) to form the new party Alliance 90/The Greens.

are formulated and decisions taken within the parliamentary groups. In the 14th electoral term (1998–2002), the PDS also achieved the status of a parliamentary group (*Fraktion*) after having been a grouping (*Gruppe*), a smaller body of party members with almost the same rights as a parliamentary group, in the Bundestag since 1990. After power changed hands in October 1998, the new governing coalition of SPD and Alliance 90/The Greens was faced with opposition parties on the Right and Left of the political spectrum (the CDU/CSU and FDP on the one hand and the PDS on the other), the first such scenario since the 1950s. In the 2002 general election, the PDS failed to achieve the five per cent of the votes needed for representation in parliament. The Opposition to the governing coalition of SPD and Alliance 90/The Greens was thus formed by the Centre-Right CDU/CSU and FDP groups alone. There were also two non-attached PDS Members who won constituency seats. In the 16th Bundestag, which was elected in 2005, the large parliamentary groups of the CDU/CSU and SPD sustained a coalition government, while the small groups – the FDP, Alliance 90/The Greens and The Left Party – the former PDS – formed the Opposition. After the general election of 2009, the reins of government were back in the hands of a Centre-Right coalition of CDU/CSU and FDP, while the Opposition comprised three parties – the SPD, Alliance 90/The Greens and The Left Party. The consequence of the altered party constellation was that parliamentary consultation processes became more difficult. Although all of the parties had come out against a Grand Coalition before the 2013 general election, following a lengthy process of exploratory discussions and negotiations another Grand Coalition of CDU/CSU and SPD materialised after all in the autumn of 2013. For the first time, the FDP was absent from the Bundestag. Moreover, the Opposition groups – Alliance 90/The Greens and The Left Party – commanded only 20 % of the seats in total, which made for hard bargaining on parliamentary minority rights.

The rights of minorities in the Bundestag have been gradually strengthened, particularly since the parliamentary reforms of 1969/70. There are no specific opposition rights as such. The rights of the Opposition were chiefly strengthened by virtue of measures to enhance the rights of parliamentary groups and minorities, which took account of the requirements of a multi-party parliament.

Under the Rules of Procedure of the Bundestag, each Member of Parliament possesses the following rights:

– the right to move amendments to bills at the committee stage and at second reading; in the case of other items presented to Parliament with only one reading, amendments may be tabled at the single reading;

– the right to engage in the work of parliamentary committees;

– the right to ask the Federal Government for oral and written answers to specific questions;

– the right to participate in debates and votes;

– the right to make statements on debates, on votes and on matters not included in the agenda and to raise points of order;

– the right to inspect all files in the safekeeping of the Bundestag administration or a parliamentary committee;

– the right to move an amendment to the agenda after the opening of a plenary sitting but before the first item has been called;

– the right to move that a question about to be put to the vote be separated into parts.

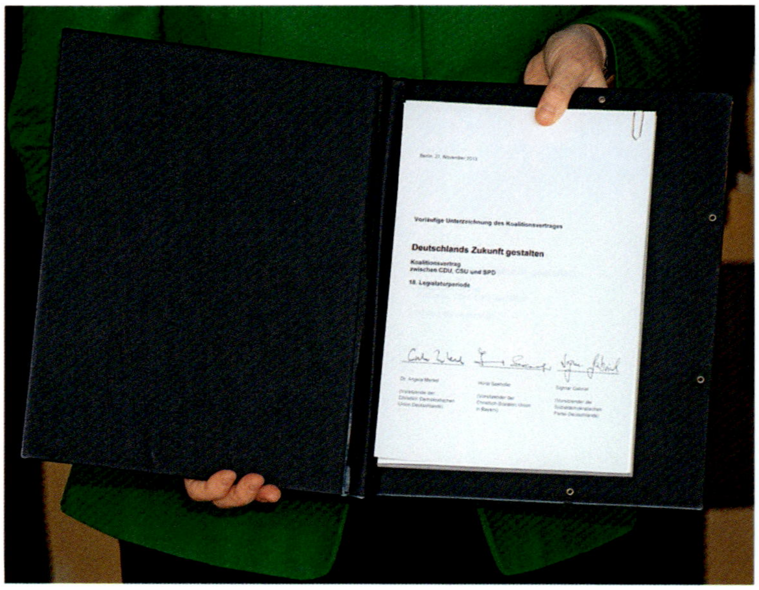

On 27 November 2013, following lengthy exploratory soundings and a binding vote by the SPD membership, the chairpersons of the three coalescing parties – (left to right:) Sigmar Gabriel (SPD), Angela Merkel (CDU) and Horst Seehofer (CSU) – sign the agreement establishing a Grand Coalition.

The rules of procedure of the parliamentary groups and the constraints of parliamentary practice, however, can also effectively restrict these rights. This applies especially to participation in debates, which is largely determined by the rules laid down by each group or its parliamentary secretaries. Amendments tabled by individual Members scarcely feature at all. Anyone tabling a motion without having consulted his or her parliamentary group is generally considered to be offending against the principle of group solidarity.

Individual Members do not have the right to initiate legislation. As part of the parliamentary reform process in 1969/70, a quorum of five per cent of the Members of the Bundestag was laid down for most types of parliamentary motion and for the exercise of other minority rights. Apart from amendments, all initiatives (proposals) require the support of a parliamentary group or of a corresponding number of Members. Under the existing rules, various minority rights cannot be exercised unless at least 25 % of Members support motions to that effect. These included the right to require the appointment of a Committee of Inquiry or a Study Commission or to insist on the lead committee holding a public hearing. For the 18th electoral term, an addition was made to the Bundestag Rules of Procedure to ensure that the opposition groups could exercise these rights jointly, even though the two groups together hold only 127 of the 631 seats. The support of only 120 Members from any parliamentary group or groups is now needed, for example, to require the appointment of a committee of inquiry.

If Members wish to launch an initiative, they must begin by seeking support within their own parliamentary group. In so doing, they have to be prepared for complex decision-making structures and for an often circuitous succession of work processes and information channels. They must take account of the division of responsibilities within the hierarchically structured group and the sensitivities of group officials. An individual's potential role and influence depend on factors such as his or her status within the parliamentary-group hierarchy, the support he or she enjoys from the various group and party factions and, last but not least, whether he or she is considered responsible for addressing a particular issue.

The structure and decision-making processes of parliamentary groups

The organisation of the Bundestag and its parliamentary groups is based on a strict division of responsibilities. Structures of this type were adopted as a means of dealing with the diversity and complexity of the Bundestag's legislative and oversight functions. The responsibilities assigned to the specialised parliamentary committees and the corresponding working groups established by the parliamentary groups are largely based on the departmental structure of the government. The increasingly specialised nature of the work of these bodies has made coordination more and more essential. Strategic coordination of the manifold activities of Parliament is as necessary as it is difficult. The process of reaching decisions within a parliamentary group not only involves the chairperson and the executive; a major role is also played by the working groups, and numerous informal coordination and advisory bodies are also involved in the process before a general meeting of the parliamentary group can take the final decision.

The structures and decision-making processes of the various parliamentary groups have much in common, but they also differ markedly in some respects. The main differences occur between the large and small groups. Needless to say, whether a group is in government or opposition also influences its working methods.

The regular meetings of parliamentary-group bodies take place on Mondays and Tuesdays of sitting weeks. This means that they precede the meetings of the parliamentary committees, which are held on Wednesdays, and the plenary sittings, which take place from Wednesday to Friday.

Working groups

In the large parliamentary groups, i.e. those of the SPD and CDU/CSU, working groups (*Arbeitsgruppen*), comprising the members of the parliamentary group who belong to a particular Bundestag committee, are the basic units where the bulk of political activity takes place. In the small groups, namely those of the FDP, Alliance 90/The Greens and The Left Party, the working groups are still known as *Arbeitskreise* and are wider in scope. The far smaller number of Members in those groups is reason enough for this choice of structure. The *Arbeitskreise* of these parliamentary groups are each responsible for the spheres of activity of two or more parliamentary committees.

In the large parliamentary groups, a specialised system of rapporteurs has been developed. The individual members of the working groups look after particular areas of political activity, generally for the whole electoral term, and normally act as their group's rapporteur on that area of activity within the parliamentary committee. This specialisation, percolating right down into the working groups, has become a characteristic feature of the decision-making process. Both of the large parliamentary groups expect their new members to begin by familiarising themselves with a specialised area and to prove themselves as rapporteurs. Such a highly refined system of rapporteurs cannot develop within small groups, whose members have to cover a far wider range of policy areas; this is reflected in a heavy workload. On the other hand, the individual Members from these groups have a better chance to make their mark in Parliament and in the public domain and to familiarise themselves with the content of several ministerial portfolios.

Concerning the leadership of the working groups and the way their work ties into that of the parliamentary group as a whole, there are marked differences between the CDU/CSU and the SPD. In both cases, the chairs of the working groups are their spokespersons within and outside the parliamentary group. Whereas the SPD working-group chairpersons also speak for the parliamentary group on the relevant parliamentary committee, however, these duties are split in the CDU/CSU group, where the deputy chairs of the working groups are responsible for coordinating the work of the parliamentary-group members in committee.

The main priorities for the working groups are the preparation of the next committee meeting and of the plenary debates for the current week's sittings; they also discuss internal initiatives and formulate opinions on proposals presented by the government, by rival parliamentary groups and by other bodies within their own group. Lastly, the working groups of the majority groups discuss planned government projects. If the plenary agenda includes a debate on a topic that falls within the remit of the working group, speakers are designated to address the House on behalf of the parliamentary group.

Interest groups and wings within the parliamentary groups

In the CDU/CSU parliamentary group there are also six 'sociological groupings': a group representing employees' interests, the SME Circle, a women's group, a young Members' group, a group of Members responsible for expellees, repatriates and German minorities and a local-government group. The influence of these groups has a firm institutional basis: they elect their own executives, employ staff and are funded from the parliamentary group budget. The chairs of these 'sociological groupings', like those of the committee working groups, are also *ex officio* members of the group executive. The political weight of these groupings varies widely and may be roughly equated with that of the associations within the national party organisation, with which they are closely linked through dual membership and interlocking organisational structures. A very prominent role is played in the decision-making process by the group representing employees' interests and the SME Circle. These two organised interest groupings meet regularly during sitting weeks.

In the SPD parliamentary group no organised interest groups have developed, but the group has traditionally had two high-profile political wings, the 'Parliamentary Left' and the 'Seeheim Circle' on the Centre-Right of the group spectrum. A third wing, the Berlin Network, whose adherents regard themselves as pragmatic reformists, was formed by a group of younger Members after the general election of 1998. At their regular meetings, each of the wings deliberates on its strategy for the forthcoming meeting of the parliamentary group as well as discussing issues on the current political agenda.

Regional groups

The CDU/CSU and SPD Members of the Bundestag from the various *Länder* form regional groups; the members of the smaller parliamentary groups do likewise, albeit on a less formal basis. The most significant of these is the group of CSU parliamentarians from Bavaria. Since 1976, agreements have been concluded at the start of each electoral term on the continuation of the joint CDU/CSU parliamentary group, within which the CSU is guaranteed a considerable degree of organisational autonomy. The two parliamentary parties jointly elect only the group chairperson. He or she has a first deputy, who is the elected chair of the group of CSU parliamentarians. The first parliamentary secretary, who is chosen by the CDU, is dependent on continuous coordination with his or her "deputy" from the CSU, who is also parliamentary secretary of the CSU. The other group office-holders are elected in accordance with the ratio of CDU to CSU Members of the Bundestag.

The CDU Members from the various *Länder* also form regional groups. Although they carry less weight than the group of CSU parliamentarians, their influence on the decision-making process of the joint parliamentary group should certainly not be underestimated. The 'mood' in the regional groups acts as a kind of 'seismograph' for the parliamentary-group executive and is also closely observed by the Federal Chancellor when the relevant parliamentary group is in government.

The SPD Members also form regional groups on the basis of their *Länder* of origin, but these bodies play a minor role in the overall decision-making process within the parliamentary group. They do have considerable influence, however, on the composition of bodies within the SPD parliamentary group and have a significant say on many matters of regional policy. The Members from the eastern federal states coordinate their work in various ways. Since 2002 the parliamentary group of the SPD has had an eastern regional group, comprising the SPD Members from six *Länder*.

Volker Kauder
(CDU/CSU)
Chair of the parliamentary group
since 2005

Thomas Oppermann
(SPD)
Chair of the parliamentary group
since 2013

Dietmar Bartsch
(The Left Party)
Co-chair of the parliamentary group
since 2015

Katrin Göring-Eckardt
(Alliance 90/The Greens)
Co-chair of the parliamentary group
since 2013

Anton Hofreiter
(Alliance 90/The Greens)
Co-chair of the parliamentary group
since 2013

Sahra Wagenknecht
(The Left Party)
Co-chair of the parliamentary group
since 2015

Management of parliamentary groups

Formally, the general meetings of parliamentary groups are the key appointment and decision-making bodies. Their final decisions, however, are shaped in advance at the various stages of a hierarchically structured decision-making process. This is unavoidable, given the complexity of political issues, the pressure of time and the size of the parliamentary groups. The discussions at the group meetings are therefore preceded, in most cases, by a coordination process in several steps. The aim of this preparatory treatment is to guarantee the best possible harmonisation of views and systematic groundwork, but it is only partly achieved in practice. An important part is played in this process by the extended group executive at its Monday meetings and by the managing executive committee. These bodies are responsible for the political leadership and management of the parliamentary groups.

The hustle and bustle of the sitting weeks ensure that the parliamentary secretaries play a highly influential role as 'managers of the parliamentary groups'. This is especially true of the first parliamentary secretaries, who are responsible for planning the work of the Bundestag and organising plenary sittings and group meetings.

The managing executive committee of each of the large parliamentary groups – the CDU/CSU and the SPD – comprises the group chairperson and his or her deputies (eleven and nine in number respectively) as well as five CDU/CSU and four SPD parliamentary secretaries; in the CDU/CSU parliamentary group it also includes two legal advisers and the spokesperson of the CDU regional groups. The deputy chairs are responsible for the spheres of activity of the working groups – in most cases more than one – and their role involves coordination as well as taking initiatives. The CDU/CSU parliamentary-group executive has the spokespersons of the working groups – currently 21 in number – and of the six 'sociological groupings' as well as 15 elected associate members. The extended executive of the SPD group comprises the members of the managing executive committee as well as other elected members, who number 25 at the time of writing. Only some of the spokespersons of the SPD working groups are on the executive. Whether the benefits of broad representation outweigh the difficulties involved in coordinating such large bodies is a moot point.

The composition of the group executives of the small parliamentary groups is similar to that of the managing executive committees of the major parliamentary groups, although the group of Alliance 90/The Greens is headed by two co-chairs. The executives of The Left Party and Alliance 90/The Greens thus comprise the group chairperson or co-chairpersons, their deputies and the parliamentary secretaries. The political coordination of the five working groups in the case of Alliance 90/The Greens and their leadership in the case of The Left Party are the task of deputy group chairpersons. The Vice-President (deputy speaker) of the Bundestag from the group is also on the executive; the Left Party group executive, moreover, includes the party chairpersons if they are Members of the Bundestag.

None of the parliamentary groups elects its senior leaders for the entire electoral term, but the chances of mid-term promotion to the leadership team are slim. The group executive and, in the first instance, the managing executive committee, where one exists, deal with the preparation of the plenary sittings and the general group meeting as well as with items from the working groups. The agendas for the executive meetings are usually more or less the same as those for the following day's general meeting, and indeed the preparation of the general meeting is the main task of the executive meetings. Considerable importance attaches to the resolution of conflicting interests between working groups. As a rule, items will only stand a chance of being accepted if the working groups have reached prior agreement on them. Topical problems are also discussed at the meetings of the groups and their executive committees, and discussions on matters of principle are conducted in connection with wider issues. As a result of these discussions, important preliminary decisions are taken and political choices made. This applies to a greater extent, in fact, to the major opposition group. The managing executive committee is now the main controlling body in the two largest parliamentary groups.

Informal coordination channels within groups and coalition bodies

In addition to the bodies prescribed by the groups' rules of procedure, there are other coordination channels. For example, regular talks are held among the group spokespersons on the various parliamentary committees to discuss the agenda. They also meet to coordinate procedural approaches and substantive positions. In the CDU/CSU group, the meetings of the working-group chairs and of the members of the managing executive committee before the parliamentary group meeting perform a key function. The same applies to the Tuesday lunchtime meetings of the SPD committee spokespersons, held since 2005 and attended by the spokespersons of the working groups (committee spokespersons) and the First Parliamentary Secretary (Chief Whip). Like the lunchtime forums of the CDU/CSU group, they serve to improve coordination and to ease the workload of the group meeting but can also serve as an additional instrument of political guidance, particularly when the group is in government.

There are also various informal coalition bodies. Alongside the work of the federal cabinet and before its meetings, top-level coalition discussions have taken place since the 1970s – at least in phases – in the Coalition Committee, known prior to 1998 as the Grand Coalition Deliberations or Grand Coalition Forum, which acts in practice as a key decision-making forum, even though the resolutions adopted at its meetings only have the formal status of recommendations. The leading representatives of the government, the parliamentary groups in the governing coalition and their party organisations take part in the meetings of this committee.

At the time of the Centre-Right coalition of CDU/CSU and FDP from 1982 to 1998, these top-level coalition discussions were held regularly on the Tuesday morning of sitting weeks, before the parliamentary group meetings and the Wednesday meeting of the cabinet. By contrast, the eight-member Coalition Committee' established by the 'Red and Green' coalition agreement of 1998 between the SPD and Alliance 90/The Greens was not initially intended to meet on a regular basis and was only convened at infrequent intervals. The coalition agreements of 2002, 2005 and 2009, however, laid down that the Coalition Committee would meet regularly, whereas the coalition agreement of 2013 made no such stipulations. In practice, however, these meetings were held at irregular intervals on an *ad hoc* basis. While the importance of the Coalition Committee temporarily waned during the SPD-Green Government, it came to play a major role again in the special circumstances of the Grand Coalition of 2005–2009 and continued to do so during the coalition of CDU, CSU and FDP that was back in power from 2009 to 2013. As well as in the Coalition Committee, important decisions are taken in the smaller circle of party chairpersons or of party and group chairs, including the chair of the CSU regional group where appropriate. A significant role in the coordination of the parliamentary work of coalitions is played by the meeting of the leading politicians from the groups in the governing coalition (the chairpersons and first parliamentary secretaries) that is held every sitting week.

Wir stecken bis zum Hals
im Kapitalismus.
Heiner Müller
DIE LINKE.
AJAX

Other coalition discussions take the form of frequent preparatory working sessions between the office-holders and specialists in the various policy areas. The government and the groups of the governing coalition are thus bound together at several different levels and in various forms. The privileged position of the leading politicians in government, parliamentary groups and political parties – many of whom have dual roles – is reinforced and perpetuated by their participation in the work of these important coalition bodies.

The general meeting of the parliamentary group

The general meetings of the parliamentary groups are their principal electoral and decision-making bodies. In principle, this is the forum where all Members of Parliament have the opportunity to inform themselves about government and group policies in general and to influence the development of these policies. Meetings of the major parliamentary groups normally open with the chairperson's political report. If the group is the senior partner in the governing coalition, there may also be a report by the Federal Chancellor. The reports deal with significant political developments, analyse and assess any conflicts within the party or its parliamentary group and between the coalition partners and express opinions on matters which are the subject of dispute with the group's political rivals.

Previous double page: Inside the meeting rooms of the various parliamentary groups. Top left: CDU/CSU; bottom left: The Left Party; top right: SPD; bottom right: Alliance 90/The Greens.

In addition, the reports reiterate policy guidelines. The reports are normally followed by a discussion, which is sometimes very wide-ranging.

It goes without saying that these general meetings also deal with preparations for the current week's plenary sittings. They formally determine who will speak for the group on each agenda item, although any disputes on this point will, as a rule, have been resolved in advance. Detailed and often lively discussions are held on major legislative proposals and other items. In the groups of the governing coalition, the focus is mostly on legislative initiatives and government policy statements, while the opposition groups tend to deal with initiatives from their working groups (draft laws, major interpellations, motions and amendments). Reports on government drafts are usually presented by the competent ministers themselves. In principle, all Members of Parliament are naturally entitled to voice their opinions on any topic at their group's general meetings. In practice, the discussions are dominated by the leading representatives of the working groups responsible for the topic being debated as well as of the interest groupings and, of course, by members of the Government and a few leading group and party figures.

The newly elected Presidium of the 18th Bundestag following the constituent sitting. In the centre is Norbert Lammert (CDU/CSU), President of the Bundestag; the Vice-Presidents are, from left to right, Johannes Singhammer (CDU/CSU), Claudia Roth (Alliance 90/The Greens), Edelgard Bulmahn (SPD), Ulla Schmidt (SPD), Petra Pau (The Left Party) and Peter Hintze (CDU/CSU). The number of vice-presidents is not prescribed. Since 1994, however, the Rules of Procedure have laid down that every parliamentary group is to provide at least one vice-president.

Organisation and decision-making processes of the Bundestag

A considerable part of the work of the Bundestag is not performed in public plenary sittings but in bodies which generally meet behind closed doors. Besides the permanent parliamentary committees and the parliamentary groups, these are bodies and office-holders concerned primarily with coordination and steering functions, such as the President of the Bundestag, the Presidium and, above all, the Council of Elders. The parliamentary groups also influence the work performed in the plenary chamber of the Bundestag and in these other bodies.

Constitution of the Bundestag and election of the Presidium

The German Bundestag is a permanently operational organ of the Constitution. Under Article 39 of the Basic Law, the term for which it is elected does not end until a new Bundestag convenes. The first sitting of the new Bundestag is chaired initially by the oldest Member, who opens the sitting with an address that is designed to heal the 'wounds' of the electoral campaign. After the election of the new President of the Bundestag, the senior Member no longer has an official role to perform.

The work of the Bundestag is governed by the discontinuity principle. Since this means that the rules of procedure apply only to the electoral term for which they were adopted, a set of rules must be adopted at the start of each term, as prescribed by Article 40 of the Basic Law. The rules of procedure for the previous term are normally reaffirmed with scarcely any amendments. Any major amendments have usually been made towards the end of an electoral term. Parliamentary minorities are particularly dependent on the establishment of procedural rules. Where the rules of procedure or statutory provisions governing parliamentary rights and responsibilities are to be amended, it is important to seek consensus, or at least a large parliamentary majority. Derogations from the rules of procedure in individual cases are possible with the consent of a two-thirds majority of the Members in attendance.

The President of the Bundestag and his or her deputies, of whom there are six at the present time, are elected by a simple majority of the Members of the Bundestag at the constituent sitting for the duration of the electoral term. The President and Vice-Presidents together form the Presidium of the Bundestag. According to parliamentary custom, it is the prerogative of the largest parliamentary group to propose the President of the Bundestag. Before the election, agreements are reached in talks between the parliamentary groups, which makes the result more or less a foregone conclusion. Until now, the candidate nominated by the largest parliamentary group has invariably been elected, usually by a majority in excess of 75 % of the Members' votes. In accordance with a revised version of the Rules of Procedure, each parliamentary group has nominated at least one Vice-President since 1994. While the second-largest group had been able

President by age Heinz Riesenhuber (CDU/CSU) delivers the opening address at the constituent sitting of the 18th Bundestag on 22 October 2013.

At the constituent sitting of the 18th Bundestag on 22 October 2013, President by age Heinz Riesenhuber (CDU/CSU) was in the chair until Norbert Lammert (photo), who presided over the Bundestag during its 16th and 17th electoral terms, was re-elected President of the Bundestag.

Erich Köhler
(CDU/CSU)
1949–1950

Hermann Ehlers
(CDU/CSU)
1950–1954

Eugen Gerstenmaier
(CDU/CSU)
1954–1969

Kai-Uwe von Hassel
(CDU/CSU)
1969–1972
Vice-President of the Bundestag
1972–1976

Annemarie Renger
(SPD)
1972–1976
Vice-President of the Bundestag
1976–1990

Karl Carstens
(CDU/CSU)
1976–1979

Richard Stücklen
(CDU/CSU)
1979–1983
Vice-President of the Bundestag
1976–1979

Rainer Barzel
(CDU/CSU)
1983–1984

Philipp Jenninger
(CDU/CSU)
1984–1988

Rita Süssmuth
(CDU/CSU)
1988–1998

Wolfgang Thierse
(SPD)
1998–2005
Vice-President of the Bundestag
2005–2013

Norbert Lammert
(CDU/CSU)
seit 2005
Vice-President of the Bundestag
2002–2005

to secure only one vice-presidential post since 1994, it provided two Vice-Presidents in the 16th electoral term (2005–2009), when the formation of a Grand Coalition created a new situation, and again in the 18th term, from 2013. The Rules of Procedure of the German Bundestag make no provision for the President or a Vice-President to be voted out of office.

Duties of the President and Presidium of the Bundestag

The President of the Bundestag is the representative of the directly elected Parliament. In terms of protocol, he or she ranks second only to the President of the Federal Republic. On behalf of Parliament, the President of the Bundestag administers the oath of office prescribed by Articles 56 and 64 of the Basic Law to the President of the Federal Republic, the Federal Chancellor and the federal ministers. As the representative of the Bundestag, the President is the official addressee and sender of all Bundestag correspondence with the Bundesrat and the Federal Government. He or she naturally uses the services of the Bundestag administration (the parliamentary secretariat and the President's office) for this purpose. The President is required to sign and, where appropriate, implement the resolutions of the Bundestag and to forward them to the appropriate addressees.

The President's role as representative of the Bundestag gives rise to numerous political and social obligations. For example, he or she receives delegations from home and abroad, groups of foreign parliamentarians and visitors from the worlds of politics, culture and business.

The President of the Bundestag exercises the proprietary rights and police powers in the Bundestag buildings. The administration of the Bundestag, which currently comprises some 2,600 persons, is subject to the supreme authority of the President. The administration works under the direction of the Secretary-General of the German Bundestag, who is the effective head of administration. Lastly, the President has some decisions to take on points of order; in practice, he generally discusses these in the Presidium and often in the Council of Elders too.

The President conducts the business of Parliament and maintains order in the House. Most of his or her powers which are listed in the Rules of Procedure relate to this function. To ensure the orderly conduct of parliamentary business, he or she can call Members to order and direct speakers who digress or exceed their allocated speaking time to discontinue speaking. In practice, the President and Vice-Presidents alternate in the chair every two hours during plenary sittings. This virtual equality of responsibility for the conduct of plenary sittings has considerably enhanced the standing of the Presidium since the 1960s.

The Presidium has few legal powers, and these lie primarily in the right to take decisions on the appointment and dismissal of civil servants and employees of the Bundestag administration. In parliamentary practice, the Presidium deals with all major requests and problems referred to the President or the Vice-Presidents; although it is not the legal decision-making instance, it is often the Presidium which effectively decides on these matters. The Presidium will generally aim for consensus in its rulings and agreements. Most matters, however, are discussed again by the Council of Elders. The actual 'power' of the President largely depends on the influence he or she can bring to bear as chair of

Presidents of the Bundestag since 1949: voting results and period in office

Elect. Term	President	Period in office	Votes cast	Votes in favour	%[a]
1st	Erich Köhler, CDU/CSU	07.09.1949–18.10.1950	402	346	86.1
	Hermann Ehlers, CDU/CSU	19.10.1950–06.10.1953	325	201	61.8
2nd	Hermann Ehlers, CDU/CSU	06.10.1953–29.10.1954	500	466	93.2
	Eugen Gerstenmaier, CDU/CSU	16.11.1954–15.10.1957	409[b]	204[b]	49.9[b]
3rd	Eugen Gerstenmaier, CDU/CSU	15.10.1957–17.10.1961	494	437	88.5
4th	Eugen Gerstenmaier, CDU/CSU	17.10.1961–19.10.1965	504	463	91.9
5th	Eugen Gerstenmaier, CDU/CSU	19.10.1965–31.01.1969	508	385	75.8
	Kai-Uwe von Hassel, CDU/CSU	05.02.1969–20.10.1969	457	262	57.3
6th	Kai-Uwe von Hassel, CDU/CSU	20.10.1969–13.12.1972	517	411	79.5
7th	Annemarie Renger, SPD	13.12.1972–14.12.1976	516	438	84.9
8th	Karl Carstens, CDU/CSU	14.12.1976–31.05.1979	516	346	67.1
	Richard Stücklen, CDU/CSU	31.05.1979–04.11.1980	469	410	87.4
9th	Richard Stücklen, CDU/CSU	04.11.1980–29.03.1983	515	463	89.9
10th	Rainer Barzel, CDU/CSU	29.03.1983–25.10.1984	509	407	80.0
	Philipp Jenninger, CDU/CSU	05.11.1984–18.02.1987	471	340	72.2
11th	Philipp Jenninger, CDU/CSU	18.02.1987–11.11.1988	514	393	76.5
	Rita Süssmuth, CDU/CSU	25.11.1988–20.12.1990	475	380	80.0
12th	Rita Süssmuth, CDU/CSU	20.12.1990–10.11.1994	650	525	80.8
13th	Rita Süssmuth, CDU/CSU	10.11.1994–26.10.1998	669	555	83.0
14th	Wolfgang Thierse, SPD	26.10.1998–17.10.2002	666	512	76.9
15th	Wolfgang Thierse, SPD	17.10.2002–18.10.2005	596	357	59.9
16th	Norbert Lammert, CDU/CSU	18.10.2005–27.10.2009	607	564	92.9
17th	Norbert Lammert, CDU/CSU	27.10.2009–22.10.2013	617	522	84.6
18th	Norbert Lammert, CDU/CSU	ab 22.10.2013	625	591	94.6

[a] Votes in favour of the elected President as a percentage of all votes cast
[b] In the third round of voting

the Council of Elders and the Presidium. Unlike the British Speaker, the Presidents of the Bundestag and, to an even greater extent, their deputies remain active members of their party and parliamentary group, sometimes in leading positions. They continue to represent the political interests of their constituencies, participate in election campaigns and can take part in votes in the Bundestag.

The Council of Elders and inter-group planning

Within the structure of the Bundestag, the Council of Elders is the main coordinating and steering body. It comprises the members of the Presidium plus 23 other Members of Parliament appointed by the parliamentary groups in proportion to their relative strengths. The dominant role is played by the parliamentary secretaries of the groups, who are generally all members of the Council of Elders.

Its main task is to reach agreement on the agenda and schedule of debates for the forthcoming plenary sittings. The Council and other inter-group meetings of first parliamentary secretaries can only arrive at such agreements if a consensus can be established among the parliamentary groups. In the case of most proposals, agreement is reached in advance by the first parliamentary secretaries, and the Council of Elders is merely notified of what the first parliamentary secretaries have agreed on behalf of their groups. The aim of this practice is to ensure that the plenary sittings run as smoothly as possible. If no agreement can be reached, the government majority does have the option of setting the agenda largely by majority decision. This, however, is regarded as unparliamentary practice and does not often occur. Nevertheless, the governing groups can use this option as a means of applying pressure at the parliamentary secretaries' meetings. At the same time, the parliamentary secretaries of the opposition groups can avail themselves of important minority rights. For example, they can secure the discussion of their own proposals after three weeks, even against the will of the majority.

The Council of Elders quite often deals with specific incidents which occurred in plenary. It can criticise decisions, but it cannot reverse them. In practice, it addresses virtually all points of order relating to plenary debates. If it cannot reach agreement on an interpretation of the Rules of Procedure, the matter is referred to the Committee on the Scrutiny of Elections, Immunity and the Rules of Procedure, which takes a fundamental decision on the interpretation of the Rules of Procedure.

Lastly, the Council of Elders also exercises the responsibility of the Bundestag for managing its own affairs in domains such as the allocation of space, building work and the structure and distribution of duties of the Bundestag Administration. Only when performing these tasks is it a decision-making body, acting by majority vote. In order to deal with the wide range of matters it is required to administer on behalf of the Bundestag, the Council of Elders has established several commissions.

Permanent committees

The bulk of parliamentary work is done by the permanent committees, of which there are currently 23 with 14 to 46 members each. While a total of 253 plenary sittings took place during the 17th electoral term from 2009 to 2013, there were 2,600 committee meetings over the same period. Without the division of

Permanent committees of the Bundestag, 18th electoral term

No.	Name of committee	No. of members	No. of members from each parliamentary group CDU/CSU	SPD	A. 90/The Greens[a]	The Left Party	Chair
1	Scrutiny of Elections, Immunity and the Rules of Procedure	14	7	5	1	1	Dr J. Wadephul (CDU/CSU)
2	Petitions	26	12	8	3	3	K. Steinke (The Left Party)
3	Foreign Affairs	37	18	11	4	4	Dr N. Röttgen (CDU/CSU)
4	Internal Affairs	37	18	11	4	4	A. Heveling (CDU/CSU)
5	Sports	18	9	5	2	2	D. Freitag (SPD)
6	Legal Affairs and Consumer Protection	39	19	12	4	4	R. Künast (A. 90/The Greens)
7	Finance	37	18	11	4	4	I. Arndt-Brauer (SPD)
8	Budget	41	20	13	4	4	Dr G. Lötzsch (The Left Party)
	Auditing	17	8	5	2	2	B. Hagedorn (SPD)
9	Economic Affairs and Energy	46	22	14	5	5	Dr P. Ramsauer (CDU/CSU)
10	Food and Agriculture	34	17	11	3	3	A. Gerig (CDU/CSU)
11	Labour and Social Affairs	41	20	13	4	4	K. Griese (SPD)
12	Defence	32	16	10	3	3	W. Hellmich (SPD)
13	Family Affairs, Senior Citizens, Women and Youth	36	17	11	4	4	P. Lehrieder (CDU/CSU)
14	Health Committee	37	18	11	4	4	Dr E. Franke (SPD)
15	Transport and Digital Infrastructure	41	20	13	4	4	M. Burkert (SPD)
16	Environment, Nature Conservation, Building and Nuclear Safety	36	17	11	4	4	B. Höhn (A. 90/The Greens)
17	Human Rights and Humanitarian Aid	16	7	5	2	2	M. Brand (CDU/CSU)
18	Education, Research and Technology Assessment	34	17	11	3	3	P. Lips (CDU/CSU)
19	Economic Cooperation and Development	21	10	7	2	2	D. Wöhrl (CDU/CSU)
20	Tourism	18	9	5	2	2	H. Brehmer (CDU/CSU)
21	Affairs of the European Union[b]	34	17	11	3	3	G. Krichbaum (CDU/CSU)
22	Cultural and Media Affairs	18	9	5	2	2	S. Ehrmann (SPD)
23	Digital Agenda	18	7	5	2	2	J. Koeppen (CDU/CSU)

[a] Alliance 90/The Greens
[b] Fifteen Members of the European Parliament also belong to this committee as non-voting members.

Meeting of the Bundestag Committee on Internal Affairs. Within the Bundestag, the committee deals with all aspects of home-affairs policy and with federal administrative matters that are not assigned to any other specialised parliamentary committee.

Meeting of the Budget Committee of the Bundestag on 19 February 2014. Besides deliberating on the annual Budget Act, the committee is also responsible for overseeing the implementation of the budget (parliamentary scrutiny). According to parliamentary custom, the chair of this committee is always a member of the largest opposition group.

responsibilities among these specialised committees, the Bundestag would be unable to process properly the numerous and often complex government proposals on almost every aspect of political and social life. This applies not only to the committees' role in the legislative process but also to the scrutiny of the Government and its vast administrative machinery.

According to the Rules of Procedure of the German Bundestag, the committees are 'bodies responsible for preparing the decisions of the Bundestag', but in fact most of their recommendations for plenary decisions have the character of decisions in their own right.

The appointment of the Foreign Affairs Committee, the Defence Committee and the Petitions Committee are prescribed by Articles 45a and 45 c of the Basic Law, and since 1992 the revised version of Article 45 has prescribed the appointment of a Committee on the Affairs of the European Union. On the basis of ordinary law or the Rules of Procedure of the German Bundestag, the Budget Committee and the Committee on the Scrutiny of Elections, Immunity and the Rules of Procedure are also established, while all other permanent committees are set up by virtue of inter-group agreements.

Since about the mid-sixties, the committee structure has largely reflected the organisational structure of the Federal Government, each committee corresponding to one of the federal ministries; the committees are generally appointed for the duration of the electoral term. The portfolios of the Interior Ministry and the Ministry of Finance are each covered by two parliamentary committees, one of which – the Budget Committee – is accorded special status.

The committees that do not correspond to this model are the Committee for the Scrutiny of Elections, Immunity and the Rules of Procedure and the Petitions Committee, which are also appointed for the duration of the electoral term. The same applies to the Committee on the Affairs of the European Union and the committees that cut across departmental portfolios, namely the Tourism Committee, the Committee on Human Rights and Humanitarian Aid and the Committee on the Digital Agenda, created in 2014. Another relative newcomer is the Committee on Cultural and Media Affairs, which was established following the appointment of a minister of state (commissioner) for that area of activity under the direct authority of the Federal Chancellor. The composition of the committees and the appointment of a chairperson are determined on the basis of the relative strengths of the parliamentary groups. The appointment of committee members is a matter for the groups, as is their recall. Non-attached Members of Parliament are appointed by the President to serve as consultative members of a committee. At the beginning of each electoral term, the parliamentary groups conclude agreements on the number, size and titles of the committees. If these agreements are duly concluded, the plenary vote is a mere formality.

The number of committees to be chaired by members of each parliamentary group is governed by the relative strengths of the groups. The selection of chairpersons is determined internally by the groups. The decision as to which committees are to be chaired by members of each group has usually been taken at inter-group meetings. If the parliamentary groups cannot reach agreement, they resort to a method of proportional allocation whereby rank-order numbers are assigned to the groups on the basis of a mathematical formula and chairs are then allocated in sequence. While the use of this allocation method was a rare exception until the early nineties, it was applied on three consecutive occasions in 1994, 1998 and 2002. According to parliamentary custom, the chairperson and vice-chair of a committee belong to different groups. Another unwritten rule is that the Budget Committee is always chaired by a member of the Opposition.

The task of the specialised committees is to ease the burden on the plenary chamber caused by the deluge of items to be deliberated on in Parliament and to enhance the ability of the Bundestag to legislate and to scrutinise the activities of the government in a competent manner. The way they perform this task also affects the Opposition's prospects of establishing their credentials in plenary and in the media as a genuine alternative to the government of the day.

The committees are bound to deal with the matters referred to them without delay. Once a matter has been referred to committee, the House cannot take a decision on it until it has received a report and recommendation from the lead committee, i.e. the committee to which the matter has been referred. The minority is armed with an effective instrument for the avoidance of delays, in that each parliamentary group, or five per cent of the Members of Parliament, can demand an interim report from the committee ten sitting weeks after the referral of an item and can insist on a plenary debate; the effect of this provision is chiefly preventive.

Since 1969, committees have had the right to address matters within their own sphere of competence without an item having been specifically referred to them. This right to deal with issues on their own authority gives them the opportunity not only to respond to items but also to take action and address wider issues in context. However, the committees do not have the right to initiate legislative proposals or to recommend plenary decisions on matters that have not been referred to them. Committee members may, however, initiate proposals and questions through their parliamentary groups.

The committees meet regularly on the Wednesday of each sitting week. In addition, each parliamentary group has the right to request a special meeting during sitting weeks. The agenda for each meeting is agreed by the group spokespersons on the committee; the committee chair also takes part in these discussions. These spokespersons' discussions also serve to determine the organisation and content of committee meetings.

The committees generally conduct their business in a fair and cooperative manner. After a brief presentation by a rapporteur or departmental civil servant, the committee engages in open debate, and contributions are normally kept short.

In the Bundestag committees, as in the corresponding working groups within the parliamentary groups, specialisation has been encouraged, and a system of rapporteurs has been developed with a view to enabling committees to study legislative proposals in detail and to act professionally in their scrutiny of the executive. In the working groups of the major parliamentary groups, the remit of the relevant committee is divided among the regular committee members, who currently number between 5 and 22. Members generally look after their respective specialised areas for a lengthy period of time and will normally report on any pertinent items both in committee and in plenary. In practice, the appointment of a rapporteur is made in consultation with the spokespersons of the parliamentary groups and the

Committees' public hearings on legislative bills

Electoral term	Subjects discussed in public hearings	of which matters relating to particular legislative initiatives		Total bills	of which bills discussed in public hearings	
	Number	Number	%	Number	Number	%
12th	177	123	69.5	800	152	19.0
13th	236	135	57.2	923	186	20.2
14th	303	183	60.4	864	222	25.7
15th	249	132	53.0	643	174	27.1
16th	372	252	67.7	905	270	29.8
17th	554	249	44.9	844	317	37.5

prospective rapporteur, whose agreement is essential. Particularly in labour-intensive 'legislation committees', the groups are keen to pave the way for decisions and iron out acute procedural problems in talks between their respective rapporteurs.

Each committee may appoint subcommittees for major projects, unless one third of its members object.

Civil servants from the federal and *Land* ministries regularly attend committee meetings, often in large numbers. The competent officials from the federal ministry or, if the matter under examination is particularly important, parliamentary state secretaries or even ministers address the committee on individual agenda items. Article 43(2) of the Basic Law lays down that the members of the of the Federal Government and of the Bundesrat may attend all meetings of the Bundestag committees and have the right to be heard at any time. The same applies to persons representing them, such as departmental civil servants. For its part, a committee may demand that any member of the Federal Government appear in person before it to speak and answer questions. Such a demand, however, requires a majority decision. Ministers generally try to cultivate good relations with 'their' respective parliamentary committees.

In every electoral term since 2004, the Bundestag has appointed a Parliamentary Advisory Council on Sustainable Development to perform an important task that cuts across ministerial portfolios. The Council, which has 17 members at the time of writing, is subject to the Rules of Procedure governing permanent committees. The Council is responsible for general parliamentary oversight of the Federal Government's sustainability policy. Its mission is to ensure that legislative action is compatible with environmental, economic and social sustainability and that vital resources are preserved for future generations. The Council presents the relevant lead committee with advisory opinions and recommendations as well as reporting to the House at plenary sittings. Repeated calls have been made for due consideration of the Council's views.

Since 1952, the committees of the Bundestag have been able to conduct public hearings of experts, representatives of special-interest groups and other sources of information. Ample use is made of this means of obtaining information and overseeing developments. In addition, numerous non-public hearings still take place. Public hearings are now conducted regularly when major legislative proposals are presented or are being prepared and are also used to examine or develop other projects, such as new programmes or strategies. Most hearings are held on the initiative of the Opposition, a unique development in Western Europe which has its roots in the enshrinement in 1969 of a minority right to demand hearings. In the case of referred items, the lead committee is obliged to hold a hearing at the request of one quarter of its members or, in the 18th electoral term, on the motion of its opposition members.

The actual impact of public hearings varies quite widely and depends largely on the stage in the decision-making process at which they are conducted. About two thirds of hearings deal with government bills. In such cases, the governing parties are often more or less concerned with the aim of justifying the proposals and fending off criticism. A more open approach to questioning is normally adopted at hearings conducted on the basis of reports, expert opinions, motions and the exercise of a committee's right to examine issues on its own initiative. Such hearings can form the basis of legislative activities in the immediate or more distant future. Some of them play a major role in the formulation of party programmes, in focusing the public debate on issues that have been receiving insufficient attention and in assessing the impact of existing regulations.

Great importance attaches to the selection of the invited experts. It is standard practice to invite a limited number of experts, each parliamentary group nominating a number of experts proportionate to its size.

Besides numerous internal briefing sessions and specialised talks between working groups or rapporteurs and experts or senior members of associations, the parliamentary groups also conduct their own public hearings and conferences. These events have developed into a common means whereby opposition groups obtain information and insight and engage in high-profile scrutiny of government activity.

Needless to say, the debates conducted in committee also generate impetus. Governments, however, rarely acknowledge that their bills incorporate suggestions from the other side of the House unless such acknowledgement is necessary for tactical reasons. The decision-making process is primarily characterised by a clear divide between the governing majority and the opposition groups, not only in the plenary chamber but in committee too. After what is usually a civilised and businesslike debate, the majority groups will normally vote in accordance with a prior decision taken at their group meetings. Group members are expected to vote *en bloc*, and they generally do. Group positions can, however, be influenced by previous debates in committee.

Apart from public hearings, the permanent committees do not normally meet in public. For many years, there has been a feeling that this contributes to a lack of visibility for the Bundestag's work. Since 1969, the parliamentary committees have had the option of admitting the public to meetings dealing with certain categories of items, but they have rarely exercised this option. Similarly, scarcely any use has been made of the opportunity introduced in 1995 to conduct what are known as "extended public committee deliberations". Instead of a specialised debate in the plenary chamber to conclude the deliberation process at second reading, this procedure involves a joint public debate by the members of the lead committee and the other committees that have been asked for an opinion on the matter in question. As a rule, the plenary sitting then confines itself to the formal vote. This was designed as a means of allowing more time for detailed plenary debates on major issues and raising their public profile.

Plenary sittings of the Bundestag

Decisions of the Bundestag can only be taken by the whole House. A wide range of issues is publicly debated in the plenary chamber of the Bundestag. Broader public awareness of parliamentary debates stems chiefly from the general debates connected with the presentation of the budget and government policy statements, but considerably less public attention is focused on debates on major areas of government policy, in which a number of important items are often discussed in a single debate. The numerous short specific debates in which the competent specialists from the committees seek to summarise the position of their respective groups in concentrated form are usually only followed by specialised audiences. These are the debates, however, which largely determine the course of sitting days in the plenary chamber. To these may be added the special forms of public scrutiny and debate in plenary, namely the debates on matters of topical interest, ministerial question-and-answer sessions and question time.

Federal Chancellor Angela Merkel delivering a government policy statement in the Bundestag chamber on 13 March 2014. Besides legislative bills and government policy statements, other occasions for plenary debates include Major Interpellations, motions for resolutions and reports from committees of inquiry, study commissions and the Petitions Committee.

Plenary debates can be initiated for a wide range of reasons. The main task of the Bundestag is to discuss draft legislation and the federal budget. However, there are also large numbers of independently tabled motions, government policy statements, major interpellations and motions for resolutions, government reports, reports compiled by committees of inquiry, study commissions and the Petitions Committee, EU items and more besides.

The following factors affect the way in which the plenary deals with proposals:

- the stage of the deliberation process an item has reached,
- whether decisions can be taken on the matter, and
- whether the item has been tabled by the government side or the opposition side of the House.

The scheduling, total duration and structure of debates are negotiated by the parliamentary secretaries and are formally agreed by the Council of Elders. Quite frequently, the parliamentary secretaries also reach inter-group agreements after the Council of Elders has met. This procedure avoids the need for time-consuming procedural debates in plenary. If no agreement is reached and the governing coalition makes use of its right to set the agenda by majority decision, stormy exchanges often ensue in the chamber.

Since the late 1960s, the opposition groups have enjoyed greater equality of opportunity in the debating chamber. In 1969, for example, the principle of paying due regard to the arguments for and against the motion under debate was explicitly enshrined in the Rules of Procedure of the German Bundestag. The right conferred by Article 43 of the Basic Law on members of the Federal Government or the Bundesrat to be heard at any time may still be exercised, but since the seventh electoral term it has been subject to an agreement which lessens its impact. Since then, a precise formula has been agreed at the start of each term for the distribution of speaking time between the government side (the Federal Government and the parliamentary groups of the ruling coalition) and the Opposition. This means that unduly lengthy speeches by those who enjoy the right to be heard at any time diminish the speaking time available to the members of their own parliamentary group. This arrangement took account of the close link between the Government and the parliamentary groups in the governing coalition as well as allowing for the fact that there might not be a single opposition group but two or more independent groups in opposition. Since the start of the 16th electoral term in 2005, quotas of speaking time have been agreed for each of the two groups of the governing coalition. The speaking times of representatives of the Federal Government and the Bundesrat are counted as part of the time allocation of the relevant parliamentary group. In practice, the parliamentary groups designate the speakers who are to argue their case in plenary. Non-attached Members are allocated speaking time in accordance with guidelines laid down by the Council of Elders.

Reform drives always include calls for livelier and more argumentative debating. A useful step in this direction is the fact that, since the 1980s, brief interventions to put questions to the speaker have no longer counted as speaking time, and good use is made of the option to give Members leave to make brief remarks on the subject under discussion. With a view to increasing public interest in detailed plenary debates on major issues, a 'plenary core time' was introduced in 1995 as part of a parliamentary reform package and has largely proved effective. During that core time, on the Thursday morning of each sitting week, which is to be kept clear of other appointments, two major issues are debated as a rule in the expectation of the largest possible turnout of Members. As far as the establishment of thematic priorities, the turnout and media attention are concerned, expectations have indeed been fulfilled to a great extent. Apart from altering the structure of its own work and debates, the Bundestag has very limited scope to influence the nature and extent of media reporting of parliamentary activity. Reporting on the work of the Bundestag in the key media – daily newspapers and weekly magazines – has decreased. The wide-ranging and informative *Phoenix* current-affairs and documentary channel that has been operated jointly by television broadcasters ARD and ZDF since 1997 transmits most of the plenary debates from the Bundestag and some of the public hearings. Viewing figures, however, are very low. Another down side is that, since the niche channel was created, live Bundestag debates have become extremely rare in the mainstream ARD and ZDF schedules, and summary reports on the day's plenary proceedings are now largely absent. As an alternative to Phoenix, viewers can watch all plenary debates live or later, on demand, including those not transmitted by Phoenix, on parliamentary TV at The importance of the Internet as a means of external projection and as an internal working tool is steadily increasing. The Bundestag website provides comprehensive information on current debates, plenary sittings and individual Members and offers a wide range of research options. In addition, the parliamentary groups and almost all Members of the Bundestag maintain their own websites. The Bundestag's in-house network, the Intranet, also plays a significant role in work processes and decision-making processes for Members and parliamentary groups, as do the groups' own Intranet pages, which are tailored to reflect the positions and priorities of each group but are not publicly accessible.

Functions of the Bundestag

The Bundestag performs the customary functions of representative assemblies in a parliamentary democracy. These are the appointment and dismissal of the Government, the adoption of legislation, including the budget, scrutiny of the Government and the administrative apparatus, articulation of interests and political positions and ensuring that the process of political decision-making takes place in public and on the basis of transparency. The Bundestag is empowered to make the final decision on legislative matters. In practice, however, tasks of the Bundestag cannot be attributed to just one of these functions; Members on the government side, moreover, perform these tasks differently to their counterparts in the opposition groups.

Formation and dissolution of the Federal Government

In contrast to most Western European countries, the formal election of the Head of Government by Parliament in Germany precedes the appointment of the cabinet. The Bundestag elects the Federal Chancellor by secret ballot without a debate. All

Federal Chancellors elected under Article 63 of the Basic Law have obtained the necessary absolute majority in the first round of voting, although the majority has been slender in several instances. In each case, the incumbent President of the Federal Republic proposed the candidate who could rely on majority support in the Bundestag. If no absolute majority materialises in the first vote, the Bundestag can elect a candidate in the second or third round who has been proposed by one quarter of the Members of the Bundestag. If voting goes to a third round, a relative majority is sufficient.

In most elections to the Bundestag, the parties have committed themselves to a particular coalition and a prospective Federal Chancellor beforehand, and so the voters have been able to vote for or against a coalition and Chancellor. Hence the majority in the Bundestag, by formally electing the Chancellor, is merely ratifying the voters' choice. Since the 1983 election, however, only the CDU/CSU and FDP have unequivocally proclaimed their intention to form a coalition, whereas the SPD avoided formally committing itself to an electoral alliance with Alliance 90/ The Greens until 2002. Prior to the 2005 and 2013 elections, no party had expressed support for the formation of the Grand Coalition of CDU/CSU and SPD that governed from 2005 to 2009 and has been in power again since 2013.

After the multi-party coalitions of the first two electoral terms, the demise of the smallest parties and the development of a bipolar system with three to five parties, a coalition comprising one of the two main parties and a smaller partner became the norm. Only three Chancellors have ever been voted out of office in general elections – Kurt-Georg Kiesinger in 1969, Helmut Kohl in 1998 and Gerhard Schröder in 2005. All other changes have come about in the course of a electoral term through the termination of the coalition agreement by one of the coalition partners and/or pressure from the Chancellor's own party for him to step down. The 1998 election was the first general election to send both of the previous governing parties intoopposition.

Since coalition governments are the norm, the extensive constitutional powers of the Federal Chancellor and the autonomy of his or her party are more or less drastically curtailed in practice. The decisions on the Government's programme and the

Following the announcement of the composition of the new Federal Government, its members have taken their seats on the government benches in the Bundestag chamber. First row, right to left: Angela Merkel (CDU/CSU, Federal Chancellor), Sigmar Gabriel (SPD, Federal Minister for Economic Affairs and Vice-Chancellor), Frank-Walter Steinmeier (SPD, Federal Minister for Foreign Affairs), Thomas de Maizière (CDU/CSU, Federal Minister of the Interior), Alexander Dobrindt (CDU/CSU, Federal Minister of Transport), Wolfgang Schäuble (CDU/CSU, Federal Minister of Finance) and Andrea Nahles (SPD, Federal Minister of Labour). Second row, right to left: Peter Altmaier (CDU/CSU, Head of the Federal Chancellery and Federal Minister for Special Tasks), Hans-Peter Friedrich (CDU/CSU, Federal Minister of Agriculture), Ursula von der Leyen (CDU/CSU, Federal Minister of Defence), Manuela Schwesig (SPD, Federal Minister for Family Affairs), Hermann Gröhe (CDU/CSU, Federal Minister of Health), Heiko Maas (SPD, Federal Minister of Justice), Barbara Hendricks (SPD, Federal Minister of the Environment) and Johanna Wanka (CDU/CSU, Federal Minister of Education and Research). Third row, left: Gerd Müller (CDU/CSU, Federal Minister for Economic Cooperation and Development).

Angela Merkel on the government front bench after being sworn in as Federal Chancellor on 17 December 2013. In her third legislative term as Chancellor, Angela Merkel once more leads a Grand Coalition, as she did when she was first elected Federal Chancellor in 2005. From 2009 to 2013 a coalition of CDU/CSU and FDP formed the Federal Government.

In the Bundestag on 27 June 2005, Federal Chancellor Gerhard Schröder tabled a confidence motion with the aim of obtaining early elections. In the debate on the motion, which took place on 1 July, he cited his Government's restricted viability as the reason for his action. Two months previously in North Rhine-Westphalia, the only remaining *Land* government formed by the SPD and Greens had been voted out of office; the SPD itself, moreover, was in conflict over Agenda 2010. The confidence motion needed 301 votes to be carried but received only 151, and so Parliament was dissolved on 21 July.

composition of the cabinet are not taken until the coalition talks, which can be long and arduous. The talks comprise rounds of negotiations involving leading government, parliamentary-group and party representatives as well as small discussion circles. Once the discussions on the substance of the coalition's programme have been concluded, the bureaux, executive committees and parliamentary groups of the participating parties formally adopt the coalition agreement. Since 1998 the final decision has lain with party congresses. After the 2013 general election, the SPD leaders, having previously rejected the option of a Grand Coalition, made their participation in such a government dependent on the consent of the party rank and file in a members' poll, which was an unprecedented step.

Although the new Government does not officially unveil its programme until the government policy statement is made to the Bundestag by the new Federal Chancellor, the programme essentially reflects the terms of the coalition agreement.

The Bundestag has no legal say in either the appointment or the dismissal of federal ministers, even though they are accountable to Parliament. Under Article 64 of the Basic Law, the formal power of appointment and dismissal lies with the Head of Government. However, a Federal Chancellor could scarcely keep a minister in office if a majority of the Bundestag approved a resolution calling for his or her dismissal.

In practice, the distribution of government posts is determined in negotiations between the prospective Chancellor and the leading politicians of the planned coalition. This also applies to the demarcation of ministerial portfolios, which is formally the prerogative of the Chancellor. The choice of people to fill the various posts, on the other hand, is largely left to the relevant party. Only in the choice of the federal ministers and parliamentary state secretaries from his or her own party can the Chancellor designate play a decisive role. Even then, he or she must try to ensure that the wings of the party, interest groups, women, regional groupings and religious faiths are adequately represented.

Unlike the parliamentary state secretaries, the Federal Chancellor and the federal ministers need not be Members of the Bundestag, although since 1998 an exceptional rule has applied to parliamentary state secretaries (ministers of state) at the Federal Chancellery. Most of the federal ministers who have been appointed, however, have been career politicians with many years' experience in party politics and, as a rule, a seat in the Bundestag.

Parliamentary state secretaries, introduced in 1967, have the task of easing the workload of the federal ministers and the Chancellor in their senior political posts by assuming responsibility for certain areas of activity, particularly in Parliament. Since the 1980s they have considerably outnumbered the federal ministers. Since the parliamentary state secretaries also regard themselves primarily as representatives of the Government, this means that a considerable percentage of Members of Parliament from the governing groups are subject to government discipline (13.8 % in 2009). At the same time, they also fulfil an important intermediary function in Bundestag committees and in the working groups established by the parliamentary groups of the governing coalition.

Vote of no confidence, motion for a vote of confidence and dissolution of Parliament

In the course of an electoral term, the Bundestag can only bring about a change of chancellor and government if it elects a new Federal Chancellor by an absolute majority (constructive vote of no confidence – Article 67 of the Basic Law). The political stability of the Federal Republic cannot, however, be primarily ascribed to this rule but rather to the development of a relatively stable party system. In fact, there have only ever been two motions for a constructive vote of no confidence: the first, in 1972, was intended to unseat Willy Brandt, but it failed, while the second, in 1982, succeeded in deposing Helmut Schmidt in favour of a coalition of the CDU/CSU and the FDP under Helmut Kohl.

Only the Federal Chancellor can be the subject of a constructive vote of no confidence. The Bundestag, however, may also adopt a majority resolution calling for the dismissal of individual ministers or explicitly censuring the conduct of government members or even of the entire Federal Government. Such a resolution is not very likely to succeed, however, in a parliamentary system of government. If such a motion for the dismissal of a minister did win majority support, the decision of Parliament would not legally bind the Federal Chancellor, but by disregarding a majority vote, the latter would run the risk of a (further) loss of confidence. Throughout the history of the Federal Republic, 16 motions calling for the dismissal of government ministers and 26 motions of censure have been tabled. Although none of them has been carried, when used sparingly, they have nevertheless given the Opposition a means of exerting pressure with a high public impact.

The German Constitution has made the dissolution of Parliament considerably more difficult than it is in most of the other parliamentary systems in Western Europe. In the course of an electoral term, it is only permissible through the collaboration of the Head of Government, the parliamentary majority and the Head of State (Basic Law, Article 68). One case in which the President of the Federal Republic may dissolve the Bundestag is if a Federal Chancellor has been elected with the votes of fewer than half the Members of the Bundestag. During the lifetime of a Parliament, the Federal President may dissolve the Bundestag if the Federal Chancellor asks for a vote of confidence, loses the vote and requests the dissolution of the Bundestag. On three occasions – in 1972, 1982 and 2005 – fresh elections have been brought about by such a motion for a vote of confidence. In 1982, there was fierce controversy as to whether the use of this device at a time when the Government demonstrably enjoyed the support of a stable majority in Parliament was unconstitutional, although such action was held to be politically legitimate. No less controversial was the dissolution of the Bundestag which Federal Chancellor Gerhard Schröder sought and which Federal President Horst Köhler granted in July 2005. In a bid to avoid such constitutional controversies, there have been repeated proposals that the Bundestag should be empowered to dissolve itself if two thirds of its Members so decide.

Only on two occasions have Federal Chancellors tabled a motion for a vote of confidence with a view to securing the support of the groups in the governing coalition. In February 1982, Helmut Schmidt sought such a vote in order to shore up his crumbling alliance with the FDP. In November 2001, Gerhard Schröder became the first Federal Chancellor to link a parliamentary decision on a substantive issue with a vote of confidence. The issue was the participation of German Bundeswehr troops in the anti-terrorism mission Operation Enduring Freedom. Although the consent of the Bundestag was not in doubt, given that the CDU/CSU and FDP opposition groups supported deployment in principle, the Federal Chancellor used the motion for a vote of confidence as a means of rallying a majority of the coalition groups behind the government position, which he succeeded in doing.

Further parliamentary powers of appointment

Besides electing the Federal Chancellor and its own President and Vice-Presidents, the Bundestag also enjoys other powers of appointment. It elects the Parliamentary Commissioner for the Armed Forces, the Federal Commissioner for Data Protection and, on the basis of a proposal from the Federal Government, the President and Vice-President of the Federal Court of Audit. It also elects the Parliamentary Oversight Panel, which is responsible for parliamentary oversight of the federal intelligence services.

The Bundestag provides half the members of the Federal Convention, which normally meets once every five years to elect the President of the Federal Republic. The other half are elected by the parliaments of the *Länder* on the basis of proportional representation. Acting on a proposal from its Committee for the Election of Judges of the Federal Constitutional Court, comprising 12 Members of Parliament, the Bundestag elects half of the constitutional judges without debate by a two-thirds majority of votes cast. Until the Federal Constitutional Court Act was amended in June 2015, the election of these judges was incumbent on the Committee itself. The Bundesrat elects the other half. A Committee for the Election of Judges, comprising 16 ministers from the *Länder* and an equal number of members elected by the Bundestag, decides on the composition of the supreme federal courts. The Mediation Committee is a joint body comprising 16 Members of the Bundestag and 16 members of the Bundesrat which meets behind closed doors to resolve legislative conflicts when convened on demand by the Bundestag, the Bundesrat or the Federal Government (Basic Law, Article 77).

Lastly, the Bundestag sends or appoints members to a number of controlling and monitoring bodies of the executive, such as the Deutsche Welle Broadcasting Council, the Governing Council of the German Federal Film Board and the Rail Infrastructure Advisory Council.

The Bundestag is also represented in several international organisations. It elects 18 members to the Parliamentary Assembly of the Council of Europe, is represented by 13 members in the Parliamentary Assembly of the Organisation for Security and Co-operation in Europe (OSCE) and sends delegations to the Inter-Parliamentary Union (IPU) Assemblies. Lastly, mention should also be made in this context of the contacts maintained with other national parliaments through the numerous bilateral parliamentary friendship groups.

Legislation

Under Article 70 of the Basic Law, the *Länder* have the right to legislate unless the Basic Law explicitly confers legislative power on the Federation. In some 'traditional' areas, such as foreign, defence and monetary policy, the Federation has exclusive legislative jurisdiction. In addition, it has made very full use of the comprehensive catalogue of powers available to it under the rules governing concurrent legislation in Articles 72 and 74 of the Basic Law, a catalogue that has been considerably widened by constitutional amendments. These have mainly been based on the provision of Article 72 of the Basic Law whereby federal legislation may be justified by the need to maintain 'equivalent living conditions throughout the federal territory'. The few remaining legislative powers of the *Länder* lie chiefly in the domains of education and culture, police law and local government.

The *Länder*, on the other hand, are primarily responsible for the implementation of both state and federal legislation, most of which they execute 'in their own right', to quote Article 84 of the Basic Law. This system of 'administrative federalism' has a profound impact on the federal legislative process. For one thing, the efforts of the federal legislature to assess the impact of its laws depend on feedback from the *Länder*. For another, this prompts the Government and Parliament to make their statutory provisions as detailed as possible in order to guarantee uniform application of the law by the *Länder* and local authorities.

The federal system of government has gradually become more unitary with the aid of the Bundesrat. On the one hand, the Parliaments of the *Länder* have been weakened. On the other hand, the representatives of the *Land* governments represented in the Bundesrat and their senior civil servants have become more closely involved in the enactment of federal laws and statutory instruments.

Amendments to the Basic Law require the affirmative vote of two thirds of the Members of the Bundestag and two thirds of the votes of the Bundesrat (Basic Law, Article 79), which means that they need the consent of the major opposition party and of a large majority of the *Land* governments. By 2005, a total of 51 laws amending numerous provisions of the constitution had been adopted. Fundamental decisions such as the adoption of the constitutional provisions governing public finances and the emergency constitution were taken in the special circumstances that obtained under the Grand Coalition of CDU/CSU and SPD from 1966 to 1969, while other significant revisions were the result of lengthy wrangling. After the unification of Germany, efforts to enact more fundamental constitutional amendments were thwarted by the failure to obtain a two-thirds majority in the Joint Commission on the Constitution, comprising an equal number of members from the Bundestag and Bundesrat, or in the Bundestag itself. The constitutional amendments were largely confined to adjustments necessitated by the Maastricht Treaty (Article 23 of the Basic Law) and a certain strengthening of the rights of the *Länder*. By contrast, the numerous further-reaching amendments proposed by the opposition parties (introduction of referendums, stronger powers for Parliament and the Opposition and definition of the social aims of the state) were rejected. In the summer of 2006, the reform of the federal system carried by the Grand Coalition involved the largest-ever package of constitutional amendments. State legislatures were strengthened by the transfer of numerous powers to the *Länder*.

Under Article 24 of the Basic Law, sovereign powers may be transferred to intergovernmental institutions by means of a law without the consent of the Bundesrat. Since 1992, however, the transfer of sovereign powers to institutions of the European Union under Article 23 of the Basic Law has been subject to the same rule as constitutional amendments, requiring a two-thirds majority of the Bundestag and Bundesrat.

The development of the interventionist welfare state from the 1950s led to a considerable increase in the volume of legislation, mostly in the form of specialised and detailed laws and, above all, government statutory instruments. In accordance with the

Basic Law, the constitutional precept of administrative legality goes hand in hand with the democratic right of legal certainty. Accordingly, the Federal Constitutional Court has consistently ruled that all important decisions must be made by the legislature itself. An average of more than a hundred laws were enacted every year during that period. The vast majority were acts amending or adjusting previous legislation, generally several statutes at a time; this is a visible sign of the close interdependence of legal provisions. The Federal Government, a federal minister or the government of a *Land* can only enact statutory instruments if they are empowered to do so by a law which specifies the content, purpose and scope of the authorisation it confers (Basic Law, Article 80). Legislation has undergone considerable change through the emergence of a multi-tiered system in which ever greater importance attaches to the European level.

Legislative initiatives and the drafting of government proposals

Legislative proposals may be presented to the Bundestag by the Federal Government, the Bundesrat, a parliamentary group or five per cent of the Members of the Bundestag. Individual Members, in other words, cannot table draft legislation. Unlike many other parliamentary systems, however, the German system makes no fundamental distinction between the treatment of bills initiated by Parliament and government bills. Initiatives launched by individual Members without the support of a parliamentary group scarcely feature at all. Bills presented by the Bundesrat require the prior approval of a majority of its members.

Most bills are presented by the Federal Government, which has access to the necessary administrative personnel. Nevertheless, whereas governments were presenting two thirds of all legislative proposals in the 1970s, this share has fallen to about half, a development that has been primarily due to the presence in parliament of another opposition party. The dominance of the Government is most clearly demonstrated by the high percentage of adopted legislation initiated by the Government and the parliamentary groups in the governing coalition: in the last six electoral terms, from 1990 to 2013, the figures were 73 % and 14.1 % respectively. As a rule, the bills initiated by the parliamentary groups in the governing coalition are also drafted by, or at least in collaboration with, the departmental civil service. On the other hand, government proposals can also stem from political momentum generated by the groups on the government side of the House.

Vital legislative impetus often emanates not only from the bodies with formal responsibility for initiating legislation but also from party bodies, trade unions, business associations and other interest groups or from academic institutes, the mass media, citizens' initiatives, the courts – especially the Federal Constitutional Court – and the churches.

Bills tabled by opposition groups, which are certainly numerous – there were 168 in the 17th electoral term – stand little chance of adoption. In the seven terms from 1983 to 2013, only five out of a total of 1,177 bills introduced by opposition groups obtained a parliamentary majority. In view of the close link between the majority groups and the Government in a parliamentary system, the very slim prospect of success for opposition bills is hardly surprising, which does not mean that they cannot have an indirect effect. The drafting of bills is nevertheless useful for the opposition groups, which generally consider it their responsibility not only to criticise government policy but also to formulate alternatives. This is all the more important when the political balance in the *Länder* enables the opposition groups to exert influence through the Bundesrat.

Bills adopted by the Bundestag, broken down by initiators and voting patterns 8th to 12th electoral terms

	8th term 1976–80		10th term 1983–87		11th term 1987–90		12th term[a] 1990–94	
	No.	%	No.	%	No.	%	No.	%
Adopted by the Bundestag	354	100.0	320	100.0	369	100.0	507	100.0
Government proposals	288	81.4	237	74.1	267	72.4	346	68.3
Bundesrat initiatives	15	4.2	32	10.0	15	4.1	28	5.5
Bundestag initiatives	39	11.0	42	13.1	68	18.4	92	18.1
SPD-FDP coalition	16	4.5						
CDU/CSU-FDP coalition			31	9.7	53	14.4	59	11.2
SPD-Alliance 90/ The Greens coalition								
CDU/CSU	9	2.5	–	–	–	–	–	–
SPD	–	–	–	–	1	0.3	2	0.4
Alliance 90/The Greens[b]			–	–	–	–	–	–
The Left Party[c]							–	–
CDU/CSU, SPD[g]	–	–					–	–
CDU/CSU, SPD, FDP	–	–	11	3.4	12	3.3	29	6.1
CDU/CSU, SPD, FDP, and Alliance 90/The Greens			–	–			2	0.4
SPD, CDU/CSU, and Alliance 90/ The Greens								
SPD, Alliance 90/The Greens, FDP								
Cross-party[d]	14	4.0	–	–	2	0.5	–	–
Non-attached[h]								
Joint initiatives (Fed. Govt/Bundestag, Fed. Govt/Bundesrat or Bundestag/Bundesrat)	12	3.4	9	2.8	19	5.1	41	8.1
Adopted by recorded vote	17	4.8	23	7.2	26	7.0	31[e]	6.1
Adopted unanimously	218	61.6	50	15.6	64	17.3	170[f]	33.5
Promulgated laws	339		320		366		493	

Bills adopted by the Bundestag, broken down by initiators and voting patterns
13th to 17th electoral terms

	13th term 1994–1998		14th term 1998–2002		15th term 2002–2005		16th term 2005–2009		17th term 2009–2013	
	No.	%	No.	%	No.	%	No.	%	No.	%
Adopted by the Bundestag	566	100.0	559	100.0	400	100.0	616	100.0	553	100.0
Government proposals	403	71.2	394	70.5	281	70.3	488	79.2	434	78.5
Bundesrat initiatives	36	6.4	22	3.9	17	4.3	19	3.1	17	3.1
Bundestag initiatives	102	18.0	108	19.3	85	21.3	89	14.4	88	15.9
SPD-FDP coalition										
CDU/CSU-FDP coalition	79	14.0							71	12.8
SPD-Alliance 90/The Greens coalition			93	16.6	–	19.0			–	–
CDU/CSU	–	–	–	–	–	–	–	–	–	–
SPD	1	0.2	–	–	–	–	–	–	–	–
Alliance 90/The Greens[b]	1	0.2	–	–	76	–	–	–	–	–
The Left Party[c]	–	–	–	–	–	–	–	–	–	–
CDU/CSU, SPD[g]	3	0.5	–	–	–	–	70	11.3	–	–
CDU/CSU, SPD, FDP	12	2.1	–	–	–	–	4	0.6	3	0.5
CDU/CSU, SPD, FDP and Alliance 90/The Greens	5	1.1	7	1.3	5	1.3	8	1.3	10	1.8
SPD, CDU/CSU and Alliance 90/The Greens			2	0.5	3	0.8	2	0.3	–	–
SPD, Alliance 90/The Greens, FDP			1	0.4	1	0.3	–	–	–	–
Cross-party[d]	–	–	3	0.5	–	–	2	0.3	2	0.4
Non-attached[h]	1		2				3	0.5	2	0.4
Joint initiatives (Fed. Govt/Bundestag, Fed. Govt/Bundesrat or Bundestag/Bundesrat)	25	4.4	35[i]	6.2	17	4.3	18	2.9	14	2.5
Adopted by recorded vote	43[e]	7.6	41	7.3	23	5.8	40	6.5	44[e]	8.0
Adopted unanimously	159[f]	28.1	210[f]	37.6	No vote		No vote		No vote	
Promulgated laws	552		549		385		612		543	

[a] Bundestag of united Germany from the 12th electoral term
[b] The Greens until 3 October 1990
[c] PDS up to and including the 15th term; represented in the Bundestag from 4 October 1990 as a result of unification; 12th term PDS/LL; insufficient representation in the 15th term to form a parliamentary group
[d] 'Cross-party' refers to initiatives sponsored by all parliamentary groups and smaller groupings.
[e] Excludes recorded votes in mediation proceedings.
[f] Includes a high percentage of acts of consent to international agreements, which have become more numerous since the 12th term.
[g] In the 16th term the CDU/CSU and the SPD formed a Grand Coalition.
[h] Initiatives launched by Members not belonging to a parliamentary group
[i] Includes eight bills based on committee recommendations.

Note: The difference between the sum of the individual figures and the indicated total is due to the merging and splitting of bills.

In the early days of the Federal Republic, the Bundesrat introduced few legislative proposals, but since the 1970s it has been responsible for more than ten per cent of all bills presented to the Bundestag. Some five per cent of the laws that have been enacted were initiated by the Bundesrat.

Initiatives for government bills, particularly for the adaptation of existing laws, are often launched by specialised divisions of government ministries; only in the case of major or politically controversial issues are initiatives expressly launched by the political leadership.

Even when the ministry draft is being developed, diverse exchanges of information and coordination processes are often taking place already within the government department in question, with other ministries and frequently with representatives of associations too. Increasing importance also attaches in this context to academic policy advice in the form of expert opinions, commissions and hearings. The impact-assessment requirements for proposed legislation were tightened when they became part of the revised Joint Rules of Procedure of the Federal Ministries in the year 2000.

Once the senior management team at the ministry have adopted the draft, it is formally transmitted to all other relevant government departments for their opinion. In certain circumstances, the appropriate specialised bodies and associations, ministries in the *Länder* and associations of local authorities as well as the offices of the parliamentary groups are also 'officially' informed. After requests for amendments have been considered, and possibly acted upon, and after a legal examination by the Ministry of Justice, the draft is then forwarded to the Federal Chancellery for consideration at one of the next cabinet meetings. In the case of major proposals, the fundamental policy decisions are often taken by the coalition committee rather than in cabinet.

The Bundesrat has six weeks to state its opinion on government bills adopted by the Federal Cabinet and generally compiles a very detailed opinion. The Federal Government then transmits the unaltered bill to the Bundestag, along with the opinion of the Bundesrat and the Government's counterstatement; only in rare cases does the Government dispense with transmission to the Bundestag.

Parliamentary discussion of bills

Bills introduced in the Bundestag are traditionally considered in three stages (readings); only acts of consent to international agreements (Article 59 of the Basic Law) are adopted after two readings. As a rule, a meeting of the Council of Elders and talks held by the parliamentary secretaries of the various groups determine when a bill is to be dealt with in plenary, whether a plenary debate is planned and, if so, how much time is to be allocated to it. If the groups of the governing coalition determine the procedure by majority decision, this normally draws protests from the Opposition.

The first reading of a bill of any real political significance is generally accompanied by a plenary debate. This compels the parliamentary groups to adopt a position internally and make that position public at an early stage in the process. At this point, however, there is no vote on the merits of the proposal or indeed a definition of the principles underlying the bill which would be binding on the committees, as is customary in some other parliamentary systems.

At the end of the first reading, the bill is referred to a lead committee – the committee responsible for its passage through Parliament – and usually to several other committees asked for their opinion. In the case of government proposals, primary responsibility is normally assigned to the committee corresponding to the ministry that has drafted the bill. The House will almost always accept the referral proposals agreed by the Council of Elders or based on subsequent inter-group agreements. If a parliamentary group does not agree with the choice of committees or believes the bill should not be referred to committee at all, a formal vote must take place in the plenary chamber. Appointing a committee to steer a proposal through the parliamentary process is certainly more than a mere formality and can even be crucial on occasion. Although this lead committee is supposed to take account of the opinions submitted to it by the other committees, the fact remains that the ultimate decision lies with it.

In general terms, it may be said that the sooner the majority groups start trying to influence the formulation of a bill, the more likely they are to succeed. Once a piece of draft legislation reaches the committees, the parliamentary groups have already more or less adopted their stance.

In committee, about two thirds of bills undergo amendment, but these amendments are seldom designed to call into question the political aims of the proposal. The amendments are frequently adjustments necessitated by recent developments or Bundesrat proposals which the Federal Government has endorsed.

At the committee stage, the opposition groups have few means of directly influencing bills presented by the government or the parliamentary majority. Their influence becomes far greater, however, if *Land* governments of their own political hue command a majority in the Bundesrat. Even in these circumstances, however, amendments made to bills on the basis of opposition motions tend to be fairly rare.

The extent to which the Government or parliamentary majority is willing to compromise with the opposition parties will have been signalled at first reading, particularly through its response to the recommendations made by the Bundesrat, and will certainly become clear during the parliamentary groups' and coalition bodies' preparations for the committee stage. Consideration of options proposed by the Bundesrat majority in the development of government drafts often ensures that bills are ready at an early stage for presentation to the Bundesrat or leads to their withdrawal. In this respect the legislative process can in some ways come to resemble democratic bargaining.

The concluding deliberations in plenary cannot take place before the second day after the distribution of the recommendation for a decision and the report from the lead committee, unless the parliamentary groups agree to waive the time limit. In the case of the numerous bills that are treated as financial proposals, the report from the Budget Committee must also be available before the start of the concluding deliberations. Where such bills have been initiated by the parliamentary groups or five per cent of the Members of the Bundestag, the Federal Government must also be given the opportunity to state its opinion. Only when the report has been received or when a four-week time limit has elapsed can the proposal be put on the agenda.

In practice, the second and third readings of bills are combined under a single agenda item. There is normally a general debate, which may also cover motions for amendments and resolutions. A decision to dispense with the debate requires the approval of all parliamentary groups. Quite often, however, the time available within the schedule of debates will only permit a brief technical discussion of the proposal.

The general debate is followed by the discussion of particular details and the votes at second reading. A separate vote may be taken on the individual provisions, or there may be a single vote on the whole bill as adopted in committee; amendments and, where appropriate, the resolution recommended by the lead committee are also put to the vote. Any Member of Parliament may table an amendment. In practice, however, they are almost exclusively an instrument of the parliamentary groups. The Opposition generally uses them to present in public its ideas that were rejected in committee, but such amendments are normally voted down. The second reading is often a complex process. Members with no experience of the specific matter in question rely on the specialists and on signals from the parliamentary secretaries at voting time. The third reading and final vote normally follow immediately. If all parts of a bill are voted down at the second reading, the third reading does not take place.

Procedure in the Bundesrat and signature

After bills have been adopted by the Bundestag, the President of the Bundestag transmits them to the Bundesrat without delay. If the governments of the *Länder*, represented in the Bundesrat, raise objections, the Bundesrat is authorised by Article 77 of the Basic Law to demand that a mediation committee be convened, which it did in 894 cases in the first 17 electoral terms, mainly with regard to bills requiring the consent of the Bundesrat. It will not come as a surprise that this right has been exercised chiefly at times when the Bundesrat and Bundestag have had majorities of different political persuasions. The Federal Government and the Bundestag too have occasionally initiated the mediation procedure. The Mediation Committee, comprising 16 members each from the Bundestag and Bundesrat, meets behind closed doors. In most cases, the Mediation Committee has reached agreement on amendments, and these have then been adopted, as a rule, by both the Bundestag and Bundesrat.

When the Bundestag adopts legislation for which the consent of the Bundesrat is not required, the Bundesrat may, if the Mediation Committee has been unsuccessful, lodge an objection within two weeks, which an absolute majority of the Members of the Bundestag may decide to reject – and usually does. Laws requiring consent, on the other hand, cannot be adopted without the express approval of the Bundesrat. The Bundesrat, to be sure, can also immediately reject a law for which its consent is required, but this rarely happens. Its only means of obtaining amendments at this stage is through the convening of the Mediation Committee. If the latter's proposal for the amendment or repeal of legislation is adopted by the Bundestag, the Bundesrat must make a decision.

Laws only require the consent of the Bundesrat where the Basic Law so prescribes. Contrary to the expectations of the Parliamentary Council, well over half of all laws since the end of the 1950s have required the consent of the Bundesrat. This development, albeit unintended, was made possible chiefly by the terms of Article 84 of the Basic Law, whereby the consent of the Bundesrat is required in cases where federal laws contain provisions

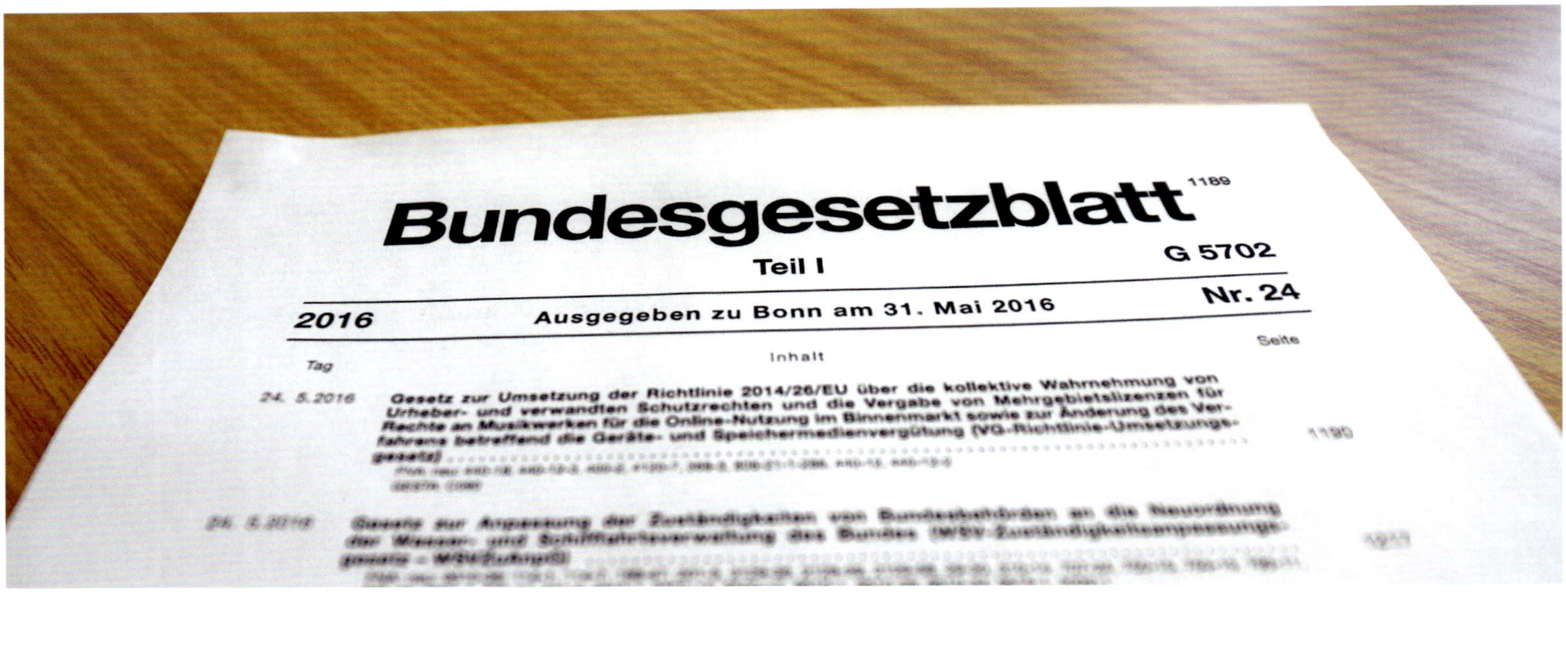

relating to their implementation by the authorities of the *Länder*, which they frequently do. The constitutional amendments adopted as part of stage one of the reform of the federal system in 2006, particularly the amendment of Article 84 of the BasicLaw, did bring about a sharp fall in the percentage of laws that required the consent of the Bundesrat, which amounted to only 38.3 % in the 17th electoral term (2009–2013). It remains to be seen, however, whether this trend will continue when opposing parties command majorities in the Bundestag and Bundesrat.

In order to enter into force, a law must be signed by the President of the Federal Republic without delay and promulgated in the Federal Law Gazette. The President may not withhold his or her signature for political reasons but may do so for legal reasons if the legislative process has failed to comply with the constitution in some way.

Treaty legislation and parliamentary decisions on force deployments abroad

The increasing interdependence of foreign and domestic policy also impacts on the work of the Bundestag. Foreign policy has become increasingly wide-ranging and complex. In a context of globalisation and European integration, it reaches far beyond the traditional fields of peacemaking, security and external trade and encompasses to an ever greater extent areas that were once purely internal matters. Almost all German government ministries now have to deal with international agreements that require the consent of the Bundestag in the form of implementing acts, and their corresponding Bundestag committees are likewise involved as lead committees or as committees asked for an opinion.

The role of the Bundestag was reinforced by a judgment delivered in 1994 by the Federal Constitutional Court, which ruled that prior constitutive approval of the Bundestag had to be obtained for every operational deployment of German armed military forces abroad. While it was decided not to amend the Basic Law to this effect, at the end of 2004, after ten years of practice without a legal basis, the Bundestag, adopted a legislative instrument known as the Parliamentary Participation Act (*Parlamentsbeteiligungsgesetz*). Since the judgment of the Federal Constitutional Court, more than 100 decisions have been adopted on the deployment of armed military forces abroad; about two thirds of these concerned the continuation of existing deployments. Though often preceded by a fierce war of words, deployment decisions have generally been carried by a large majority of the Bundestag.

Parliamentary discussion of EU documents and influence on EU legislation

The development of the European Community and the founding of the European Union has resulted in a substantial transfer of legislative powers to the Community (the EC and EU). In more recent times, this process has been driven forward by the Single European Act of 1986/87, the Maastricht Treaty (1992/93), which established the European Union , the 1997 Treaty of Amsterdam and the Treaty of Lisbon, which entered into force on 1 December 2009. The powers that were forfeited by national parliaments as a result of these developments created a serious democratic deficit, although this has been tempered since the time of the Single European Act by considerable increases in the legislative powers of the European Parliament and by enhanced information and participation rights for national parliaments. The number of EU proposals forwarded to the Bundestag, which

For a law to be valid, it must be promulgated in the Federal Law Gazette (*Bundesgesetzblatt*), which is published by the Federal Ministry of Justice in Bonn and administered by the *Bundesanzeiger* publishing office. The public promulgation medium of the Federal Republic of Germany is the successor publication to the *Reichsgesetzblatt*, which was published from 1871 to 1945. It has been appearing since the promulgation of the Basic Law (Federal Law Gazette, 1949, p. 1).

v. Marschall
CDU/CSU

The Committee on the Affairs of the European Union deals with all matters relating to government policy on Europe. In the past, such matters have included the introduction of the euro, the abolition of internal borders, accession negotiation with potential new EU members and the euro rescue package. Over the last few years the committee has further gained in importance, partly through the Treaty of Lisbon.

was already large, has continued to rise over the past ten years. Some 25,000 documents relating to EU matters reach the Bundestag every year. The political significance and the impact and reciprocal effects of individual EU documents are often hard to gauge. The bulk of these documents concern EU legislative acts, a distinction being made between regulations, directives and decisions. Regulations have general application. They are binding in their entirety and are directly applicable in all Member States. Decisions are binding on the Member States, enterprises and individuals that they specify. Directives set binding objectives for all or some of the Member States but leave it to national authorities to determine the form and methods to be used to achieve the prescribed result (Article 288 of the Treaty on the Functioning of the European Union). It is not unusual for difficulties to arise when Member States transpose what are often highly detailed directives by means of national laws and regulations. About two thirds of the laws that apply in Germany are European legislative acts. In addition, a large percentage of federal laws are influenced by European initiatives.

The Federal Government is required to inform the Bundestag "comprehensively and at the earliest possible time" (Article 23(2) of the Basic Law) of matters concerning the European Union. The Act on Cooperation between the Federal Government and the German Bundestag in Matters concerning the European Union (EUZBBG) also stipulates that this information should be provided "continuously" and, in principle, in writing. "The notification shall cover, in particular, the Federal Government's decision-making process, the preparation and course of discussions within the institutions of the European Union and the opinions of the European Parliament, of the European Commission and of the other Member States of the European Union as well as the decisions that have been taken. The same shall also apply to all preparatory bodies and working groups" (section 3 EUZBBG). Matters concerning the European Union also encompass international agreements and intergovernmental arrangements "if they supplement, or are otherwise closely related to, the law of the European Union" (section 1).

The Federal Government must also provide the Bundestag with an opportunity to state its position before participating in legislative acts of the EU and must "take that position into account" during the negotiations (Article 23(3) of the Basic Law). Such statements of position are still a rarity. Nevertheless, the large number of motions for resolutions that Bundestag committees table on EU documents testifies to the intense scrutiny and influence to which the Federal Government is subjected. New organisational structures were needed to deal competently with the growing volume of documents. The expansion of the former European Affairs Division of the Bundestag Administration into the European Affairs Directorate and the prioritisation procedure that was formally introduced in 2008 greatly improved the conditions for appropriate participation by Bundestag Members and parliamentary groups in European decision-making. Since then, the referral of EU documents to committee has been subject to new rules, which are designed to ensure concentration on politically important projects.

It remains to be seen whether the new rules will lead to a sustained reinforcement of the role of the Bundestag in the political decision-making process in the realm of EU affairs and thereby lend the process greater legitimacy.

A specific political role is played by the Committee on the Affairs of the European Union, which, besides 34 Members of the Bundestag, currently includes 15 German Members of the European Parliament, who can take part in the committee's deliberations but have no voting rights. The EU Affairs Committee is responsible for fundamental matters of European integration; as a committee whose remit cuts across ministerial portfolios, it deals especially with European projects covering various different policy areas. Lastly, as the specialised committee on European matters, it also deals with proposals that have implications for government policy on European integration, typically with a view to delivering an opinion. The transposition of EU directives that have already been adopted, on the other hand, is a matter for the competent specialised committees.

Parliamentary scrutiny and communication

The process of reaching political decisions is subject to a wide range of oversight mechanisms. Their effectiveness depends to a great extent on whether they are transparent and whether they initiate reflection and responses among the public at large.

Besides the reviewing of executive activity, prior and ongoing scrutiny have come to play a considerably more significant role. Parliamentary scrutiny cannot be effective if it only begins after the Federal Government, with its huge administrative apparatus, has already prepared, or even implemented, draft legislation and other projects in consultation with major associations.

Opposition and government groups exercise scrutiny differently. The formal instruments of oversight with the highest public profile are used predominately by the opposition groups. In the five electoral terms from 1994 to 2013, for example, those groups accounted for more than 95 % of all major interpellations and about 99 % of all minor interpellations addressed to the Federal Government. The purpose of these interpellations is to obtain factual information, but their chief purpose is to expose the intentions and shortcomings of government policy and lay them open to criticism. In addition, they offer the Opposition an opportunity, which it takes in many different ways, to present and justify alternative positions. The key criterion of their effectiveness is the public response they evoke.

The groups of the governing coalition, on the other hand, seldom make use of the formal oversight mechanisms to scrutinise government activity. As a rule, they seek to give the Government the opportunity to portray its policies in a favourable light.

Summoning members of the Federal Government

Under Article 43 of the Basic Law, the Bundestag and its committees may require the presence of the Federal Chancellor and of each individual federal minister, who are then bound to answer questions from the House or the relevant committee. Conversely, members of the Government or the Bundesrat may attend all sittings of the Bundestag and meetings of its committees and have the right to be heard at any time. Motions for a summons to the plenary may be tabled by the parliamentary groups or by five per cent of the Members of Parliament. The decision to summon a member of the Government, however, can only be made by a majority, which blunts the impact of this instrument of parliamentary scrutiny.

Number of questions, question times, debates on matters of topical interest and questions addressed to the Federal Government

	1st term 1949–53	2nd term 1953–57	3rd term 1957–61	4th term 1961–65	5th term 1965–69	6th term 1969–72	7th term 1972–76	8th term 1976–80	9th term 1980–83
Major Interpellations	160	97	49	35	45	31	24	47	32
Minor Interpellations	355	377	411	308	488	569	480	434	297
Oral questions	392	1069	1536	4786	10733	6966	12925	11826	4971
of which urgent questions	–	–	2	33	198	135	74	49	13
Written questions	–	–	–	–	–	4107	5572	11641	9413
Question times	16	44	96	178	223	176	168	135	79
Debates on matters of topical interest	–	–	–	2	17	8	20	9	12
Reports from cabinet meetings and questions addressed to the Fed. Gov.	–	–	–	–	–	–	8	–	–

	10th term 1983–87	11th term 1987–900	12th term 1990–94	13th term 1994–98	14th term 1998–02	15th term 2002–05	16th term 2005–09	17th term 2009–13	all terms
Major Interpellations	175	145	98	156	101	65	63	54	1377
Minor Interpellations	1006	1419	1382	2070	1813	797	3299	3629	19134
Oral questions	7028	4034	4160	3540	3299	2515	2703	6164	88702
of which urgent questions	41	39	55	34	83	37	111	107	1011
Written questions	15836	16117	16661	14905	11838	11069	12789	20141	150093
Question times	142	107	121	79	68	52	67	71	1822
Debates on matters of topical interest	117	126	103	103	141	71	113	131	973
Reports from cabinet meetings and questions addressed to the Fed. Gov.	3	32	44	41	61	42	59	69	358

Since the creation of the Bundestag, 100 motions to summon government members have been tabled, almost all of them from the ranks of the Opposition. Twenty-three of these motions have actually been carried. The occasional interest of opposition groups in summoning ministers is explained by the fact that the Government is forced to explain itself and is subjected to public criticism when competent ministers are absent from plenary debates on key political issues. The indirect preventive effect of occasional summonses is no less important than their public impact and their successful outcome.

Interpellations and Question Time

The right to ask questions is one of the classic powers of scrutiny vested in parliaments and their members. The Rules of Procedure contain specific provisions governing major and minor interpellations, Question Time and individual written questions. One purpose of these instruments is to obtain information which Members of Parliament need for their legislative and supervisory activity in committee and plenary, but they also serve as a 'direct' means of scrutinising the activities of the Government or the parliamentary majority. They do this by providing an opportunity to subject government policy to critical examination in public and to present alternatives, thereby compelling the governing majority to justify its position.

Among the high-profile information and oversight mechanisms in routine parliamentary procedure, the major interpellation is surely the most significant. Major and minor interpellations are written questions which may be submitted to the Government by any parliamentary group or a sufficient number of Members of Parliament. At the request of a parliamentary group, a major interpellation must be placed on the agenda following receipt of the reply or if the Federal Government refuses to reply to it or fails to do so within three weeks.

The major interpellation is particularly useful as a means of eliciting a fundamental and detailed political opinion on major issues from the Government. What gives this instrument its cutting edge is the fact that it enables parliamentary groups to force a plenary debate. As is only to be expected, the oversight and communication mechanism of the major interpellation is used primarily by opposition groups. Most of these interpellations relate to major issues of political importance.

Unlike major interpellations, minor interpellations attract only a written reply, for which the normal time limit is 14 days. They may not be placed on the agenda for debate. Minor interpellations provide an opportunity to obtain a reply to requests for information within two weeks and to demand a statement of the Government's position. They are submitted almost exclusively by opposition groups.

Every Member of Parliament has the right to address brief individual questions to the Federal Government for oral or written reply. In sitting weeks a two-hour period of Question Time takes place. Members make ample use of their right to ask questions. Even the proceedings at Question Time, however, are subject to a certain degree of coordination within the parliamentary groups.

Individual Members ask far more questions requiring a written answer than oral questions; the former account for some 80 % of all questions submitted (20,141 out of 26,305 in the 17th electoral term). Another factor is that some of the oral questions on the Question Time schedule can only be answered in writing, partly for want of time.

The questioners ask for specific factual information. The overwhelming majority of questions, however, are designed to prompt the Government to reveal and explain its assessment of political developments and statements as well as its intended action and current plans.

Question-and-answer session

For decades there was repeated criticism of the fact that the Federal Government made its first report on the proceedings and content of cabinet meetings to the Federal Press Association rather than the plenary assembly of the Bundestag and that it opted for individual interviews with cabinet members as its preferred channel of communication with the general public. In order to reduce this information gap in favour of the executive in the mass media, there were calls for many years for the Federal Government to report regularly to Parliament. After some experience of such reporting had been gathered, a ministerial question-and-answer session was established in the Rules of Procedure of the Bundestag in 1990.

The question-and-answer session takes place regularly on Wednesdays after the cabinet meeting and is supposed to last for 30 minutes as a rule. At the beginning, a member of the Federal Government is given five minutes' speaking time on request, and ministers generally exercise this right. The important point is that the Members of Parliament need not confine their questions to the preceding cabinet meeting but can ask about any matter falling within the responsibility of the Government. In practice, however, most or even all of the session is devoted to a single item from the preceding cabinet meeting. Moreover, the criticism has been levelled at the way in which questions are often answered superficially and evasively. The question-and-answer session has not fully lived up to expectations, and new reforms are therefore being considered.

Left: Omid Nouripour (Alliance 90/The Greens) and Gregor Gysi, chair of the parliamentary group of The Left Party, addressing the House at the special sitting of 1 September 2014 on the situation in Iraq. Right: Thomas Oppermann, chair of the SPD group, delivers a speech during the special sitting on the Bundestag on the result of the referendum on continued British membership of the EU on 28 June 2016.

Debates on government policy statements

The term 'government policy statement' is associated primarily with the comprehensive presentation of the Government's legislative programme at the start of the electoral term or after the formation of a new government. In the course of a electoral term, however, the Federal Chancellor and federal ministers also deliver government policy statements on specific issues. These are an important instrument in publicly presenting and ensuring support for government policy. Under Article 43 of the Basic Law, the Government may make a statement to the Bundestag at any time. During the last electoral term, from 2009 to 2013, a total of 51 such statements were made. These statements primarily concern international relations, foreign and security policy, EU affairs and economic relations. About a third of government policy statements are now devoted to internal affairs. Policy statements are used to demonstrate the ability of the Government to act decisively; to emphasise Germany's international presence and its standing in the global community and to determine the political issues of the day and the timing of their discussion by Parliament. For the parliamentary majority, they serve to ensure that the Government is always one step ahead of the Opposition in terms of media coverage.

Government policy statements are generally the occasion for a major debate, which often lasts for several hours and is dominated by the contributions of leading members of the parliamentary groups and of the Government. The reply to the policy statement is normally delivered by the head of the largest opposition group or one of his or her deputies. Policy statements and the ensuing debates are closely observed by the mass media. They are also a means whereby the Chancellor can commit recalcitrant coalition partners and wings of parliamentary groups to a common government policy line. This pressure to display unity in public is rendered all the more effective by the fact that Members often have to vote on motions for resolutions, which may be done immediately after the debate, not infrequently by recorded vote. Some motions for resolutions are referred to committee, which means that they will have to be dealt with again in plenary at a later date.

Debates on matters of topical interest

By introducing debates on matters of topical interest in 1965, the Bundestag equipped itself with a means of addressing topical issues quickly and conducting political debates on those issues with brief contributions.

In debates on matters of topical interest, individual Members may not speak for more than five minutes in order to guarantee a lively exchange of arguments. The absence of motions and decisions on the matter in hand is intended to keep the discussion process as open-ended as possible. The duration of the debate is limited to one hour.

Federal Government policy statements

Electoral term	1st	2nd	3rd	4th	5th	6th	7th	8th	9th	10th	11th	12th	13th	14th	15th	16th	17th	1st–17th
Federal Chancellor	25	7	4	7	16	14	20	19	13	25	24	19	16	32	13	16	26	296
Federal Ministers	2	8	4	3	8	11	18	3	3	24	14	16	30	28	10	18	25	225
Total	27	15	8	10	24	25	38	22	16	49	38	35	46	60	23	34	51	521

Question time with Minister of State Michael Roth on 19 March 2014. In Bundestag sitting weeks, question time always takes place on Wednesdays from 1.30 to 3.30 p.m. During question time, Members of Parliament put questions to the representative of the Federal Government and receive an oral reply. The questions must be received by the President of the Bundestag by 12 noon on the preceding Friday; urgent questions in the public interest may also be submitted up to 12 noon on the day before question time. Each Member of the Bundestag may submit a maximum of two questions per sitting week, and the questioner as well as any other Member may ask two supplementary questions, provided they are connected with the original question.

Debates on matters of topical interest come about as the result of an inter-group agreement in the Council of Elders or at the request of a parliamentary group or of five per cent of the Members of the Bundestag. Until 1980, a parliamentary minority could not insist on a debate on a matter of topical interest unless it was dissatisfied with the answer given by a representative of the Federal Government to an oral question – an option that is still available. The fact that more debates have been held on matters of topical interest since then – a total of 905 took place between 1983 and 2013 – is due to the rivalry between two opposition groups after the change of government in 1982/83 and to the keen interest of the Green parliamentary group in this means of scrutiny, which can be spontaneously activated and has a high public profile.

The subjects debated are diverse, covering virtually the entire spectrum of political activity. Debates on mattersof topical interest often focus on recent incidents at home and abroad or on controversial decisions and political statements. The mass media report regularly and comparatively extensively on these debates. The scope they offer for a politically fruitful discussion, however, is not always fully exploited. Where all parliamentary groups agree that there is a need to discuss a particular issue, increasing use has also been made of an instrument known as the 'agreed debate', which is likewise conducted independently of any specific motion for a decision.

Substantive motions

One extensively used means of carrying out political scrutiny and taking political initiatives is the substantive motion, which can take the form of an autonomous motion or a motion for a resolution and can serve to bring about a 'simple' parliamentary resolution. In addition to participation in the legislative process, this is another means available to the parliamentary groups to initiate parliamentary resolutions. Such a decision, while not legally binding on the Government, is regarded as politically binding. The vast majority of autonomous motions deal with substantive political issues. Since the Rules of Procedure do not restrict their content, they are highly versatile instruments.

Motions for a resolution give the parliamentary groups a means of expressing their opinion in written form, in addition to their oral contributions, and of bringing about the adoption of a parliamentary resolution on government reports and statements, on major interpellations and legislative bills and on other items. Like other submissions to the House, autonomous motions and motions for a resolution must be signed by a parliamentary group or by five per cent of the Members of Parliament. The number of autonomous motions and motions for resolutions has risen considerably since 1983, when a second opposition group entered Parliament. In the 17th electoral term, from 2009 to

2013, 88 % of the 1,918 autonomous motions and 94 % of the 383 motions for resolutions were tabled by the Opposition. The chances of the opposition groups obtaining a majority for substantive motions are slim. Nevertheless, they are an indispensable and high-profile means of exercising scrutiny and exerting influence.

Each form of motion has its own specific function in the process of political opinion-forming. Autonomous motions may be placed on the agenda even though they are unconnected with any of the items under discussion. At the request of the mover of the motion, this must be done no later than three weeks after the date of distribution of the relevant printed paper. In this way, minority groups can secure debates on their own chosen issues, and they make ample use of this mechanism.

Motions for a resolution can also be referred to committee. This happens quite often to motions for resolutions on major interpellations and on government policy statements.

Especially for the opposition groups, substantive motions are an important means of presenting alternative strategies and action programmes. The governing majority is compelled not only to address these alternatives in the debate but also to show where it stands by the way it casts its votes.

Federal Government reports

Since the mid-1960s, reports from the Federal Government to the Bundestag have been a very significant means of obtaining information and opening government activity to scrutiny. Most government reports are compiled at the request of the Bundestag, which often stipulates that they are to be presented at regular intervals. Such requests arise when committees and parliamentary group bodies dealing with bills discover that they need to draw on past experience or obtain more information or when they identify a lack of planning alternatives.

About half of these reports deal with particular legislative provisions and programmes. A distinction should be made between these and the reports which are devoted to the sphere of activity of a ministry or which deal with a broad area of political activity that cuts across departmental boundaries. Examples of these are the agricultural report, the report on social affairs, the environment report, the report on state aid and the report on human rights.

Since government reports can only be requested by a majority vote, the Opposition has limited scope to exert pressure by this means. Pressure is most likely to be exerted on the government and the departmental civil service by obligations to present periodic reports at prescribed intervals. The Opposition can most expect to derive some benefit from specialists' reports produced by 'independent' government-appointed commissions whose status and reporting obligations are enshrined in law. Although the Government may express an opinion on these reports, it is duty-bound to publish them unedited. For example, the Government is regularly confronted with the annual report from the German Council of Economic Experts.

Major plenary debates are held on most reports covering one or more areas of government policy but also on many reports relating to specific measures. Some reports have also aroused widespread public discussion.

Parliamentary discussion of the budget and financial control

At first sight, budgetary primacy lies with Parliament, since the budget is adopted each year by means of an Act of Parliament, the Budget Act, since close attention is paid by parliamentarians and the general public to budget debates and since the Budget Committee is regarded as the most influential Bundestag committee. In actual fact, however, the budget clearly bears the stamp of the executive, as both practical observation and the relevant constitutional provisions show.

The presentation of the draft budget and the budget is a matter for the Federal Government alone. Once the cabinet has adopted the budget, the Federal Government transmits it to the Bundesrat in the form of a bill containing the proposed Budget Act and budget and, in order to save time, simultaneously presents it to the Bundestag (Basic Law, Article 110).

The draft budget should be presented in good time for the first reading to take place immediately after the summer recess in the first half of September and for the second and third readings in the Bundestag and the so-called second passage through the Bundesrat to be completed before the Christmas recess. In the intervening period, the Budget Committee engages in a series of intensive discussions. As a rule, the Bundestag has adhered to this timetable. This has only been possible because the members of the Budget Committee were already informed of the content of the draft budget before it was officially transmitted.

The budget speech, delivered by the Federal Minister of Finance, is followed by a debate lasting several days, in which the main focus of attention is the general debate involving leading politicians. After the budget debate, the Budget Bill and the draft budget are referred to the Budget Committee; the specialised committees can only deliver an advisory opinion, and most of them take the opportunity to do so.

The system of rapporteurs in the Budget Committee is similar to that of the other committees but has a few distinctive features. For one thing, there is an even higher degree of specialisation; for another, the flow of information between the rapporteurs and group spokespersons and the departmental bureaucracy is far more intensive, and their working contacts are far more frequent.

After the formal referral of the draft budget to the Budget Committee, detailed talks are held in the ministries, involving the rapporteurs and co-rapporteurs as well as senior civil servants from the ministry in question and from the Federal Court of Audit. Before the Budget Committee begins its deliberations, the departmental budgets and the rapporteurs' proposals are discussed by the competent working groups of the parliamentary groups and by the specialised parliamentary committees, which submit proposals for amendments in their advisory opinions. The process is concluded with a 'tidying-up' meeting of the Budget Committee, at which all outstanding decisions have to be taken.

Amendments, or at least major amendments, cannot normally be achieved unless they are supported not only by the majority groups in committee and plenary but also by the Government. Notwithstanding the specific way in which members of the

Budget Committee perceive their own role, the group structure of Parliament determines the nature of the budget process too, in that the decisions taken in advance within the parliamentary groups of the ruling coalition usually prevail in the Budget Committee.

In contrast to the traditional perception of the role of Parliament, the Bundestag also plays a part in the execution of the budget. The Budget Committee's most important means of controlling the execution of the budget is the blocking of appropriated funds. In exceptional cases, this mechanism can be used to stipulate that the disbursement of appropriated funds requires the consent of the Bundestag. Increasing use is being made of this lever, particularly in the case of procurement programmes which tie up budgetary resources beyond the current year.

In principle, all parliamentary groups agree that the budgetary sovereignty vested in the Bundestag requires effective control of the execution of the budget, but this is precisely the point at which theory and practice drift far apart. In the quest for effective control, the Auditing Committee was established as a subcommittee of the Budget Committee, but the Auditing Committee is dependent on considerable specialised input from other sources. The capacity of the parliamentary support services, however, is far from sufficient for this task, for which the Bundestag relies primarily on the assistance of the formally independent Federal Court of Audit, which provides Parliament and the Government with an increasing number of advisory services. In spite of the desirability of close collaboration with the Bundestag, and specifically with the Budget Committee, the legal status of the Federal Court of Audit is not that of an auxiliary body of the Bundestag. Its constitutional task is to submit an annual report to the Federal Government as well as to the Bundestag and Bundesrat; its members enjoy judicial independence (Article 114 of the Basic Law).

Committees of inquiry

Under Article 44 of the Basic Law, the Bundestag has the right and, upon the motion of one quarter of its members, the duty to set up a committee of inquiry to take the requisite evidence at public hearings on matters under investigation. This makes the Bundestag one of the few Western European parliaments in which a committee of inquiry can be formally established at the behest of a qualified minority. Committees of inquiry can deal with all matters for which responsibility rests with the Federal Government or the Bundestag itself. In the framework of federal competence, they can also be established to investigate cases of maladministration in areas of non-governmental activity.

In parliamentary practice, the work of committees of inquiry is focused primarily on the investigation of abuses within the Federal Government and the public administration. In several instances, however, investigations have also been conducted with the intention of bringing about improvements, as in the cases of the committees of inquiry into the Flick donations affair, the Transnuklear nuclear-waste scandal, the Commercial Coordination Department of the former GDR Ministry of Foreign Trade, security issues relating to visa policy, the Federal Intelligence Service (BND), the National Socialist Underground (NSU) terrorist group and the National Security Agency (NSA) affair.

The primary purpose of committees of inquiry in the Bundestag is to exercise parliamentary oversight of the Government. They devote themselves to establishing the facts of a particular case when the revelation of those facts is in the public interest, and they report on their findings to Parliament. The legal bases for their appointment are Article 44 of the Basic Law and the Committees of Inquiry Act 2001.

Committees of inquiry

Elec. term	Subject of inquiry	Motion tabled by	Appointment		Committee report (BT printed paper No.)	Chaired by
			Date	Sit. No.		
1st	Review of imports	Bavarian Party	02.02.1950	34	I/1596	Herbert Kriedemann (SPD)
	Review of motor-fuel consumption	SPD	10.02.1950	37	I/4675	Gerhard Schröder (CDU/CSU)
	Review of contracts awarded in the Bonn area	SPD	02.03.1950	44	I/2275 I/3626	Walther Hasemann (FDP)
	Mining disaster at Dahlbusch Colliery	KPD	22.06.1950	71	– [a]	Heinrich Imig (SPD)
	Corruption allegations relating to the vote on the seat of government (known as the *Spiegel* Committee)	Cross-party	05.10.1950	89	I/2274	Johannes Semler (CDU/CSU)
	Theft of documents in the Federal Chancellery	CDU/CSU	11.10.1951	167	– [b]	Walter Menzel (SPD)
	Irregularities in the federal administration	SPD	11.10.1951	167	– [b]	Matthias Hoogen (CDU/CSU)
	Irregularities in the foreign service	SPD	24.10.1951	170	I/3465	Max Becker (FDP)
	Employment of severely handicapped persons by federal departments	SPD	10.09.1952	228	I/4609	Maria Probst (CDU/CSU)
2nd	The case of Otto John	SPD	16./17.09.1954	43	II/3728	Gerd Bucerius (CDU/CSU)
	Pruning of *Reich* and federal legislation	CDU/CSU	28.01.1955	65	II/1404 II/3703	Matthias Hoogen (CDU/CSU)
	Incidents in the Import and Storage Centre for Fats and Oils	SPD	23.02.1956	130	II/3596	Herbert Kriedemann (SPD)
4th	The Fibag Affair	SPD	21.03.1962	21	IV/512 IV/639	M. Hoogen (CDU/CSU)
	The phone-tapping affair	SPD	23.10.1963	91	IV/2170	H. Schmitt-Vockenhausen (SPD)
5th	HS.30 procurement[c]	FDP	16.03.1967	99	V/4527	H.-J. v. Merkatz (CDU/CSU)
	State of the German intelligence services	SPD	13.11.1968	194	V/4208	M. Hirsch (SPD)

Committees of inquiry

Elec. term	Subject of inquiry	Motion tabled by	Appointment of committee Date	Sittings	Committee report (BT printed paper No.)	Chaired by
6th	The Paninternational airline	CDU/CSU	01.10.1971	139	VI/3830	W. Rawe (CDU/CSU)
7th	The Steiner and Wienand affair	CDU/CSU	15.06.1973	43	7/1803	F. Schäfer (SPD)
	The Guillaume affair	CDU/CSU	06.06.1974	105	7/3246	W. Wallmann (CDU/CSU)
8th	Tapping of a telephone conversation with Franz Josef Strauss	CDU/CSU	26.01.1978	69	8/3835	W. Althammer (CDU/CSU)
9th	The case of Lt.-Col. Klaus-Dieter Rauschenbach	CDU/CSU	09.10.1981	57	– [d]	H.-J. Jentsch (CDU/CSU)
10th	The Flick donations affair	SPD	19.05.1983	8	10/5079	M. Langner (CDU/CSU)
	Counter-espionage during Friedrich Zimmermann's period of office as Federal Minister of the Interior	SPD	03.10.1985	162	10/6584	G. Jahn (SPD)
	The *Neue Heimat* housing company	CDU/CSU, FDP	05.06.1986	219	10/6779	H. G. Hüsch (CDU/CSU)
	Sale of submarine plans to South Africa	Greens, SPD	10.12.1986	255	– [d]	W. Penner (SPD)
11th	Sale of submarine plans to South Africa	SPD, Greens	02.04.1987	8	11/8109	H. Eylmann (CDU/CSU)
	The Transnuklear nuclear-waste scandal	CDU/CSU, FDP, SPD, Greens	21.01.1988	55	11/7800	H. Bachmaier (SPD)
12th	Activity of the GDR Bureau for Commercial Coordination	SPD, Alliance 90/Greens	06.06.1991	28	12/3462 12/3920 12/4500	F. Vogel (CDU/CSU)
	The *Treuhand* Privatisation Agency	SPD	30.09.1993	179	12/8404	O. Schily (SPD)
	Infection by HIV-contaminated blood products	SPD, CDU/ CSU, FDP	29.10.1993	186	12/6700 12/8591	G. Scheu (CDU/CSU)
13th	Plutonium smuggling	Alliance 90/Greens, SPD, CDU/ CSU, FDP	11.05.1995	35	13/10800 13/10852[e] 13/10909[e]	G. Friedrich (CDU/CSU)
	Embezzlement of GDR assets	SPD	28.09.1995	58	13/10900	V. Neumann (SPD)

Committees of inquiriy

Elec. term	Subject of inquiry	Motion tabled by	Appointment of committee Date	Sittings	Committee report (BT printed paper No.)	Chaired by
14th	Donations to political parties	SPD, Alliance 90/ Greens	02.12.1999	76	14/9300	V. Neumann (SPD)
15th	Electoral fraud	CDU/CSU	20.12.2002	17	15/2100	K. U. Benneter (SPD)
	Visa policy as a security risk	CDU/CSU	17.12.2004	32	15/5975	H.-P. Uhl (CDU/CSU)
16th	Activities of the Federal Intelligence Service (BND)	FDP, Left Party, Alliance 90/Greens	07.04.2006	33	16/13400	S. Kauder (CDU/CSU)
	Hypo Real Estate (HRE) Crisis[f]	FDP, Left Party, Alliance 90/Greens	26.03.2009	214	16/14000	Dr H.-U. Krüger (SPD)
17th	Gorleben nuclear-waste storage facility	SPD, Left Party, Alliance 90/Greens	26.03.2010	35	17/13700	Dr M. Flachsbarth (CDU/CSU)
	The National Socialist Underground (NSU) terrorist group	CDU/CSU, SPD, FDP, Left Party, Alliance 90/Greens	26.01.2012	155	17/14600	S. Edathy (SPD)
18th	Surveillance activity of the U.S. National Security Agency (NSA)	CDU/CSU, SPD, FDP, Left Party, Alliance 90/Greens	20.03.2014	23	–[g]	Dr P. E. Sensburg (CDU/CSU)
	Operation Spade	Left Party, Alliance 90/Greens	02.07.2014	45	18/6700	Dr E. Högl (SPD)
	The National Socialist Underground (NSU) terrorist group (II)	CDU/CSU, SPD, Left Party, Alliance 90/Greens	11.11.2015	135	–[g]	C. Binninger (CDU/CSU)
	Cum/ex trades	Left Party, Alliance 90/Greens	19.02.2016	157	–[g]	Dr H.-U. Krüger (SPD)

[a] No concluding meeting held by the committee
[b] The procedure was not formally concluded.
[c] The HS.30 is a type of armoured fighting vehicle.
[d] The inquiry was not completed by the end of the electoral term.
[e] Dissenting reports were drawn up by the SPD group (13/10852) and the PDS group (13/10909).
[f] On the economic plight of Hypo Real Estate Holding AG in the autumn of 2008
[g] Not yet concluded at the time of going to print

Since 2001, there has been a Committees of Inquiry Act (*Untersuchungsausschussgesetz*), the first law governing the activities of these bodies. Special procedural rules had previously been adopted by the Bundestag in each electoral term.

The reports that committees of inquiry are required to present to the plenary assembly of the Bundestag generally contain not only factual evidence but also political appraisals and often proposals for improvements too, such as new legislation. There is no risk involved in this. The customary channels of communication with the organs of the parliamentary groups, which are maintained by members of committees of inquiry too, largely guarantee adherence to the 'party line'. Other bodies are not bound by the factual findings, assessments and recommendations of committees of inquiry, although a majority vote certainly carries considerable weight with the executive. In practice, committees of inquiry are almost invariably used as political weapons, particularly in the struggle between the ruling majority and the opposition groups. This, of course, does not rule out the intention of promoting the common good.

Committees of inquiry are high-profile instruments of parliamentary scrutiny, and most of them are therefore requested and secured by opposition parties. Of the 43 committees of inquiry that have hitherto been set up, 31 were requested by an opposition group, five were requested by a group in government, and the other seven were jointly requested by government and opposition groups. In the committees' investigations, however, the battle lines are not always drawn between the opposition and government groups.

The composition of committees of inquiry is also determined by the relative strengths of the parliamentary groups, and the committee members are appointed and dismissed by the groups. The relative strengths of the groups is also taken into account in the appointment of a chairperson.

A notable innovation introduced by the Committees of Inquiry Act is the option of appointing an investigator. The committee of inquiry has the right and, upon the motion of one quarter of its members, the duty to appoint an investigator at any time. The investigator, who acts 'independently' in the fulfilment of his or her mandate, is appointed within three weeks by a two-thirds majority of the members present. By conducting detailed preliminary investigations, he or she is intended to facilitate the work of the committee of inquiry.

Gathering evidence is likewise designed as a minority right. Evidence is to be gathered if one quarter of the members of the committee of inquiry so request. Gathering evidence involves examining witnesses, hearing the testimony of experts, inspecting files and obtaining information, opinions and reports. There has been repeated wrangling in the past between committees of inquiry, or at least their opposition minorities, and the government of the day, and even between committees and the courts, over refusals to release files. Gathering evidence is extremely labour-intensive as a rule. The files examined by the committee of inquiry into the Flick affair, for example, ran to a total of more than 100,000 pages. A large part of the time devoted to parliamentary inquiries is normally taken up by the examination of witnesses and experts.

The Bundestag is not empowered to appoint committees of inquiry to investigate matters relating to military defence. Its investigative powers in this field have been vested in the Defence Committee. If the Defence Committee decides to make a specific matter the subject of investigations, it has the powers of a committee of inquiry. If one quarter of its members demand such investigations, it has the duty to conduct them (Basic Law, Article 45a). In practice, the Defence Committee has used these powers sparingly.

A report compiled by a committee of inquiry is adopted by majority vote. Whereas the 'factual' part of committee reports is often endorsed by the opposition groups too, they arrive at divergent assessments and make different proposals in their dissenting opinions. One notable exception was the committee of inquiry into the NSU during the 17th electoral term from 2009 to 2013, in which consensus unquestionably prevailed. Equipped with an effective set of controls, committees of inquiry are certainly able to investigate the consequences of political decisions and to encourage innovation through their administrative and legislative proposals.

The public effect of such scrutiny is crucially dependent on the opportunities people have to form a judgement on the basis of objective and focused media reporting.

The Petitions Committee

The Petitions Committee of the Bundestag operates as a special kind of monitoring body. Article 17 of the Basic Law guarantees everyone the right to address written requests or complaints to the competent authorities (public authorities or international agencies) and to the legislature. Ample use is made of this right. Over the past few years, the annual number of petitions received has ranged from 15,000 to 18,000. There have also been numerous mass petitions and collective petitions, each submitted with a list of signatories. Mass petitions are large numbers of submissions on the same matter, the text of which is completely or largely identical. Since 2005 it has also been permissible to submit petitions electronically, using a web form (epetitionen.bundestag.de).

Many petitions addressed to the Bundestag relate to specific exceptional cases for which no provision has been made in laws and administrative regulations; many deal with acts or omissions by the public administration which are regarded as unjust or injurious. In such cases, petitions to Parliament may be the only feasible recourse, because they are not subject to administrative rules or time limits. For this reason, the parliamentary petition system is often described as the 'nation's gripe box'.

The right of petition also enables individuals to submit requests, in other words to approach Parliament with suggestions and proposals, particularly with regard to legislation. The public make wide use of this option. About two fifths of the petitions received are submissions on federal legislation. This aspect of the right of petition, focused on the common good, has played an increasingly important role since the emergence of citizens' initiatives in the 1970s. The petitions procedure has been improved over the course of time, and the means open to people to influence the actions of the public authorities have been placed on stronger legal foundations.

A public meeting of the Petitions Committee takes place in the Paul Löbe Building. The committee is responsible for dealing with petitions addressed to the Bundestag. It possesses various powers to enable it to establish relevant facts, including the right to summon and hear witnesses and experts. The committee deals with individual and public petitions.

Under Article 45c of the Basic Law, the Petitions Committee is responsible for dealing with requests and complaints addressed to the Bundestag. The President of the Bundestag must refer all petitions to the Committee. If, however, a petition concerns a subject under debate in one of the specialised committees, the Petitions Committee is required to request the comments of the relevant committee; in practice, the majority of such petitions relate to draft legislation.

In order to allow the Petitions Committee to prepare decisions on complaints, the Federal Government and the federal authorities are required to transmit files, provide information and allow access to their facilities. The significant point is that the Petitions Committee can enforce this right directly against the federal authorities. Only some of the committee's new powers have been exercised, and it has exercised them to a limited extent. The heavy demands on Members' time are one of the reasons for this; another is that the powers can only be used with the approval of a majority of the committee.

Considerable importance attaches to the essential groundwork performed by the committee service of the Bundestag administration (Petitions and Submissions Directorate). Even Members who are willing to participate wholeheartedly in the work of the Petitions Committee soon find themselves close to the limits of their capacity, because they usually also belong to a specialised committee, which is generally their first priority.

The Petitions Committee only deliberates and decides on individual cases that are technically or politically complex and votes on consolidated lists of all the other petitions, a purely formal act. The Petitions Committee reports to the Bundestag on the petitions it has dealt with and makes recommendations for decisions in the form of monthly consolidated summaries. These are almost always the subject of a single blanket vote without debate. The Petitions Committee also submits an annual written report to the Bundestag setting out the focal points of its work.

The Bundestag, however, has the right to refer petitions to the Government, which gives it an additional and by no means ineffective means of overseeing the actions of the Government and the administrative machinery. A petition may be referred to the Government 'for remedial action', 'for re-examination' or 'as background material', but the outcome of such referrals often fails to live up to expectations.

Another important function of petitions is their contribution to performance testing. They frequently expose defects in legislation. This direct feedback and stimulus from the public at large is important and indeed indispensable. Special importance attaches in this context to the large number of collective and mass petitions, in which active citizens join together to put their requests and complaints regarding matters such as legislation to the Petitions Committee and Parliament. The special arrangements adopted in June 2005 have placed greater procedural emphasis on the purpose and political import of collective and

Since 2005, it has also been possible to submit petitions online in the form of e-petitions.

mass petitions. In the case of petitions signed by at least 50,000 people within the space of four weeks, petitioners are heard at an open committee meeting, a procedure that has been put into practice on numerous occasions. This is subject, of course, to the consent of the petitioners and to the proviso that the committee does not reject such a hearing by a two-thirds majority of its members in attendance. Since 2005, it has also been possible to submit, sign and discuss public petitions on the Bundestag website in a participation-friendly procedure that was simplified and made permanent in 2008. Extensive use is now made of these mechanisms. If the individual mass petitions and the signatures appended to collective petitions and public petitions are taken into account, some 1.8 million persons subscribed to a petition to the Bundestag in 2010.

The Parliamentary Commissioner for the Armed Forces

In 1956, following the Scandinavian example, the German Bundestag's Parliamentary Commissioner for the Armed Forces was established as an ombudsman with a particular sphere of responsibility. The Commissioner's duties are laid down in the Act on the Parliamentary Commissioner for the Armed Forces (*Gesetz über den Wehrbeauftragten*).

The Bundestag or its Defence Committee can instruct the Parliamentary Commissioner to examine particular cases, but this power has seldom been exercised. The Parliamentary Commissioner acts on his or her own initiative if, in the exercise of his or her right of troop inspection, through reports from Members of the Bundestag or submissions from members of the armed forces or in any other way, the Commissioner becomes aware of circumstances indicating a violation of the fundamental rights of military personnel or of the principles of leadership development and civic education. In practice, this is the Commissioner's main task.

Great importance attaches to submissions which the Parliamentary Commissioner for the Armed Forces receives from service personnel, which currently exceed 6,000 a year. Every serviceman and servicewoman has the right to communicate directly with the Parliamentary Commissioner without going through official channels. The Commissioner, in other words, is another institution for the receipt of petitions and complaints. Like the Petitions Committee, the Parliamentary Commissioner for the Armed Forces also has to submit a general report to the Bundestag every year; this report is normally the subject of a plenary debate. The Commissioner and his or her staff regularly play an active part in the meetings of the Defence Committee and maintain close contacts with the members of the relevant bodies of the parliamentary groups.

The Parliamentary Commissioner for the Armed Forces, Hans-Peter Bartels (SPD), in conversation with troops during his visit to the German NATO Response Force combat unit in Münster in 2015. In his function as an auxiliary organ of the Bundestag in its exercise of parliamentary oversight of the Bundeswehr, the Commissioner is entrusted with the task of ensuring that the fundamental rights of all service personnel are respected and that the principles of leadership development and civic education are applied in military training.

The Parliamentary Commissioner for the Armed Forces is elected by secret ballot by a majority of the Members of the Bundestag for a five-year term and may be re-elected. The Office of the Parliamentary Commissioner, with a staff of about 50, is part of the Bundestag Administration and assists the Commissioner in his or her activity.

Study commissions

Since 1969 there has been the possibility of appointing a study commission to prepare decisions on significant and wide-ranging issues. In their composition, powers and functioning, study commissions are a distinctive type of committee. Academics and other experts, such as representatives of associations, work with parliamentarians on these commissions and enjoy equal participatory and voting rights. To date, 36 study commissions have been established with the task of analysing complex developments and drawing up proposals for strategic measures. Among the focal points of their work have been new technology and its environmental, economic and social implications. The subjects examined by the most recent study commissions have included the protection of mankind and the environment, the future of the media, economic globalisation, the future of active citizenship, the ethical and legal aspects of modern medicine, culture in Germany and the Internet and digital society.

Parliamentary Commissioners for the Armed Forces

Name	Party	Period in office	Voting result (% of the House in favour of appointment)
Helmut von Grolmann	–	1959–1961	88.2
Hellmuth Guido Heye	CDU	1961–1964	By acclamation
Matthias Hoogen	CDU	1964–1970	59.3
Fritz Rudolf Schulz	FDP	1970–1975	53.7
Karl Wilhelm Berkhan	SPD	1975–1980	90.1
Karl Wilhelm Berkhan	SPD	1980–1985	91.6
Willi Weiskirch	CDU	1985–1990	84.5
Alfred Biehle	CSU	1990–1995	55.9
Claire Marienfeld-Czesla	CDU	1995–2000	71.1
Willfried Penner	SPD	2000–2005	77.8
Reinhold Robbe	SPD	2005–2010	51.3
Hellmut Königshaus	FDP	2010–2015	64.8
Hans-Peter Bartels	SPD	2015–	84.3

The Bundestag is required to set up study commissions at the request of one quarter of its Members. Almost all such decisions taken by the Bundestag, however, have actually been backed by a large majority, sometimes after hard bargaining to thrash out a compromise among the parliamentary groups.

The size of the commissions and the number of parliamentary members is negotiated by the parliamentary groups on a case-by-case basis. They generally comprise equal numbers of Members of the Bundestag and external specialists.

Study commissions are designed to provide what is probably the most intensive form of direct policy advice that exists at the federal level. They allow direct exchanges of information and ideas and can initiate communicative two-way learning processes in the longer term. One of the main keys to success is that the political parties and the Government have not already committed themselves to specific positions before a commission is appointed. The extent to which the reports of study commissions can affect political decision-making processes also depends on successfully creating awareness among the other organs of the parliamentary groups and the specialised committees and generating public discussion.

Technology assessment

Study commissions, however, are appointed for only a limited time. For this reason, after years of discussion, a permanent advisory capacity was established in 1990 for the impact assessment of new technology. Its task is to assess the opportunities and risks that technological developments are likely to bring and to map out response and strategic planning options for political decision-makers. It is the task of the Bundestag Committee on Education, Research and Technology Assessment to arrange for technology assessments and to analyse and evaluate them for the Bundestag. It may commission institutions outside the Bundestag to conduct technology assessments. Since 1990 this has been the task of the Office for Technology Assessment of the German Bundestag (TAB), which has conducted more than 160 studies to date. The TAB gives the committees and parliamentary groups the opportunity to obtain advice independently of interest groups and government departments. On the whole, it is observable that the influence of technology assessment reports on parliamentary decision-making has been growing. The findings of the TAB, however, have received insufficient attention in the public debate.

Parliamentary and constitutional reform

Discussions about reform have accompanied the Bundestag ever since its creation. Although divergence of aims has prevented any major parliamentary reform since the 1969s, the Bundestag has responded to new challenges and has managed, in numerous small steps, to effect significant procedural changes. Some of these changes have been eminently innovative; collectively, they represent a significant institutional adaptation achievement. Reform efforts have proceeded chiefly from the belief that the Bundestag should be both a 'working parliament' and a 'debating parliament', that it should be both the 'workshop of democracy' and the hub of political debate.

Constituent meeting of the Study Commission on the Internet and the Digital Society in a meeting room in the Paul Löbe Building on 5 May 2010. These commissions comprise Members from all parliamentary groups and external experts, all of whom enjoy equal rights.

Bundestag study commissions

Elec. term	Subject of study	Motion tabled by	Date of appointment/Bundestag sitting	Committee membership (Bundestags members, experts)	Chaired by	Commission report
6th	Foreign cultural policy	(1) CDU/CSU 2) Foreign Affairs Committee	18 March1970 39th sitting	5:4	B. Martin (CDU/CSU)	VI/3825 (Z)
	Questions relating to constitutional reform	(1) C. O. Lenz and CDU/CSU (2) SPD, FDP (3) Legal Affairs Committee	8 October 1970 70th sitting	7:12[b]	F. Schäfer (SPD)	VI/3829 (Z)
7th	Foreign cultural policy	Cross-party CDU/CSU, SPD, FDP	22 February 1973 17th sitting	5:5	B. Martin (CDU/CSU) M. Schulze-Vorberg (CDU/CSU)	7/4121
	Constitutional reform	Cross-party CDU/CSU, SPD, FDP	22 February 1973 17th sitting	7:14[b]	F. Schäfer (SPD)	7/5924
	Women and society	(1) CDU/CSU (2) JFG Committee[c]	8 November 1973 64th sitting	5:5	H. Timm (CDU/CSU)	7/5866 (Z)
8th	Women and society	Cross-party CDU/CSU, SPD, FDP	5 ay 1977 25th sitting	5:5	U. Schleicher (CDU/CSU)	8/4461
	Future nuclear-energy policy	(1) SPD, FDP (2) CDU/CSU (3) FT Committee[d]	29 March1979 145th sitting	7:8	R. Ueberhorst (SPD)	8/4341
9th	New information and communication technology	(1) SPD, FDP (2) Committee on Internal Affairs	9 April 1981 31st sitting	9:7 9:7	C. Schwarz-Schilling (CDU/CSU) C. Schwarz-Schilling (CDU/CSU)	9/2442 (Z) 9/2442 (Z)
	Youth protest in a democratic state	(1) SPD, FDP (2) FJG Committee[e]	26 May 1981 38th sitting	7:5	M. Wissmann (CDU/CSU)	9/1607 (Z) 9/2390
	Future nuclear-energy policy	SPD, FDP	26 May 1981 38th sitting	7:8	H. B. Schäfer (SPD)	9/2001 (Z) 9/2130 (Z) 9/2438f
10th	Opportunities and risks of genetic engineering	(1) SPD (2) The Greens (3) FT Committee[d]	29. June 1984 78th sitting	9:8	W.-M. Catenhusen (SPD)	10/6775
	Technology assessment and evaluation: creating conditions for technological development	(1) CDU/CSU, FDP, The Greens (2) SPD (3) FT Committee[d]	14 March 1985 126th sitting	9:8	J. Bugl (CDU/CSU)	10/5844 10/6801 (Z)

Elec. term	Subject of study	Motion tabled by	Date of appointment/Bundestag sitting	Committee membership (Bundestags members, experts)	Chaired by	Commission report
11th	Risks of AIDS and effective ways of reducing them	(1) SPD (2) CDU/CSU, FDP (3) The Greens (4) JFFG Committee[g]	8 May 1987 11th sitting	9:8	H.-P. Voigt (CDU/CSU)	11/2495 (Z) 11/7200
	Structural reform of statutory health insurance	(1) SPD (2) The Greens	4 June 1987 16th sitting	9:9	K. Kirschner (SPD)	11/3267 (Z) 11/6380
	Precautions to protect the earth's atmosphere	1) CDU/CSU, FDP (2) The Greens (3) UNR Committee[h]	16 October 1987 34th sitting	11:9[i]	B. Schmidbauer (CDU/CSU)	11/3246 11/7220 11/8030
	Shaping technological development: technology assessment and evaluation	(1) The Greens (2) SPD (3) FDP (4) FT Committee[d]	5 November 1987 36th sitting	9:8	J. Rüttgers (CDU/CSU)	11/4606 11/4607
	Future education policy – Education 2000	(1) SPD (2) The Greens (3) BW Committee[j]	9 December 1987 48th sitting	9:8	E. Kuhlwein (SPD)	11/5349 (Z) 11/7820
12th	Protecting the earth's atmosphere	(1) CDU/CSU, FDP (2) CDU/CSU, SPD, FDP, Alliance 90/ The Greens	25 April 1991 23rd sitting	13:13[k]	K. Lippold (CDU/CSU)	12/2400 (Z) 12/8300 (Z) 12/8359 (Z) 12/8600
	Protection of humanity and the environment – assessment criteria and prospects for environment-friendly material cycles in an industrial society	(1) SPD (2) UNR Committee[h]	14 February 1992 77th sitting	13:13[l]	E. Schwanhold (SPD)	12/5812 (Z) 12/8260

Bundestag study commissions

Elec. term	Subject of study	Motion tabled by	Date of appointment/Bundestag sitting	Committee membership (Bundestags members, experts)	Chaired by	Commission report
	History and consequences of the SED dictatorship	(1) SPD (2) Alliance 90/Greens (3) CDU/CSU, FDP (4) CDU/CSU, SPD, FDP	12 March 1992 82nd sitting	16:11	R. Eppelmann (CDU/CSU)	12/7820
	Demographic change – challenges posed to the individual and politics by our ageing society	(1) SPD (2) CDU/CSU, FDP	16 December 1992 114th sitting	16:11	A. Fuchs (SPD)	12/7876 (Z)
13th	Protection of humanity and the environment – objectives and framework for sustainable development	CDU/CSU, SPD, Alliance 90/Greens, FDP	1 June 1995 41st sitting	11:11[m]	E. Schwanhold (SPD) M. Caspers-Merk (SPD)	13/7400 (Z) 13/11200
	Demographic change – challenges posed to the individual and politics by our ageing society	CDU/CSU, SPD, Alliance 90/Greens, FDP	1 June 1995 41st sitting	11:11[m]	W. Link (CDU/CSU)	13/1146 (Z)
	Overcoming the consequences of the SED dictatorship in the process of German unification	(1) CDU/CSU, Alliance 90/Greens, FDP (2) SPD (3) WIG Committee[n]	22 June 1995 44th sitting	11:11[m]	R. Eppelmann (CDU/CSU)	13/8700 (Z) 13/11000
	Future of the media	(1) SPD, Alliance 90/ Greens (2) PDS (3) CDU/CSU, FDP (4) WIG-Committee[n]	7 December 1995 77th sitting	11:11[m]	S. Mosdorf (SPD)	13/6000 (Z) 13/8110 (Z) 13/11001

Elec. term	Subject of study	Motion tabled by	Date of appointment/Bundestag sitting	Committee membership (Bundestags members, experts)	Chaired by	Commission report
	So-called sects and psycho-groups	1) SPD 2) WIG-Committee[n]	9 May 1996 104th sitting	11:11[m]	O. Schätzle (CDU/CSU)	13/8170 (Z) 13/10950
14th	Globalisation of the world economy – challenges and responses	SPD, CDU/CSU, Alliance 90/Greens, FDP	15 December 1999 78th sitting	13:13	E. v. Weizsäcker (SPD) E. v. Weizsäcker (SPD)	14/6910 (Z) 14/9200
	Future of civic activities	SPD, CDU/CSU, Alliance 90/Greens, FDP	15 December 1999 78th sitting	11:11	M. Bürsch (SPD)	14/8900
	Demographic change – challenges posed to the individual and politics by our ageing society	SPD, CDU/CSU, Alliance 90/Greens, FDP	16 December 1999 79th sitting	11:11	W. Link (CDU/CSU)	14/8800
	Sustainable energy in the context of globalisation and liberalisation	SPD, CDU/CSU, Alliance 90/Greens, FDP	17 February 2000 87th sittingg	13:13	K.-D. Grill (CDU/CSU)	14/7509 (Z) 14/9400
	The law and ethics of modern medicine	SPD, CDU/CSU, Alliance 90/Greens, FDP	24 March 2000 96th sitting	13:13	M. v. Renesse (SPD)	14/5157 (Z) 14/7546 (Z) 14/9020 (Z)
15th	The ethics and law of modern medicine	SPD, CDU/CSU, Alliance 90/Greens	20 February 2003 28th sitting	13:13	R. Röspel (SPD)	15/3700 (Z) 15/5050 (Z) 15/5858 (Z) 15/5980
	Culture in Germany	SPD, CDU/CSU, Alliance 90/Greens, FDP	3 July 2003 56th sitting	11:11	G. Connemann (CDU/CSU)	15/5560 (Z)
16th	Culture in Germany	CDU/CSU, SPD, FDP, Left Party, Alliance 90/ Greens	15 December 2005 8th sitting	11:11	G. Connemann (CDU/CSU)	16/7000
17th	The Internet and the Digital Society	CDU/CSU, SPD, FDP, Alliance 90/Greens	4 March 2010 27th sitting	17:17	A. E. Fischer (CDU/CSU)	17/12550
	Growth, well-being and quality of life – paths to sustainable economic activity and social progress in the social market economy	CDU/CSU, SPD, FDP, Alliance 90/Greens	1 December 2010 77th sitting	17:17	D. Kolbe (SPD)	17/13300

[a] Reference number of the Bundestag printed paper; (Z) = interim report
[b] Seven of whom are *Länder* representatives appointed by the Bundesrat
[c] Committee on Youth, Family Affairs and Health
[d] Committee on Research and Technology
[e] Committee on Family Affairs, Youth and Health
[f] Progress report
[g] Committee on Youth, Family Affairs, Women and Health
[h] Committee on the Environment, Nature Conservation and Nuclear Safety
[i] Eleven experts from 7 December 1988
[j] Committee on Education and Science
[k] In addition, the PDS/LL and Alliance 90/The Greens groupings each provided one non-voting Member of Parliament
[l] In addition, the PDS/LL and Alliance 90/The Greens groupings each provided one Member of Parliament and one appointed expert as non-voting members
[m] In addition, the PDS grouping provided one Member of Parliament and one appointed expert as non-voting members.
[n] Committee for the Scrutiny of Elections, Immunity and the Rules of Procedure

Since the 1960s, the rights of the minority have been progressively strengthened, reflecting the importance attaching to an effective Opposition in a parliamentary democracy. The powers of the Opposition were chiefly strengthened through the extension of the rights of parliamentary groups. In this way the Bundestag has prepared itself well for its development into a five-party or six-party Parliament in which competition takes place both between and within the government and opposition camps.

Procedural reforms have ensured that, unlike the parliamentary systems in some other countries of the European Union, the German system does not treat bills and other proposals initiated by opposition groups any differently from those emanating from the Government or from the groups of the governing coalition.

The objectives of the reform of the federal system which the Grand Coalition carried through Parliament in the summer of 2006 were to transfer legislative powers and assign them more clearly and to reduce considerably the number of laws that required the consent of the Bundesrat, the ultimate goal being to enhance the effectiveness of both the Bundestag and the state parliaments and to improve the quality of legislation. It has not yet proved possible, however, to satisfy the repeated demands for provisions requiring the Federal Government to provide information and release files to parliamentary minorities, which would likewise have to be enshrined in the Basic Law.

The Bundestag and its parliamentary groups have gradually been responding to the growing diversity and complexity of the tasks of government which have resulted in part from technological developments, the European integration process and globalisation. This response is reflected in increasingly narrow specialisation and in the addition of more staff, information technology and oversight instruments. The advent of the Internet and of the Bundestag and group Intranet as well as the wealth of information and means of interaction that are now available to Members have changed their working methods quite profoundly.

The Bundestag has taken only small steps to accommodate the growing public interest, observable since the 1960s, in participation and communicative involvement in political decision-making processes. A series of new rules have been introduced for the purpose of improving the communicative capacity and transparency of the Bundestag. Not all of them, however, have been implemented as originally intended. Efforts to raise public awareness of parliamentary decision-making processes remain an arduous and unending task in view of the extensive changes to the media structure that have occurred since the 1980s. In order to strengthen the public role of the Bundestag, ministerial question-and-answer sessions and 'plenary core time' – reforms that had long been mooted – were introduced, but at best they have only partly fulfilled expectations. This applies in particular to the option of holding public committee meetings and to extended public committee deliberations, which have rarely taken place. Practical improvements are still being sought. New forums and new forms of public participation and debate may serve to forge a productive link between citizens' initiatives and the parliamentary decision-making process. The revised petitions system which was introduced in 2005 and which has proved its worth, particularly as regards mass petitions and public petitions, is a shining example. Less successful, on the other hand, have been the attempts to include in the Constitution an element of direct democracy at the national level, even though these were largely similar high-profile efforts to link Parliament productively with active citizens. This is especially true of the 2002 proposal for a three-stage instrument of direct democracy, comprising a popular initiative, a petition for a referendum and a referendum, the first such proposal ever made by parliamentary groups of a ruling coalition.

Appropriate reforms cannot be achieved unless the individual steps in the reform process are properly coordinated with each other. Moreover, the future will continue to hold formidable challenges for Members of Parliament. What is expected of them is a strategic, long-term, forward-looking policy. This need is all the more urgent at a time when social, environmental and political problems and their implications are becoming ever more diverse, far-reaching and complex.

“To the German People” – the Reichstag building then and now

Hans Wilderotter

At the start of the plenary sitting on 20 October 1871, Dr Eduard von Simson, President (Speaker) of the Reichstag, expressed his "satisfaction" that "the establishment of a provisional Reichstag building now enables us to pursue our transactions in this new elegant and serviceable accommodation, free from the manifold inconveniences of our previous situation". The President expressed his thanks to the architects and asked the honourable Members of the House to rise to their feet as a token of their approval – which they duly did: as the Minutes state, "The House rose".

This new building that provided the Reichstag with a temporary home was the fruit of the same decision that initiated the construction of its new permanent seat in Berlin's *Spreebogen*, the area south of an arc in the westward course of the River Spree.

This decision was taken at the end of the first debate on a new building, held on 19 April 1871 in the chamber of the Prussian House of Representatives, which played host to the new parliament during its first session from mid-March until mid-June 1871. Parliament asked the Imperial Chancellor to appoint a Commission with a mandate to plan an architectural competition for the new building and to choose a suitable site; since it would probably take years to complete the new building, the Commission was also instructed to propose measures to eliminate "the deficiencies of the present temporary arrangement".

The Commission, which comprised government representatives, members of the Reichstag and officials from the Prussian building administration, proposed, as a transitional solution, the construction of a new temporary building on land belonging to the

This wood engraving, dating from 1872, shows a sitting of the Reichstag in the former premises of the Royal Prussian Porcelain Manufactory at number 4 Leipziger Strasse. The building served as a temporary seat until 1894.

In 1871 a competition was launched to find a suitable design for the planned Reichstag building. Architect Ludwig Bohnstedt won the competition, but the search for an appropriate site proved very difficult, and his plans were never implemented. A coloured steel engraving by J. Ubmach dating from 1871 shows the winning entry.

Royal Porcelain Manufactory at number 4 Leipziger Strasse. This proposal was adopted by a clear majority on 15 June, at the last sitting before the summer recess, enabling the construction work to begin on 26 June 1871. By working round the clock, the builders managed to complete their task in time for mid-October.

The Commission had decided to roof the courtyard between the building facing the front street, the side wing and the rear building for use as a plenary chamber. Rather than use the external courtyard walls of these three buildings, it was decided to build a separate half-timbered architectural structure in the courtyard – a 'building within a building', as it were. The plenary chamber was designed like an amphitheatre, with a total of 400 gently tiered Members' seats arranged in a semicircle. This seating arrangement was entirely new in German parliamentary history and was modelled on the French National Assembly in the Palais Bourbon. The semicircular seating layout faced a longitudinal wall, in the middle of which stood the podium on which the Presidium sat and the rostrum from which Members addressed Parliament. To each side of these, lower than the Presidium but on a higher level than the front tiers of the Members' seats, were two rows of seats for the Bundesrat. The seating was upholstered with light-brown leather, and each Member had a writing desk.

For those who lived through the Bismarck era, that was the Reichstag building. By the time Parliament moved into the later building on Königsplatz, today's Platz der Republik, the first Imperial Chancellor had long been in retirement. Planned as a transitional solution that would last a few years, the temporary fragile building on the site of the porcelain works housed the German Reichstag for 23 years.

The politics of siting and planning the new Reichstag building

The reasons why it took so long to plan and construct the new building were neither technical nor economic but entirely political. Between the parliamentary majority on the one hand and the Government on the other there were considerable differences of opinion on the status and relative importance of Parliament in the institutional structure of the new state; closely connected with this was the question of the way in which the Reichstag should project itself architecturally.

The parliamentary majority wanted to see the construction of a building designed to make the importance of the Reichstag publicly visible and underline its status. In contemporary public discussions, the adjective 'monumental' was used to describe such buildings. Strictly speaking, this idea of monumentality was supposed to be confined to public buildings and expressed size, visibility and appropriate architectural ornamentation. What it meant is evident from a passage dating from 1877 referring to new buildings for imperial ministries. In recent years, it read, importance had been attached "to representing, through the building, the dignity and importance of the authorities seated therein". What was appropriate for public authorities had to be only right and proper for Parliament.

The Government, by contrast, was not interested in such demonstrative parliamentary posturing, because it did not wish to see precedence being given to the role of the Reichstag; it therefore had to try to sideline the Reichstag in architectural terms. That, of course, was not expressed so bluntly. Government representatives, including Otto von Bismarck himself, repeatedly advanced the argument of what they called 'business considerations'. By this they meant that the new building should be constructed near the Imperial Chancellery and the government ministries in Wilhelmstrasse, where the lack of a sufficiently large site would ensure that it could be neither large nor prominent and so could not be monumental.

As the site for the new Reichstag building, the Works Commission selected a plot on Königsplatz, but it was already occupied by the Palais Raczynski, shown here in a photograph from 1876. Count Raczynski lived there during his visits to Berlin, and the Palais also housed his art collection. From the outset, the Count refused to make the land available for the building and could not be persuaded to change his mind.

This was clearly reflected in a statement made by the President of the Imperial Chancellery, Rudolph von Delbrück, on 29 March 1871 in response to a question submitted by Reichstag Member Johannes von Miquel (National Liberal). The Government, said Delbrück, planned to erect a debating chamber behind the building at number 74 Wilhelmstrasse, which had been purchased the previous year to provide offices for the Federal Chancellery of the North German Confederation; the entrance would be in Königgrätzer Strasse, to which the site extended.

Several Members raised objections to this plan. The most vociferous was Hans Victor von Unruh, who emphasised that the government proposal was in no way commensurate with the importance and status of the Reichstag. "A building behind the Federal Chancellery would, to some extent, be hidden. It would be a rear building with its front facade facing the Tiergarten". While it was possible, he said, to imagine quite a fine facade on Königgrätzer Strasse, sooner or later the entrance edifice would be flanked by other buildings. "A roadside building will remain a simple facade, no more than that, however pretty or ugly the apron they tie around it". According to von Unruh, "unless a building stands as freely as possible, its monumental character cannot come to the fore".

It was therefore only logical that, at the decisive sitting on 19 April 1871, a Member of the Reichstag, August Braun, tabled a motion stating that "the construction of a monumental House of Parliament" was "a requirement for the German nation". In the explanatory statement for his motion, Braun declared "that, if a new House of Parliament be built", it should "not merely be makeshift accommodation but should rather be executed in a grand monumental style". For the sake of compromise, however, the decision taken at the end of this debate excluded any reference to monumentality and was worded as follows: "The construction of a Reichstag building that is commensurate with the tasks of the German Reichstag and a representation worthy of the German people is an urgent requirement".

Be that as it may, the Commission which was appointed by virtue of this decision and which began by seeking an interim arrangement interpreted its mandate so broadly that the term "a monumental House of Parliament" found its way back into favour. At the end of the specifications for the architectural competition, which were presented to the Reichstag on 24 November 1871, was the following formulation: "The competing projects should not only be designed to offer the most expedient solution to the pending task but should also embody the idea of a parliamentary building for Germany in a monumental manner". If, however, a monumental building had to be as free-standing as possible, as Hans Victor von Unruh had declared in the House on 29 March, only one potential building site could fit the bill.

The Commission had found that site. In the very first sentence of the programme for the architectural competition, it informed the architects – who, after all, had to know the location of the site to which their plans were to relate – that the building would be "on the eastern side of Königsplatz". After lengthy discussions, the programme was adopted by a majority vote and was published during the week before Christmas. By the expiry of the time limit for competition entries on 15 April 1872, designs had been submitted by 101 architects' offices, slightly more than 30 of which were from abroad, because a decision had been taken to make the competition international.

Once it was clear that the preferred site would not be available to the Works Commission, the search began for an alternative, and the searchers' attention was drawn to the land containing Kroll's Establishment, shown here in a lithograph produced around 1845. The company was in financial difficulties, and so the owner was prepared to sell. Despite its proximity to Königsplatz, however, a majority of the Commission voted against the site.

The first prize was awarded to Ludwig Bohnstedt from Gotha, and four firms of architects came second equal, including Scott & Scott from England. None of the contributions, however, had met with unbounded enthusiasm on the part of the jury. Although Reichstag Member Franz Duncker, in his report to the House on 12 July, stated that there was reason to be pleased with the outcome of the competition, since "results have been obtained for certain of the dispositions in the final building", he conceded that the competition had not led "for the moment to a definitive result", because none of the designs "would lend themselves to unamended implementation". That even applied to Bohnstedt's winning design. The task now, said Duncker, was to "produce a definitive construction plan". In particular, there was a need to establish clarity concerning "the site required for this purpose and its acquisition", because "before we can arrive at a definitive construction plan, we must have complete certainty regarding the site itself".

The uncertainty about the envisaged site stemmed from the fact that the Commission had settled on its choice at an early stage and had evidently shrugged off warnings of potential difficulties. The site earmarked for the new building, in fact, was already occupied by the villa belonging to Count Athanasius Raczynski, which also included a publicly accessible gallery where the Count's art collection was exhibited, some artists' studios and a dwelling used by the Count during his stays in Berlin. The whole venture depended on the Count's willingness to sell his properties.

Raczynski, however, had no intention of selling. He had already made his refusal public in August 1871 in the foreword to a catalogue for an exhibition of paintings he was hosting; this foreword was read out by Ernst Lieber at a Reichstag sitting on 24 November 1871. Lieber wanted to make his fellow Members aware that the location specified in the first sentence of the competition notice presented by the Commission could well pose problems. The fact that the Count knew of the plan months before the Reichstag took its decision was down to the fact that on 15 June, when the question of provisional accommodation was on the agenda, Hans Victor von Unruh, reporting on behalf of the Commission, told the House that the Commission had already taken the decision that the new permanent seat was to be built on the square "on which the so-called Raczynski Buildings presently stand". This news naturally found its way into the press and so came to the attention of the Count.

In spite of Ernst Lieber's warnings, the Chamber adopted the wording of the competition notice proposed by the Commission, including the problematic site specification, on 24 November 1871. Nor had the situation changed by 12 June of the following year, when Franz Duncker reported to the Reichstag on the results of the competition; following several efforts made in the second half of 1872 to do a deal with the Count, the attempt ended in the realisation that there was neither a workable construction plan for the new Parliament nor a place where it could be built.

The Commission resumed its search and found another site on the same Königsplatz, opposite Palais Raczynski on the western side of the square, where Kroll's Establishment was located . This restaurant was popular among the wealthier classes as a destination for outings, offering a combination of high-class food, drink and entertainment. Since the business had been struggling with economic problems for years, the owner expressed immediate willingness to sell. The Reichstag, however, did not want to buy. When the Commission presented its report containing this proposal to the House on 19 May 1873, it triggered a heated debate. August Reichensperger, one of the leading spokesmen for the Centre Party, who had already voted against the purchase of the Kroll property in the Commission, raised aesthetic, urban-planning and financial objections. At the heart of all the reservations expressed about the Commission's proposal for the construction of the Reichstag building on the western side of Königsplatz, however, was the fear that the walk could be too long and that Members could easily catch a cold on their way to and from the building. When a recorded vote was taken on the proposal at the end of the debate, 152 Members voted for the motion rejecting the site on the west side of Königsplatz and proposing other sites, all of which shared the common feature that they could not accommodate a free-standing edifice. A total of 82 Members voted against the motion, thereby implicitly backing the Commission's proposal.

In reality, of course, the issue was not about long walks and Members' colds; it was a political protest in the guise of a vote against a building site. The fact that the parliamentary group of the Centre Party voted against the plan at this time was down to the struggle known as the *Kulturkampf* which had pitted political Catholicism and its representative organisation, the Centre Party, against a united front of Bismarck and the Liberals. The Liberals supported a series of laws through which they sought to complete the separation of church and state and so achieve a modernisation of society in the face of opposition from the Centre Party, which, in their eyes, was battling against such separation and obstructing modernisation. Bismarck, for his part, referred repeatedly to the danger to German unity emanating from the Centre Party, asserting that it was controlled from abroad, from the Vatican. Perhaps he believed in that possibility; there is a great likelihood, however, that he was more interested in marginalising the Catholic population, in creating a bogeyman against whom various political groups with quite heterogeneous interests could be mobilised to form a common front.

The Centre Party, in short, had no reason to support a pet project of the National Liberals, especially when the future Reichstag building was being invoked time and again, and in ever new flights of rhetoric, as the "monument to the achievement of unity at long last". In the eyes of those who had been marginalised as 'enemies of the Empire', however, this unity was a more distant dream than ever. There was no reason, in other words, to approve the erection of any monuments to unification, even though opposition meant supporting the efforts of the Government in general and Bismarck in particular to prevent the construction of a monumental new building.

The Commission reviewed the potential sites identified in the parliamentary decision as well as a total of more than 60 other locations but came to the conclusion that the western side of Königsplatz was the only site that actually lent itself to the construction of a monumental building. It presented this finding to the Reichstag on 25 February 1874. The fact that the Commission was once more proposing the site that had been rejected by a substantial majority in the previous year caused some consternation. At the end of the debate, another recorded vote resulted in another rejection of the Commission's proposal. This time, however, the margin was not so wide as in 1873, with 130 Members against and 120 in favour of the proposal.

No more progress was made over the next three years. On 10 July 1879, Parliament dealt with a motion that had not been tabled by the Commission but by Prussia through the Bundesrat. The new motion proposed that the land on the eastern side of

Königsplatz, which had originally been the first choice, be designated as the site for the new Reichstag building. Following the death of Count Raczynski, his son was prepared to sell the buildings on Königsplatz to the Prussian treasury. In the course of the plenary debate, however, it became apparent that a majority of Parliament could not and would not support the motion. August Reichensperger of the Centre Party was once again the most vehement opponent of the motion, which was ultimately rejected.

The fact that the rejectionist front was led once more by the Centre group on this occasion is explained by a complete reversal of the political constellation that had existed in 1873. The *Kulturkampf* had ended, and the Centre Party, which had emerged strengthened from it, had undergone a transformation, following Bismarck's break with his previous parliamentary allies, the National Liberals, from 'enemies of the Empire' to a party of government. The Imperial Chancellor had long been trying to win the support of the Liberals for his economic policy U-turn from free trade to protective barriers. The offer to make the site on the eastern side of Königsplatz available for the Reichstag building was an offer from Bismarck, a gift to the National Liberals, as it were, which he hoped would enable him to enlist the support of that party for his protectionist policy. As it emerged that this aim was unattainable but that the Centre Party was prepared to support the proposed legislation along with the Conservatives, the magnanimous offer could be withdrawn. Needless to say, the Government could not do that itself but sought and found welcome enforcers in August Reichensperger and the Centre Party, its new political confederates.

Following the death of Count Raczynski, his son was prepared to sell the Berlin property, and so the way was clear for the construction of the Reichstag building. In February 1882 a second competition was advertised, and this time the successful architect was Paul Wallot. His prizewinning design is seen here in a wood engraving dating from 1882 and based on a drawing by Gottlob Theuerkauf (1833–1911).

On 13 December 1881, more than ten years after the first negotiations on the construction of a new Reichstag building, things finally began to happen. Following a new Bundesrat initiative, which was not Bismarck's doing – in fact he refused to sign it – but which is said to have stemmed from Emperor William, a motion to construct the Reichstag building on the site of the Palais Raczynski and to take all necessary preparatory steps for that project was adopted by a large majority of the Reichstag.

In February 1882, a second competition was advertised. Unlike the first competition, this one was restricted to candidates from German-speaking countries; the prizewinners in the first competition received special invitations to take part. By the submission deadline of 10 June, 188 entries had been received. The jury was able to announce its decision only two weeks later. The winner was not one of the participating star architects but a relatively unknown Frankfurt architect called Paul Wallot.

Winning the competition did not in any way imply the immediate award of a contract. First of all, the architect had to revise the floor plans, taking particular account of the criticisms and usage requirements formulated by the Reichstag Works Commission. Once the Prussian Academy of Public Works, which had been asked for an expert opinion at the special request of the Imperial Chancellor, had signalled its approval in principle, the Reichstag Works Commission decided in December to present the plans to the Reichstag for adoption.

Before this item could be placed on the agenda, however, an unexpected objection was raised. The debating chamber was positioned too high for the Imperial Chancellor. The 60 steps that had to be climbed to reach the chamber were too much for him. None of the bodies involved in examining and appraising the plans had expressed any reservations on this point; it is not unreasonable to suppose that the Iron Chancellor was less concerned about his own and other Members' shortage of breath than about trying at least to delay the apparently inevitable. Lucius von Ballhausen, a Free Conservative Member of the Reichstag who was by no means an adversary of Bismarck but a close ally who had been observing the latter's delaying tactics on the Reichstag building issue at close quarters for many years, summed it up concisely in his comments on this episode: "For ten years he has adopted a dilatory approach to the construction, and he does not seem averse to further procrastination".

An objection from the Chancellor had to be considered, of course. Not until Paul Wallot had completely revised the floor plans again was the Reichstag able to decide "almost unanimously" on 9 June 1883 "to request the Imperial Chancellor, with the co-operation of the Parliamentary Works Commission, to arrange for the construction of the new Reichstag building, adhering as closely as possible to the floor plans designed by the architect, Paul Wallot ...".

As the content of the debate showed, Parliament's patience was at an end. The fact that the Reichstag, "after thirteen years in existence, is only now proceeding to the construction of a Reichstag building" was due, as Ludwig Bamberger stated in his contribution to the debate, referring not only to the latest crisis regarding the location of the chamber, to "particularly unfavourable circumstances with which this plan has had to contend from the very outset". These circumstances included "the disfavour with which the whole affair has been viewed from above". "If I may say so", Bamberger continued, "there is something symbolic in the fact that, of all things, the creation of the Reichstag building, the development of the internal representation of the German nation, has been dealt with so lukewarmly and has encountered manifold obstacles".

The architect, the Kaiser and the dome

After another revision, the final floor plans were completed in October 1883. The debating chamber was in the central part of the main floor, though it was positioned slightly to the east of the intersection of the two axes. It had a floor area of some 600 square metres and seats for 400 Members. The layout of the seats, the presidential podium, the rostrum and the benches for Bundesrat Members was largely modelled on the chamber of the provisional Reichstag building; the press and public galleries, which lined the chamber on three sides, as they did in the temporary seat of the Reichstag, were accessed from the mezzanine floor.

In the south-eastern quarter of the building were the premises of the Bundesrat, the Bundesrat Chamber being located in the south-eastern tower. The north-eastern quarter accommodated the offices of the Reichstag Presidium and the Reichstag Administration, while the north-eastern tower accommodated the library reading room. Opposite, in the north-western quarter, that is to say immediately to the left of the main entrance portal, were the reading and the writing room, while the south-western section to the right housed the Reichstag restaurant. In the area between the reading room, the western portal and the restaurant on the one side and the chamber and the two internal courtyards on the other was the three-part gallery, for which the architectural specifications prescribed a minimum size of 500 square metres and which we would no doubt describe today as the foyer or, to use a more parliamentary term, the lobby.

The unconventional shape of this lobby, with a rectangular space in front of each of the internal courtyards and a huge central rotunda in front of the debating chamber, stemmed from a stipulation made by the Academy of Public Works in its expert opinion on Wallot's floor plans, which formed the basis of the Reichstag's decision of 9 June 1883. The Academy found that

From 15 June 1888 to 28 November 1918, William II (1859–1941) was German Emperor and King of Prussia. He was born on 27 January 1859 as the first son of Prince Frederick William of Prussia, later Emperor Frederick III, and his spouse Princess Victoria, Princess Royal of Great Britain and Ireland, in the Crown Prince's Palace in Berlin. This image, taken by the court photographer, shows him in Berlin in 1884.

there was a "disproportion between the dimensions of the chamber on the one hand and the dome superstructure covering it, which is intended solely as an external symbol, on the other"; it feared, moreover, that the chamber might obtain insufficient light because of the dome. It therefore proposed that the building be constructed without the dome. This criticism provoked a debate during the Reichstag sitting of 9 June. Some participants, including August Reichensperger himself, who was actually opposed to domes as a matter of principle, declared emphatically that the building without the dome was unthinkable. The Reichstag Works Commission therefore took the logical decision to uphold the Academy's objection but only to the extent that it shifted the dome westward, away from the debating chamber, and repositioned it above the lobby. This meant that the planned rectangular lobby had to be redesigned and given a central rotunda.

From 1886, or perhaps earlier, the architect seems to have had growing aesthetic reservations about this shift, for he strove resolutely to have the dome restored to the position above the chamber. These efforts were extraordinarily costly and time-consuming, generating designs, expert opinions, dissenting expert opinions and then new designs. The turning point came with the approval of the Emperor, William II, who had inherited the throne on 15 June 1888, for without his approval such an intervention in the planning process would have been unthinkable. During a visit that the young Kaiser paid to Wallot in the Reichstag works office at the end of 1888, he seemed to have no reservations. The following January, however, during an audience, the Kaiser apparently tried to do some designing of his own; the architect's fierce resistance to such interference in his plans evidently aroused lasting animosity on the part of William II.

Nevertheless, on 14 January 1890 the Reichstag Works Commission took the decision to return the dome to its original position. Kaiser William II could have vetoed that decision and prevented the change in the plans but did not do so. Rumour had it that the main problem in William's eyes was the height of the dome, since it might be higher than the dome of his palace. Various calculations and comparisons that were initiated in this context, some of them by the Kaiser himself, lend a degree of credibility to this supposition. Which dome was actually higher seems never to have been definitively ascertained to this day.

It could be that Kaiser William objected to the material to be used for the dome. In his plans for the repositioned dome, Wallot naturally had to take account of the objections raised by the Academy, whose members had identified what they perceived as a lighting problem. He met these objections by forming the idea of constructing the dome in iron and glass, which seems to have caused public confusion, because it was customary for these materials to be used for railway stations and exhibition halls – utility buildings, in other words – but certainly not for prestigious edifices. Significantly, it was an expert from the Imperial Railways Department, engineer Hermann Zimmermann, who made the requisite calculations and produced the working drawings.

Domes were, naturally, symbols of authority for the traditional powers of throne and altar and featured on palaces and religious central-plan buildings. It was equally natural, however, that bourgeois institutions should emulate these signs of authority on their prestigious buildings to demonstrate their claim to a share in the exercise of power. We need not cite the Capitol in Washington or the *Palais de Justice* in Brussels; it went without saying that a building of such importance serving such a purpose would have a dome, so much so that all but a few of the entries in the two architectural competitions proposed a domed structure.

The dome which Wallot planned to locate above the chamber was the subject of a dispute. The Reichstag Works Commission wanted it to be shifted westwards to a position above the lobby. The architect vigorously challenged this decision and succeeded in having the original location reinstated.

As a rule, these domes were built of curved stone segments; the Reichstag dome, on the other hand, used the materials of modern civil engineering that were commonly used in commercial and transport structures, materials that were inextricably linked with the bourgeois society of the 19th century. In that respect, this dome was a demonstration of the claim to political power by the people's representative assembly against the dome of the imperial palace, neither simply because the Reichstag dome was built at all nor because it may have been higher but because it combined a traditional architectural symbol of power with modern materials and a modern construction. This made the dome one of the few unequivocally non-monarchic features of the Reichstag building.

A few stories circulated about the Kaiser, Paul Wallot and the Reichstag building. There can be no doubt that William's vanity was wounded by the architect's steadfast opposition, and this was reflected in his subsequent harsh treatment of Wallot.

It is entirely possible that the Kaiser actually liked the Reichstag building. Even if that were so, however, he could not admit it in the company of others or even to himself – not so much on account of the architect but primarily because it had been built for the representative assembly of the people, which he held in utter contempt. During a state visit to Italy in 1893, William II did call the Reichstag building a "pinnacle of bad taste', but behind that aesthetic verdict there probably lurked a political attitude.

The parliament building as a symbol of monarchy

After more than ten years' construction work, the Reichstag was able to take possession of the new building when it hosted its first sitting on 6 December 1894. On that occasion a scandal erupted when the President of the Reichstag, Albert von Levetzow, called on the House to rise and pay tribute to the Emperor in gratitude for the new building, and SPD Member Wilhelm Liebknecht remained seated. The matter had no consequences during the sitting, as the President had missed the incident. On 11 December, the Imperial Chancellor informed Parliament that the Public Prosecutor's Office planned to institute criminal proceedings against Wilhelm Liebknecht for lese-majesty; the Chancellor accompanied this information with a request that the House lift the Member's immunity. On the motion of the Committee on the Rules of Procedure, which had concluded that Mr Liebknecht's conduct was covered by Rule 30, according to which Members of the Reichstag could not be indicted before a court of law for statements made in the practice of their profession, Parliament rejected the request to lift Liebknecht's immunity by 168 votes to 58.

Half a year previously, on 28 May 1894, the architect had hosted a VIP tour of the building in which Baroness Spitzemberg and a group of friends took part. The Baroness, who was the widow of the former envoy of Württemberg to the Bundesrat, was quite surprised to find the building vastly overladen with ornamentation; she found the "countless coats of arms, crowns and allegorical figures" downright "ludicrous", concluding that this heraldic decoration, which primarily celebrated princes and dynasties rather than Parliament and democracy, was quite out of place in a building constructed for a Parliament elected by general suffrage. The opinion of the Baroness, who was actually a rather conservative figure, was echoed by journalist August Stein, who wrote for the liberal *Frankfurter Zeitung* and who commented laconically in 1898 that, "although it was intended for the representation of the people", the House contained "nothing but princely images and heraldic embellishments".

These two assessments applied not only to the external facades but also to the interior of the building. Symbols of monarchic power, such as crowns and sceptres, were liberally distributed on the outer walls and in the main internal reception areas as well as on stairways and in hallways. Repeated stone carvings were to be found bearing the names of the princes who ruled the individual states at the time when the Empire was founded along with the monograms of the three Emperors who had been on the throne since then. Then there were the "countless coats of arms" with which the whole building was so amply flooded that a contemporary critic was moved to write that "never had so many coats of arms been seen in any one spot". A hierarchy applied within this community of crests, for the arms of the four kingdoms – Prussia, Bavaria, Saxony and Württemberg – received preferential treatment and sometimes appeared on their own; even within that exclusive group, the arms of Prussia and Bavaria were accorded precedence over those of Saxony and Württemberg.

One of the highlights of this monarchic display was the statue of Emperor William I which rose to a height of several metres at the centre point of the lobby rotunda. Clothed in a military greatcoat and holding a small book – the Constitution of the German Empire of 1871 – the sculpted figure could not have conveyed a more explicit message: the founding of the German Empire was the result of three wars waged successfully under Prussian leadership, and the Constitution was gifted by the grace of the Prussian King.

Everyone had to pass this statue to enter the plenary chamber, where a surprise lay in wait. "There is one single area in the Reichstag Palace", said August Stein, "that does not seem imposing or even august and dignified, and it is the only area where such qualities would be appropriate, namely the debating chamber. For reasons of acoustics, the chamber was cladded with wooden panelling. Below the glass ceiling a frieze of coats of arms ran all the way along the four walls. Beneath them, on the arcade pilasters rising from the galleries, were caryatids, a total of ten figures embodying various aspects of life and areas of activity to which the legislative work of Parliament related. Since the attributes of most of these figures were unmistakably depicted, the areas to which they alluded were easily identifiable; the female figure symbolising the realm of transport and communications, for example, held a telephone receiver in her hand. Such representations were to be found in various places on and inside the building – a weak attempt to establish at least one link with the activity of Parliament. They were not specifically parliamentary, however, for a lady holding a receiver would also have been a fitting emblem for a telephone exchange.

The focus of attention was, of course, the front wall above the presidential platform and the Bundesrat benches. This wall comprised three large unadorned areas, separated and flanked by four niches containing statues, though the statues were not added until 1916. The figures were allegorical representations of the virtues of courage, justice, wisdom and humility. On and in the building, portrayals of moderation and caution, enthusiasm and truthfulness, charity and justice were encountered everywhere; there must have been half a dozen depictions of wisdom

This photograph, taken around 1900, shows the completed Reichstag building of 1894. The eye is drawn from the Victory Column on Königsplatz towards the Reichstag.

Parliamentary sitting on the opening of the Reichstag building on 5 December 1894. SPD Member Wilhelm Liebknecht caused a storm by remaining seated when the House stood to cheer the Emperor in gratitude for the new building. The Public Prosecutor's Office then initiated proceedings against Wilhelm Liebknecht, but Parliament refused to lift his immunity. At that sitting the wall areas above the presidential platform were bare. For the wood engraving, which served as a print template for illustrated newspapers, imaginary pictures were added.

View of the north side of the chamber with visitors' boxes. To ensure good acoustics, the chamber was cladded with wooden panelling. Immediately below the ceiling was a frieze of coats of arms, and the pilasters rising from the galleries were adorned with ten figures embodying various aspects of life and areas of activity which lay within Parliament's sphere of competence.

alone. These are all splendid qualities, and it was certainly hoped that they would guide Members of Parliament in their work. They were, however, even less specific than the lady with the telephone receiver, for they would not have been out of place on or inside any public building.

No doubt one of the main contributory factors to August Stein's overall impression were the three unadorned areas of wall. Since 1891 there had been plans to cover them with a wall fresco or with canvasses with subjects from modern German history. In 1895, Paul Wallot established contact with Anton von Werner, whose *Proclamation of the German Empire*, depicting the proclamation of William I as German Emperor in Versailles in 1871, was one of the iconic images of the new Empire. Since early sketches that Wallot had made of the interior of the chamber featured this proclamation as the centrepiece of that wall, establishing such contact was a logical move. The proclamation was to be flanked by a painting showing the foundation stone being laid for the Reichstag building and one showing the placing of the final stone.

This choice of motifs was consistent with the general monarchic ethos of the Reichstag building. The proclamation of the Empire in Versailles was not only an imperial but also a military occasion; there was talk of the ways in which the ceremony of 18 January 1871 had emphasised the Emperor's military role. This monarchic-military combination was no less evident in the laying of the foundation stone by Emperor William I in the open excavation on 9 June 1884 and in the setting of the final stone by William II on 5 December 1894 at the spot in the lobby rotunda where the large statue of William I would be erected in 1905. On both occasions, the Members of the Reichstag were in the background; when the ceremonial tapping of the foundation stone took place, the hammer was not passed to the President and Vice-Presidents of the Reichstag until the chiefs of the general staff had taken their turn. The procedure for the placing of the final stone was no different. A journalist from the *National-Zeitung* referred in his report to the 'golden shimmer' of military medals. It speaks volumes for the primacy of the military forces that Albert von Levetzow, the Conservative President of the Reichstag, appeared in the uniform of a *Landwehr* major. On the following day, the *Vossische Zeitung* was not alone in criticising what it considered to be a completely inappropriate choice of apparel. "Yesterday, however, the major had no role to play ...", it wrote, "but only the President of the German Reichstag, the freely elected trustee of the representative assembly of the people, and that is why we should have wished him to allude to his tenure of this high office by wearing the garb of a free man."

King William I of Prussia was proclaimed German Emperor in the Hall of Mirrors in the Palace of Versailles on 18 January 1871. This depiction of the scene on an oil painting by Anton von Werner (1843–1915) was one of the iconic images of the new Empire.

The laying of the foundation stone for the Reichstag building on 9 July 1884 was attended by many military representatives, who stood in the foreground while the Members of Parliament were pushed into the background. The central figures in the ceremony were Emperor William I and his son and grandson, who later became Emperors Frederick III and William II. This photograph shows Emperor William I preparing to tap the stone with a hammer. The strike broke the symbolic tool.

following the Battle of Sedan, when Emperor William, accompanied by the Crown Prince, Bismarck and Moltke, are reputed to have ridden across the battlefield.

The plan to commission Anton von Werner was never implemented. Not until 1903 did the matter reappear on the agenda of the Adornments Commission. How seriously such matters were taken, particularly on the Conservative side, is reflected in a comment made by Count Hugo von Lerchenfeld-Köfering, who was one of the Bavarian Plenipotentiaries in the Bundesrat and who served for many years in that capacity on the Reichstag Works Commission. In 1898 the Reichstag decided to dissolve the Commission and appoint in its place an Adornments Commission. The new body was to comprise only Members of the Reichstag, but for the sake of courtesy the Bundesrat was invited to take part in its deliberations. Although the Count regarded this parliamentary decision as an affront, he was willing to participate in order to exert influence, since "the choice of themes for the murals can have a certain political significance".

The Commission initiated a restricted competition in which five painters were invited to participate and which was won by Angelo Jank. Since the subjects of the paintings were prescribed by the Commission, on which the three Bundesrat members together with the Conservative Reichstag deputies formed a majority, there could be no doubt that the chosen themes would live up to Conservative expectations. For the main image, the Commission requested the depiction of a historically attested scene

When the paintings were hung in 1908, they provoked criticism from several quarters. To critics on the Right, the central image was not sufficiently heroic. Emperor William, in their view, looked less like a victorious commander than like a tired old man. Numerous critical observers drew attention to the fact that a French tricolour was being dragged through the mud in the picture and that the head of a slain French soldier was positioned suspiciously close to the hoof of the Emperor's horse; it was feared that these features would have diplomatic repercussions. Lastly, a good number of Members were unable to fathom what such a painting was doing in the plenary chamber of a Parliament; an event from the history of parliamentarianism, they believed, would be a far more fitting subject. National Liberal deputy Gustav Stresemann envisaged a scene from the National Assembly in St Paul's Church, Frankfurt, in 1848. Two years previously, when the Commission's choice of subjects for the paintings was announced, one Member – Count Waldemar von Oriola – had proposed, as an alternative, an episode from Germany's parliamentary history, namely the scene on 18 January 1871 when a deputation from the North German Reichstag conveyed to King William of Prussia the wish of Parliament that he accept the German imperial crown. That civil ceremony emphasised the role of Parliament in the creation of the Empire but had been consigned to oblivion by the military spectacle which took place on the same day and which was firmly rooted in the public memory, not only on account of Anton von Werner's paintings.

On 5 December 1894, ten years after Emperor William I had laid the foundation stone, his grandson, Emperor William II, placed the final stone in a ceremony recorded in this wood engraving, based on a drawing done in 1894 by William Pape. Once again, most of those in attendance are members of the military forces.

In the face of the heavy criticism from many quarters, the President of the Reichstag decided to have the paintings removed from the chamber during the Christmas recess of 1908. The vast grey areas of wall then remained permanently empty. Nothing would alter the situation that Eugen Richter, the recognised spokesman of the left-wing liberal *Freisinnige* party, described only a few weeks after Parliament had moved into the new building: "The emblems and ornamentations that have been assembled here until now would do justice to almost any princely residence or pantheon. One seeks in vain for any place where the individual character of this House as a workshop of legislation, as a seat of Parliament, is actually brought to the fore." When the deputies pressed for a monumental Reichstag building at the start of the planning stage, they could not have foreseen that they would ultimately be working in a monument to monarchy.

Difficulties with an inscription

Eugen Richter's comments no doubt extended to the inscription *Dem Deutschen Volke* ('To the German People'), which had been clearly recognisable under the tympanum of the main entrance portico on numerous representations of the main facade that had been published in the last years before the completion of the building. At the laying of the final stone and the handover of the new building to the Reichstag, there was widespread indignation when the public saw the blank frieze, devoid of any inscription. Left-wing Liberal deputy Friedrich Payer took the opportunity, at one of the first sittings in the new building, to denounce the absence of the inscription as a clear sign of the Government's lack of political trust in Parliament, saying that, "In the illustrated journals, in the drawings of the new building which the artists have been sending to us in Parliament and at home to keep us abreast of developments and on which the new Reichstag building is depicted as it should appear, not as it does appear, we have seen, above the main portal, the inscription *Dem Deutschen Volke*. When I came here, however, I did not find the inscription, and since then I have been racking my brains to establish what the absence of that inscription means." Payer, who suspected that the Bundesrat had blocked the inscription, made it unmistakably clear that this decision would do nothing to promote social harmony.

It was not the Bundesrat, however, nor was it the Kaiser, as propagated in the press. On the contrary, the initiative lay with the Reichstag Works Commission, which had discussed the matter on several occasions in 1893. One argument advanced against the planned inscription was that the German people, through their representative assembly, had approved the allocation of funds for the construction project and could not now dedicate the building to themselves. No doubt there were political motives behind this and numerous other petty objections. Since no practical alternative was found, the Commission, by a majority of its Reichstag members, voted in December 1893 to dispense with the inscription altogether.

When the building was inaugurated without an inscription and the press pinned the blame for this deficiency on the Kaiser rather than the Commission, the latter had no option but to put the matter back on its agenda. At a meeting in January 1895, it appears that not one member of the Commission spoke in favour of the original proposal, which had presumably come from Paul Wallot. Instead, as a compromise, the members agreed on the formula *Dem Deutschen Reich* ('To the German Empire'). When this outcome was submitted to the Kaiser for approval, he made a handwritten counterproposal – *Der Deutschen Einigkeit* ('To German Unity') – in the margin; thereafter the whole issue simply petered out.

It took another 20 years to resurface through an article published in the *Leipziger Tageblatt* of 5 August 1915, timed to coincide exactly with the first anniversary of the outbreak of war. The assertion that the war would not last long had now clearly been disproved, and the burdens on people at the front and at home were heavier than had ever been expected. Among many of the population, this development had led to a loss of confidence in the Government and the monarchy; in these circumstances, according to the *Leipziger Tageblatt*, the inscription could be understood as a gesture of reconciliation, as a contribution to social harmony. The Government immediately took the hint; once it was established that the Kaiser would raise no objections if the Reichstag Adornments Commission were to take a decision to affix the inscription, the process took its course. In December 1916, the inscription was affixed to the building; the letters were designed by architect and typographer Peter Behrens and were cast in the Loevy foundry, the bronze reputedly being taken from cannon captured in the wars of liberation in 1813. When the President of the Reichstag, Johannes Kaempf, announced the decision at the end of the sitting of 27 August 1915, the House responded, to quote the Minutes, with 'loud applause'.

The Reichstag building in the *Spreebogen*, 1919 to 1933

Following the end of the monarchy, the Reichstag building, which had tended to be on the periphery of the centres of power in imperial Germany, now became the starting point for all further plans to develop the political heart of the Republic and its capital city of Berlin. The Reichstag building, as architect and urban planner Hugo Häring stated in a lecture in 1927, should become the "core of the city's new political district".

Numerous designs of the facade showed the inscription *Dem Deutschen Volke* ('To the German People') on the front portico, above the main entrance. Yet there was no inscription to be seen on the finished building. Contrary to a widespread assumption, it was not the Emperor who had vetoed it but the Reichstag Works Commission. Not until one year after the outbreak of the First World War was more consideration given to the inscription, which was now intended to serve as a contribution to social harmony in the war-torn country. It was finally mounted in December 1916.

Häring's lecture was part of the fringe programme for the Great Berlin Art Exhibition, which was held from May to September 1927 and which featured a small special architectural display showing the latest Berlin development projects. These included ideas for the reshaping and redesigning of the Platz der Republik presented by three architects – Peter Behrens, Hugo Häring and Hans Poelzig. All three proposed the construction of buildings for the *Reich* ministries in the *Spreebogen* area – a government precinct with the Reichstag at its heart.

Almost simultaneously, but entirely separate from this exhibition, a competition was advertised in the summer of 1927 for an extension to the Reichstag building. This had become an urgent necessity, as for many years the work of Parliament had suffered increasingly from a shortage of space. In particular, there were insufficient offices and meeting rooms for Members; no provision had been made for such facilities in the plans, and there was nowhere in the building where they could be created. For the preparation of group, commission and committee meetings and plenary sittings, for reading printed papers, motions and bills and even for their entire, political, private and social correspondence, the 400 deputies had to use the two reading rooms and the writing room, unless they preferred to do this work at home. For the Members from the provinces, home normally meant a furnished flat rented for the duration of the parliamentary sessions in Berlin.

Since the early days in 1871, these sessions had grown steadily longer, and the parliamentary mandate had simultaneously evolved from an ostensibly honorary part-time post to a full-time occupation. The introduction of Members' remuneration in 1906 did take account of this development, albeit rather late; it gave numerous Members the means to devote themselves entirely to their parliamentary tasks, which only served to trigger another considerable increase in the need for places within the Reichstag building itself where deputies could work before, between and after sittings.

For this reason, the Budget Committee had presented the House on 2 February 1913 with a plan to develop the attic floor of the Reichstag building to provide a total of 106 offices, each of which would accommodate two to four Members. The development of this roof space was carried out in the course of 1913; more extensive plans, which could not be implemented during the war and in the years that followed, did not reappear on the agenda until 1925. By that time the shortage of working space had become even more acute, because the end of the monarchy had put the Reichstag at the centre of the power structure, not only topographically and symbolically but also politically. The additional new duties that devolved on Parliament as the representative body of the sovereign people following the birth of the Republic increased the workload of its Members, whose number, moreover, had risen by 1924 to almost 500 – about 100 more than in 1894. Accordingly, at the Reichstag sitting of 9 July 1925, the Budget Commission proposed that a plot of land to the north of the building which had been sold a few years before the war should be repurchased as the site for an extension of the building. Parliament acted on this recommendation. At the end of 1925 the plot was acquired, and more land purchases were made the following year to extend the site.

As a result, when the construction project was put out to tender in the summer of 1927, the site took the form of an irregular trapezium, which presented the competitors with some difficulties. The evident failure of all 278 participants to overcome these difficulties is reflected in the fact that the jury decided not to award a first prize and awarded only two second, two third and three fourth prizes.

Before the Reichstag Administration could restart the process, critical comments began to appear in specialised literature and in the press. At the heart of these published criticisms was a demand that any future plans for an extension should be part of a general development plan for the *Spreebogen*. The task could not be successfully performed, architecturally or otherwise, unless it were conceived from the outset as part of a government forum, a 'Forum of the Republic', designs for which had already been proposed in the contributions to the Great Berlin Art Exhibition of 1927.

Berlin City Surveyor Martin Wagner communicated this wish to Paul Löbe, President of the Reichstag, in a letter dated December 1928, combining it with an appeal to Parliament to exercise its responsibility, as the contracting authority, for ensuring that the architecture celebrated democracy. In his reply, Löbe expressed understanding for these considerations but pointed out that developing and implementing such comprehensive plans took a very long time, which the Reichstag did not have, given the need to resolve its pressing space problems. As a compromise, it was agreed to hold a kind of double competition, in which the plans for an extension would be the overriding objective; in the framework of what the programme for the architectural competition called a "competition for ideas for the design of the Platz der Republik", however, entrants were "free to make proposals for the general design of the square".

Most of the participants in this competition, which was not openly advertised but confined to the prizewinners from the first competition plus another eight invited architects, took full advantage of the opportunity to develop 'visions'. Hans Poelzig came up with the most radical proposal. Making a virtue out of necessity, he not only responded to the irregular shape of the site for the extension building but highlighted it by designing a three-sided high-rise building with its outer walls curving inward. Alongside it was the first of nine high-rise buildings for government ministries, arranged in a radial layout around the arc of the Spree and forming a semicircle together with the Reichstag extension. Martin Wagner considered Poelzig's plan to be "the only one applying the right conceptual scale to the design of the square". Gustav Lampmann, on the other hand, writing in the architecture and building journal *Zentralblatt der Bauverwaltung*, criticised the design for making the Reichstag building look "as if pushed aside".

By the time the Weimar Republic came to an end, an extension to the Reichstag building had never been realised, let alone any of the architectural visions for the Forum of the Republic within the arc of the Spree. In the last two years of the Republic, there was not only insufficient money but also a lack of political will. Democracy had failed in its quest for architectural embodiment.

It is apparent that none of the critics and writers who intervened in these debates on a Forum of the Republic within the *Spreebogen* and none of the architectural visionaries who had drawn up designs for such a complex had ever questioned whether the Reichstag building, with its profusion of monarchic symbols, was even a suitable hub for such a forum. Nevertheless, there had been initiatives, albeit entirely unconnected with the debates and visions concerning the Forum, for the purpose of at least reducing this superabundance.

In direct chronological connection with the plenary debates on the Protection of the Republic Bill, which was introduced in the wake of the assassination of Walther Rathenau, Foreign Minister of the *Reich*, and which focused in part on the use of monarchic symbols and insignia, the Reichstag appointed a subcommission on 12 July 1922 to deal with the question of removing such symbols and insignia from the Reichstag building. To this end the subcommission sought an expert opinion from the National Art Curator, Edwin Redslob, which he delivered shortly afterwards and in which he advanced artistic arguments against the removal of the monarchic symbols. "It would be grossly contrary to the spirit of the whole building", he wrote, "and would most seriously impair the general effect of the historic structure if these motifs were to be removed in particular places". With the exception of the crowns on the flagpoles, which were removed in December 1922, everything therefore remained as it was. The huge statue of Emperor William I, which had at least been veiled with large drapes during the memorial ceremony for Walther Rathenau on 27 June 1922, stood in its original place in the lobby rotunda for the entire lifetime of the Republic.

There were certainly contemporary figures who were aware of the strange contrast between the democratically elected assembly on the one hand and the monarchic appearance of the building on the other. Writer Joseph Roth, who was working as the Berlin correspondent of the left-leaning liberal *Frankfurter Zeitung*, wrote in May 1924, after attending the opening sitting of the short-lived second Reichstag term, "In December of this year, the great temple of art will be thirty years old. For decades it has been a source of annoyance to people of taste and a democratic persuasion. At its entrance is the dedication 'To the German people'. From its dome, however, seventy-five metres above street level, rises a golden crown – broad and bulky, a weight bearing no relation to the dome and disavowing that dedication. ... It is immensely difficult not to see any symbol here from the time of Kaiser William II."

The Reichstag building from 1933 to 1945

On the evening of 27 February 1933, the Reichstag building caught fire. At the scene, a 24-year-old Dutchman, Marinus van der Lubbe, was arrested and confessed to having set fire to the building. The top echelons of the National Socialist regime asserted that van der Lubbe had acted on Communist orders and that the fire was meant to be the signal for a communist coup. The former chairman of the Communist (KPD) group in the Reichstag, Ernst Torgler, and three Bulgarian Communists – Georgi Dimitrov, Blagoi Popov and Vasil Tanev – were arrested as the alleged instigators. The trial of the five suspects began on 21 September 1933 before the Supreme Court in Leipzig and ended on 23 December in the acquittal of the four Communist politicians. Marinus van der Lubbe was sentenced to death for high treason in conjunction with arson and was executed on 10 January 1934.

As is universally acknowledged today, there is no basis at all for the allegation that Marinus van der Lubbe acted on Communist orders. The question whether he acted alone or whether the operation was masterminded or aided and abetted by the National Socialists has long been the subject of bitter controversy and has never been resolved to this day.

Assertions that the National Socialists themselves were behind the arson attack were being made and circulated shortly after the event. It is not entirely implausible, of course, in view of the fact that the fire could scarcely have suited their leaders' purposes any better. On the very next day, 28 February, supposedly in response to the alleged Communist putsch attempt, an emergency decree, the Presidential Order for the Protection of the People and the State, was signed by President Paul von Hindenburg, suspending the constitutionally enshrined fundamental rights and freedoms. This Order, commonly known as the Reichstag Fire Decree, not only provided the basis for the arrest of numerous Communist and other opposition politicians in the days and weeks following the fire but also afforded a welcome opportunity, in the longer term, to use every means to pursue critics of the regime, free from the constraints of constitutional safeguards.

The photograph of the burning Reichstag that is shown here had been retouched to add the flames and clouds of smoke. According to the police report, the fire was already under control at 12.25 a.m. on 28 February 1933; when this photograph was taken, only light palls of smoke were still drifting over the building.

Shortly after 9 p.m. on 27 February the alarm was sounded in the Reichstag building when fire was discovered in the restaurant. It was extinguished quite quickly, but then outbreaks were spotted in several other places. The chamber was very soon ablaze. Because of the heat, the fire brigade could not enter the heart of the building but could only prevent the flames from spreading. The plenary chamber, in the upper part of the image, and some adjoining rooms were completely gutted by the fire.

An aerial photograph of the Reichstag building taken from the east. Behind it is Königsplatz with the Victory Column and the Kroll Opera House; next to the opera house on the right is the General Staff Headquarters, facing Alsenplatz and the Alsen Quarter; in the lower right of the image is the loop in the River Spree known as the *Spreebogen.*

This radical step on the path to dictatorship was followed on 23 March 1933 by the Enabling Act, with which Parliament, elected on 5 March, incapacitated itself by surrendering its powers to the Government of the *Reich* under the incumbent Chancellor, Adolf Hitler. It goes without saying that this Parliament was unable to hold its sittings in the burned-out plenary chamber of the Reichstag building. After its inaugural sitting, held on 21 March, the so-called 'Potsdam Day', in the Potsdam Garrison Church, the newly elected Reichstag convened in the Kroll Opera House on the western side of the square, which reverted to its former name of Königsplatz in that same month. The auditorium of that building remained the venue for a total of 18 events in the period up to April 1942. Referred to as sittings of the Reichstag, these occasions could scarcely be called genuine parliamentary sittings.

Although no more plenary sittings could be held in the Reichstag building after the fire, quite a considerable percentage of the premises had emerged unscathed. The large Reichstag Library, containing more than 300,000 volumes, remained housed in the building until 1940 and could still be used there; the same applied to the offices of the Reichstag Administration. Larger rooms that were still intact were hired out for public events. Among the most spectacular of these were two propaganda exhibitions – *Bolschewismus ohne Maske* ('Bolshevism unmasked') in the winter of 1937 and *Der ewige Jude* ('The Eternal Jew') in the winter of 1938/39, both of which drew large crowds.

The plans produced by the Inspector-General of Works for the *Reich* Capital, to which post Hitler had appointed architect Albert Speer in January 1937, made the Reichstag building a focus of public interest for a time. Central to the plans to develop Berlin into 'Germania', a world capital, was a magnificent seven-kilometre-long, 120-metre-wide boulevard ending in the *Spreebogen*, where it would culminate in a 'Great Hall of the People' a square building 315 metres in length and breadth with a dome that was to rise to a height of 290 metres. This Hall was to dominate Königsplatz, which would be extended to form a gigantic parade ground and on the western side of which a Führer's Palace was planned, exactly opposite the Reichstag building but many times larger than it.

The plenary chamber was completely gutted by the Reichstag fire. For this reason, the Parliament elected on 5 March 1933 met in the Kroll Opera House, which housed a total of 18 Reichstag sittings in the period up to and including April 1942, although these, of course, no longer bore any resemblance to genuine parliamentary sittings.

In a city built on this scale, the Reichstag building would naturally have faded into total insignificance. Nevertheless, in accordance with Hitler's wishes, plans seem to have been made initially to repair and extend the building. Although this idea never went beyond the planning stage, the building had to be cleared by its present users so that the plans could be implemented. By the end of 1939, they had been replaced by plans to construct a new Reichstag building, which would be joined to the northern end of what would now be the old building and be linked to the Great Hall on the other side; its plenary chamber was to have a floor area of 2,000 square metres. In connection with these plans, it is said that Hitler rejected Speer's proposal for the demolition of the Reichstag on the grounds that it should be left there as a monument, because that was where the National Socialists had waged their struggle against the Republic and had ultimately triumphed. To clear the way for the implementation of these plans, extensive demolition work had been taking place in the *Spreebogen* since 1938, and this was continued until 1942; thereafter, it fell to British bombers to complete the task.

The Reichstag building, where the nearby Charité hospital had set up a maternity ward in the basement air-raid shelters in 1943, was not spared during the bombing raids either. The last attacks, however, came from the Red Army, which subjected the Reichstag building to heavy artillery bombardment on 29 April 1945. The most famous testimony to this 'battle for the Reichstag' is undoubtedly the image captured by Soviet photographer Yevgeny Khaldei which shows a Red Army soldier raising the Red Flag on the roof of the Reichstag building to signal victory, although the scene was actually recreated for the camera on 2 May, when the fighting was over. The fact that this photograph was so widely disseminated, so often reprinted and even reproduced on postage stamps has to do with the Red Army regarding the Reichstag building as the symbol *par excellence* of the Nazi dictatorship. In fact, following the elimination of parliamentary democracy by that dictatorship, there could scarcely be a better representation of the temporary failure of democracy than that ruined building; though reduced to ruins by the Reichstag fire and the war, its outer walls had nevertheless withstood their ravages.

Under the National Socialists, it was intended to develop Berlin into a global capital city, to be known as *Germania*. Its central feature was to be a seven-kilometre-long north-south axis, 120 metres in width, that would culminate in the Great Hall, a monumental congress hall 315 metres wide with a dome rising to a height of 290 metres. The General Building Inspectorate, headed by Albert Speer, drafted the plans for the Grand Hall as well as producing the model pictured here.

Shortly before the end of the war, the Red Army marched into Berlin and began to bombard the Reichstag building with heavy artillery on 29 April 1945. This famous photograph, taken by Yevgeny Khaldei, of two Red Army soldiers raising the Red Flag, would later be widely disseminated in the Soviet Union. In actual fact, the scene was reconstructed, and the photograph was not taken until 2 May, when the fighting was over.

After the end of the war, the situation was so desperate that people even planted potatoes in the Tiergarten park. The Soviet War Memorial and the ruined Reichstag building can be seen in the background. The photograph dates from 1945.

The Reichstag building as a symbol of unity in divided Germany

When the war ended, the Reichstag building was a ruin. Reconstruction was out of the question. It could have come as no surprise, then, to read a report in the *Tägliche Rundschau* in December 1947 disclosing that the Building and Housing Department of the Magistracy of Greater Berlin was planning "to use the Reichstag structure as what it has essentially become, namely an extremely convenient and plentiful quarry".

As the confrontation between the power blocs led to the division of Germany and the split in the four-sector city, more and more voices began to clamour for the reconstruction of the Reichstag for political reasons. Not least because of the repeated anti-blockade and anti-division demonstrations that had been taking place on the Platz der Republik since the summer of 1948, the ruin that formed a backdrop to these events increasingly came to embody these protests and the hopes that the unity of Germany would be restored. Jakob Kaiser, who had been Federal Minister for All-German Affairs since 1949, formulated this interpretation in a speech he made at a demonstration on 1 May 1950 in front of the Reichstag building, linking it with the calls for reconstruction. "Over the past few years," he said, "the Reichstag building before us has become a symbol of the solidarity of all Berliners. Today it is becoming clearer than ever that this home of the Germans must be quickly rebuilt and developed to host the Bundestag, the Bundesrat and the Federal Government." In a plenary debate in the Bundestag on 20 June 1951 on the motion that sittings of the Bundestag be held in Berlin, the Minister reaffirmed his call, arguing that it was a matter of creating "one more symbol of our confident belief in German unity". In so doing, he endorsed the views of the previous speaker, Willy Brandt, one of the Bundestag Members for Berlin, who had stated "that a national obligation exists towards that building, the workplace of the Reichstag in the Weimar Republic, which was set on fire by the National Socialists and was sorely ravaged by the effects of war and in front of which – right next to the Soviet sector – some of the marvellous demonstrations for freedom have taken place."

In his contribution to the debate, the Minister for All-German Affairs mentioned that "very many artistic objections" had been made to reconstruction. These aesthetic reservations were expressed time and again over the years and were often accompanied by calls for demolition. To counter these objections, which focused chiefly on the historicist ornamentations but also on the symbols of monarchy, calls for reconstruction were coupled with proposals that the building be restored with "a fairly contemporary face", in other words that as many of the ornaments and symbols as possible be removed. The President of the Bundestag, Eugen Gerstenmaier, spoke repeatedly in favour of reconstruction between 1956 and 1959 but made it unmistakably clear after a visit to the ruin in March 1957 that he was not for "domes and towers and old paraphernalia".

Another option was to call for reconstruction but renounce parliamentary use of the building. This was expressed in the following terms by Willy Brandt in a plenary debate on 26 October 1955: "When all is said and done, we should ensure that the years of wrangling and arguing about the Reichstag ruin are brought to an end by modest but practical action. It is not in any way a matter of whether the future National Assembly would be able to work in the reconstructed Reichstag building or whether additional new buildings would be needed; it is a matter of a little sense of history and of determining how the reconstruction of the Reichstag building for some national purpose or other can be aptly initiated at all in practice". Brandt had invoked this 'sense of history' in the context of a debate on an SPD motion for the allocation of a budget of 350,000 deutschmarks for an urban

Occupied Germany, and Berlin in particular, became the first focal points of the fermenting Cold War. The Soviet Union responded to the currency reform in the western zones with a blockade of West Berlin that lasted from 24 June 1948 to 12 May 1949. On 9 September 1948, some 350,000 people demonstrated against the blockade on the Platz der Republik in front of the Reichstag building. Mayor Ernst Reuter called for support for the beleaguered city.

DEM DEUTSCHEN VOLKE

design competition entitled *Hauptstadt Berlin* ('Capital City Berlin') and a budget of DM 60,000 to a design competition for the restoration of the Reichstag building. The motion was carried by a large majority.

An international call for entries for the *Hauptstadt Berlin* competition in March 1957 was published in March 1957. This, of course, was partly a political gesture, designed to make it clear that the Federal Republic, even – or indeed especially – after its accession to NATO and its forging of closer links with the West, remained politically committed to the idea of reunification and was already making plans for the capital city of reunified Germany. One of the tasks for the competing architects was to envisage how the parliamentary quarter inside the arc of the Spree should look and what role the Reichstag should play there. After the end of the competition in February 1958, it became clear that almost all participants and every one of the prizewinners wanted the Reichstag building to be preserved, but none of them could imagine it as the seat of Parliament. The proposed uses ranged from the Federal Constitutional Court to a library or a museum. The competition on the restoration of the Reichstag building had been postponed so as not to influence the responses of candidates in the capital-city competition to the question of the future of the Reichstag building.

Nevertheless, the Bundestag had made funds available for the continuing removal of rubble and for measures to secure the Reichstag building and to preserve its fabric. Such work had taken place at various times in previous years, but it was stepped up in the autumn of 1957, when the *Hauptstadt Berlin* competition was not yet completed. The Federal Building Office had the southern part of the main facade restored, although this was tantamount to a partial destruction. Almost all of the architectural decoration was removed, the end result being a facade shorn of its stylistic features which was now virtually immune to any further 'artistic' objections. The dome, incidentally, had been dynamited back in 1954 for safety reasons in an operation that had taken several years to prepare.

Not until 1 July 1960 could the long-awaited competition be launched, but entry was by invitation only, with ten architects invited to participate; in January 1961, Paul Baumgarten emerged as the winner. Although the competition specifications had made it clear that the building was to serve parliamentary purposes after restoration, the requested design proposals were limited to the main entrance hall and lobby and the reception suites in the west wing. The fact that Paul Baumgarten was ultimately able to restructure the whole building and to design a plenary chamber for which no provision had originally been made was mainly due to his persistence in negotiations with the competent authorities.

The result of this reconstruction, which took ten years to complete, was the subject of a great deal of discussion and widely varying assessments. Baumgarten was credited with creating a great deal of transparency by using large quantities of glass; this, indeed, is also characteristic of the building today. The opening and glazing of the great western portal, for example, was Baumgarten's idea. On the other hand, the architect went so far in the direction of modernism with his architectural vocabulary of the 1960s as to either encase or remove almost all of the preserved historical elements in order to achieve straight lines and flush surfaces. Thanks to the gutting of part of the interior of the building, the plenary chamber was twice as large as the old one, but its almost spartan furnishings "made it look unfinished to the end of its days", as architectural historian Dieter Bartetzko remarked.

From the foundation of the Federal Republic, the aim of reconstructing the Reichstag building was pursued as a symbol of a united democratic Germany. The design was to be found by means of a competition, but between 1957 and 1959 financial resources were initially devoted to clearing rubble, making the structure safe and preserving the remaining fabric of the building.

In January 1961, architect Paul Baumgarten emerged as the winner of a restricted design competition with ten participants. The reconstruction that was carried out under his direction involved extensive use of glass, and so the transparency which marks the building today was already created in some places. At the same time, the bulk of the preserved historical ornamentation was covered or removed in favour of the straight lines and smooth surfaces that typified the architecture of the 1960s.

Even before the President of the Bundestag, Annemarie Renger, was able to take over the building officially on behalf of the Bundestag on 1 June 1973, meetings of parliamentary committees and groups had been held on numerous occasions in the reconstructed Reichstag building, beginning in 1971. Plenary sittings, however, could no longer take place there, since the occupying powers had confirmed the four-power status of Berlin in the Quadripartite Agreement of 1971, which meant that West Berlin was still not part of the Federal Republic. That plenary chamber would perform its intended function only twice – on 4 October 1990, when the first Bundestag for the whole of Germany convened for its initial sitting in the Reichstag building, and a few weeks later, on 20 December 1990, for the constituent sitting of the 12th Bundestag, which had been elected in the first free all-German elections on 2 December.

The Reichstag building for the Bundestag

On 20 June 1991, the Bundestag decided by 338 votes to 320 that the seat of parliament and government of the Federal Republic of Germany was to be moved from Bonn to Berlin. There seemed to be no doubt as to where the Bundestag would hold its plenary sittings in Berlin. The *Frankfurter Allgemeine Zeitung* surely reflected the views of the vast majority of Bundestag Members when it aired this topic on 18 September 1991 under the heading 'The Reichstag, where else?'. Finally, on 30 October 1991, the Council of Elders decided "to make a start on plans for the Reichstag building, which should be based on its permanent use for plenary sittings".

Before this decision was taken, however, and afterwards too, a number of objections were raised to the plan to use the Reichstag building to house the plenary chamber of the Bundestag. At the heart of these objections was the assertion that the Reichstag was not a suitable architectural vehicle with which to project the image of the parliamentary democracy of the Federal Republic of Germany. This argument was advanced in Parliament and in the public debate as well as during a colloquium held by the Bundestag on 14 and 15 February 1992 and attended by almost 400 architects, urban planners, historians, custodians of historic buildings and Members of Parliament on the subject of the architectural design and use of the Reichstag building.

The imposing architecture of the edifice, it was argued, perfectly mirrored the authoritarianism of the Wilhelminian empire, for whose parliament it had been built. Although that parliament had been involved in the legislative process, it could neither form nor oversee the government, and so the building was a monument to a parliamentary power deficit. The counterargument was that the ornate architecture of the building had been created precisely because the architect, Paul Wallot, like numerous Reichstag deputies, wanted it to be an unequivocal demonstration of parliamentary authority. The regretted power deficit had been reduced over the years, *de facto* if not *de jure*, and the people's representative assembly of the Empire, moreover, had been elected on the basis of a franchise that was extraordinarily democratic for its time. The building, so this argument ran, embodied democratic traditions with which the Bundestag could associate itself without any qualms.

The initial plan was only to redesign the main entrance hall, the lobby and the reception rooms in the west wing, but Paul Baumgarten managed to persuade the authorities that his brief should include a redesign of the plenary chamber, which is shown here.

The objections to the use of the Reichstag building were not sufficiently persuasive. On 19 June 1992, a design competition for the reconstruction of the Reichstag building for the Bundestag was launched. A total of 94 architects and architectural offices took part; three entrants – Santiago Calatrava, Pi de Bruijn and Sir Norman Foster – were placed first equal by the jury in January 1993. All three winners, however, went far beyond the specifications in both architectural and financial terms. For this reason the Building Commission and the Design Concept Commission that had been appointed by the Council of Elders in 1991 to take the fundamental decisions relating to the planning and logistics of moving the Bundestag to Berlin asked the three prizewinners on 12 April to revise their designs. On 1 July 1993, following the presentation of the revised designs, the Council of Elders commissioned Sir Norman Foster to continue the planning process. The British architect had presented a convincing design concept that met the needs of a modern working parliament while seeking to combine a high degree of functionality and efficiency with sensitive preservation of the historical building fabric.

Wrapped Reichstag – the art project realised by Christo and Jeanne-Claude

The reconstruction of the Reichstag building for the Bundestag cleared the way for an art project entitled *Wrapped Reichstag* that Franco-Bulgarian artist couple Christo and Jeanne-Claude had been planning, often with lengthy interruptions, since 1971. In numerous contacts with German politicians, particularly with successive Presidents of the Bundestag, the two artists received kind attention but also met with opposition. At the heart of all the arguments raised against the project was that shrouding the Reichstag building could compromise its elevated status as a symbol of German unity during the years of *de facto* division.

Once the division of Germany had ended, this argument no longer had any foundation. For this reason, the panel of experts forming the jury for the competition to reconstruct the Reichstag building for the Bundestag recommended in 1993 that the project be authorised for implementation prior to the reconstruction work. This, it said, would not devalue the building but enhance its status. "The unwrapping before its conversion into the seat of the Bundestag", the jury explained, "will highlight the beginning of the new chapter in the history of the building".

A cross-party initiative involving numerous Members of the Bundestag embraced this recommendation and tabled a parliamentary motion on 3 February 1994 headed *Wrapped Reichstag – project for Berlin*, arguing in the explanatory statement that "The Reichstag building is a noble symbol of German history and merits great respect. This is made particularly clear by the artwork. Before the start of the work to convert the Reichstag into

From 24 June to 7 July 1995, artist couple Christo and Jeanne-Claude wrapped the Reichstag building entirely in aluminised polypropylene fabric. The project was initially suggested to Christo in 1971, but although the artist began to plan it immediately, the project was thwarted time and again by resistance from the Bundestag. Not until 1994 did Parliament give its approval.

The wrapping of the Reichstag was a huge undertaking. *Verhüllter Reichstag GmbH* ('The Wrapped Reichstag Company') was created to implement the project, and ten firms produced and provided the materials. The artists ultimately needed 109,400 square metres of polypropylene fabric, 15,600 metres of blue polypropylene rope and 200 tonnes of steel for the substructure. The total cost of the project was 13 million dollars.

the Bundestag, the wrapping represents a great opportunity to highlight the caesura in the history of the German people." This motion was the subject of a lively and disputatious debate in the Bundestag chamber on 25 February 1994. After the opponents and adversaries had advanced their arguments, the House voted by 292 votes to 223 in favour of wrapping. Christo and Jeanne-Claude now had the green light.

From 24 June to 6 July 1995, the Reichstag building was in its wrapping, having disappeared under a covering of some 100,000 square metres of silvery-grey polypropylene fabric. The last week in June and the first week in July lived up to the proponents' expectations. Although the numbers visiting the wrapped building were difficult to estimate accurately, it is believed that up to five million people witnessed the spectacular event, which, as Michael S. Cullen, an American writer living in Berlin, said when reminiscing 20 years later, "magically transfigured the image of Berlin in the world, a magic that still casts its spell today". It was Cullen who first suggested the wrapping in 1971 when he sent Christo and Jeanne-Claude a picture postcard of the Reichstag building. The global impact was overwhelming and vindicated the judges of the architectural competition, who had concluded their recommendation with the following sentence: "The project will gain worldwide attention and serve as the symbol of a new open Germany".

The architect, the Members of Parliament and the dome

On completion of the wrapping action, the reconstruction work could begin in late July 1995. Before then, however, numerous lesser and greater obstacles had to be overcome, as is only natural in a project of this scale. One such problem, in fact, proved to be well nigh intractable in the course of 1994, namely the design of the roof; at one particular point in the wrangling, in April 1994, it even looked as though the cooperation between the Bundestag and the British architect was heading for an untimely end.

The cause of the dispute was the question whether or not the Reichstag building should have a dome again. This had already emerged as a bone of contention at the colloquium in February 1992. The opponents of a dome took the view that a dome would merely reinforce the ostentatious effect of the building, because domes were, after all, architectural signs of authority in pre-democratic political systems. For that very reason, the proponents argued, a dome had to be built, because it illustrated the fact that the former monarchic claim to authority in Germany now lay with Parliament; in short, the dome reinforced the authority of Parliament that was already made visible in the elaborate architecture.

In the competition specifications the dome issue was left unresolved. One of the three winners, Santiago Calatrava, had submitted a design with a dome. Norman Foster, in his entry, had provided for a transparent flat roof that rested on 25 pillars and seemed to hover above the building like a kind of baldachin or canopy. He had subsequently discarded that idea but continued to design the roof as a walkable terrace open to the public with a glazed opening in the centre through which visitors could look down into the plenary chamber. No other superstructure was planned for the roof.

In the architectural competition for the government quarter, the jury did not award a single first prize for the reconstruction of the Reichstag building but choose three designs. One of the three winning models was the work of London-based architect Sir Norman Foster. In it, he placed the Reichstag building under a 50-metre-high transparent canopy supported by 25 slender pillars.

The Reichstag building was reconstructed in accordance with the plans produced by British architect Sir Norman Foster. At first Foster was not prepared to replace the flat roof in his design with a dome, but he eventually relented. The model shows the Reichstag building from the west side with the glass dome. The right-hand side of the building, which did not feature in the original model, has been added with the aid of computer software.

On 1 July 1993, when the Council of Elders commissioned Sir Norman Foster to continue developing his plans for the reconstruction of the Reichstag building, it also instructed him to devise a "roof variant with a dome". This instruction stemmed from a decision taken by the CDU/CSU parliamentary group, an overwhelming majority of whose members advocated the dome option. The FDP, which was the junior coalition partner of the CDU/CSU in the Federal Government, had reservations about the dome, while the SPD group spoke out against a dome. The lines were essentially still drawn as they had been at the previous year's colloquium.

The architect himself expressed aesthetic, technical and financial objections to a dome. A conflict between the architect and the contracting authority, the Bundestag, represented by the Building Commission, and also among the political groups, was scarcely avoidable, and it came to a head in the spring of 1994. In February, following another request from the Building Commission, Norman Foster had presented a dome design; at the same time, however, he made it abundantly clear that he rejected this and all other possible dome ideas in principle. The reactions to his comments were polarised. Former Building Minister Oscar Schneider (CSU), a staunch advocate of the dome option, stated pointedly that the dome had to be built, since it had been "a monument to democracy". The Federal Building Minister of the time, Irmgard Adam-Schwaetzer (FDP), said that erecting a dome on the Reichstag building would be "relapsing into the architecture of the Wilhelminian era". SPD Member Gerd Wartenberg, finally, stated that a dome on the Reichstag building would be "a signal of political Restoration".

In spite of his reservations, the architect presented more design variants for a dome but also for a cylindrical roof superstructure, which was his clear favourite. In the weeks that followed, lively debates ensued in the political groups between the supporters and opponents of a dome. Not until 16 June did the process reach a temporary conclusion, when the architect presented another dome variant, though he also presented the glass cylinder, which remained his preferred option. Asked whether he was prepared to set aside his own reluctance and have a dome built, Foster replied that he would accept the decision of the Bundestag if it came out in favour of a dome. The CDU/CSU group responded to his willingness to compromise by giving up its insistence on a restoration of Wallot's original dome in favour of a "modern interpretation of the historical form". Accordingly, on 30 June the Building Commission was able to decide, by a majority of one, to commission Norman Foster "to plan the design on the basis of the dome variant", a decision that the Council of Elders endorsed by 18 votes to 5 on that same day. More time would pass, however, before the final form of the dome was determined. In the months that followed, the architect submitted 27 different dome designs, none of which won the approval of the Building Commission. The latter finally gave its consent to a design presented on 29 March 1995, which was revealed to the public on 8 May 1995.

This dome has a diameter of 40 metres at its base and stands 23 metres high. It can be accessed from the roof terrace through two entrances, one on either side. From here two ramps spiral upwards in a double helix for 230 metres to an outlook platform with an area of 200 square metres, from which visitors have a magnificent view of the centre of Berlin. As they climb to the top, inside the 3,000 square-metre glazed shell of the dome, visitors can also look down at various points and from various angles into the plenary chamber, above which the dome spreads out without an intervening ceiling.

The plenary chamber and the plenary level

At 1,230 square metres, the floor area of the plenary chamber is about twice as large as that of the old Reichstag. It is on the first floor, the main level, at which visitors enter the building through the western portal after passing the six massive columns supporting the large tympanum with its frieze bearing the inscription *Dem Deutschen Volke* ('To the German People'). The location of the chamber in the architectural centre of the building reflects the importance of the chamber, for this is where the Members of the Bundestag, the elected representatives of the sovereign people, deliberate and decide on matters that affect all of us. This is where, in its major debates, Parliament becomes the 'forum of the nation'.

Preceding double page: The 23-metre-high dome has a diameter of 40 metres at its base and is covered with a total of 3,000 square metres of glass. From two entrances on opposite sides of the roof terrace, two walkways, each 230 metres in length, spiral upwards towards a visitors' platform with a surface area of 200 square metres.

As far as was possible, Sir Norman Foster enclosed the chamber in glazed walls. In so doing, he was acting on a conviction that government should be made more accessible to the public. On the northern and southern walls of the chamber, looking out onto the two courtyards of Wallot's Reichstag building, are high arched windows with a large upper window above each. The western and eastern walls, on the other hand, are made entirely of glass.

Visitors coming from the entrance foyer into the western lobby can see the whole chamber through what may be described as a gigantic shop window. Straight ahead, in front of the eastern wall, they see the presidential podium, where the President or Vice-President who is conducting the sitting is flanked by two Members acting as secretaries. Behind this Presidium are the seats for the Secretary-General of the Bundestag and the staff of the Bundestag Administration who assist the President and his or her team during the sitting.

In front of the Presidium is the rostrum from which speakers address the House, and in front of the rostrum is the writing desk for the parliamentary shorthand writers. On the left of the Presidium, from the perspective of visitors looking through the western glazed wall, are the seats for the Government, and on the right are those for the Bundesrat. The Members' seats are arranged in a flattened half circle, a kind of semi-ellipse. Of the total of more than 700 seats for Members, the Government and the Bundesrat, three are distinguished by having higher backs. These are for the heads of the three constitutional organs involved in the legislative process, namely the President or Vice-President chairing the sitting, the Federal Chancellor and the President of the Bundesrat.

Directly underneath the dome of the Reichstag building is the plenary chamber. This means that visitors can observe proceedings inside the chamber throughout their ascent and descent of the two walkways, albeit from constantly changing perspectives. In this way, the people are placed symbolically above Parliament, which is, moreover, under their constant scrutiny.

On the eastern wall, above the Presidium, hangs the Bundestag eagle, with which millions of viewers are familiar from televised parliamentary debates. The first version of this eagle, designed by Ludwig Gies in 1953, was fixed to the front wall of the chamber, above the Presidium, in the Bundeshaus, the seat of the Bundestag in Bonn. When that chamber was demolished in 1987, the eagle, which was made of plaster, was sawn into pieces, and these were taken to the *Haus der Geschichte*, the Museum of Contemporary History of the Federal Republic of Germany. Sir Norman Foster had planned to design a new eagle for the plenary chamber in the Reichstag building and had submitted a number of sketches. After lengthy deliberations, however, the Building Commission of the Council of Elders decided to adhere to the Ludwig Gies design. The eagle that now hangs over the Presidium was therefore designed by Foster on the basis of the Bonn model. It is made of aluminium. At seven metres tall and eight metres wide, it is slightly larger than the original. Back to back with it, separated only by the glazed eastern wall, hangs an eagle designed by Foster that faces the eastern entrance, which is reserved for Members.

The basic colour of the chamber is pale grey. The fitted carpet is pale grey, as are the walls behind the Presidium, while the presidential podium itself is dark grey. A very strong splash of colour, however, is delivered by the upholstery of the seats, a bluish purple selected by Sir Norman Foster and patented as 'Reichstag blue'; Foster had originally intended a tone of pale grey for the upholstery too. His plan, as the architect himself recounts, to work chiefly with muted colours alongside grey, white and silver tones met with fierce resistance at a meeting of the Building Commission. In particular, Federal Chancellor Helmut Kohl, who attended that meeting, wanted more vibrant colours and therefore commissioned Danish designer Per Arnoldi to develop a colour scheme for the interior of the building. This scheme assigns a keynote colour to each floor, making one's present location identifiable from the colour of the doors.

Blue is the orientation colour for all areas of the plenary level that are not publicly accessible. To the left of the western portal, these restricted areas comprise the restaurant, a bistro in the corner tower and a cafeteria on the northern side as well as a reference library. To the right of the western portal, they comprise the Members' lobby for fringe discussions, the club room in the adjoining corner tower and the reflection and prayer room on the southern side.

A dominant feature of the Members' lobby is Katharina Sieverding's artwork entitled *In Memory of the Members of Parliament in the Weimar Republic who were Persecuted, Outlawed or Murdered between 1933 and 1945*. This is a large-scale five-panelled photo painting with the blazing corona of the sun as its background motif. In front of it stand three wooden tables, each with a book of remembrance. The middle book documents the fate of the 120 Members of the Reichstag who were murdered by the National Socialist regime. The other two books are devoted to the Members who were persecuted, imprisoned or forced to emigrate. The reflection and prayer room, where a brief ecumenical service of morning prayers is held on Thursdays and Fridays before the start of sittings, was designed by Düsseldorf-based artist Günther Uecker. It is presented in very light colours, its visual impact dominated by seven high wooden panels leaning against the walls, bearing abstract motifs which Uecker created as objects of meditation, using his characteristic media of nails, stones, ashes, paint and sand.

Wolfgang Thierse, President of the Bundestag, unveiling the Bundestag eagle in the plenary chamber on 17 December 1998. Norman Foster modelled it on a design by Ludwig Gies, whose eagle had hung in the plenary chamber of the *Bundeshaus*, the seat of Parliament in Bonn, from 1953 to 1987. The original is now in the *Haus der Geschichte*, the History Museum of the Federal Republic of Germany, in Bonn.

The work of Parliament is meant to be transparent, as symbolised by the large glazed walls surrounding the plenary chamber. Visitors can thus follow parliamentary proceedings at any time.

Artist Katharina Sieverding designed the memorial to the persecuted Members of the Reichstag in the Weimar Republic for the Reichstag building back in 1992. With its background motif of the blazing corona of the sun, the five-part photo painting conjures up associations with both the Reichstag fire and the global conflagration unleashed by the National Socialists as well as the subsequent rebirth of a purified, democratic Germany as a "phoenix from the ashes". This artwork is displayed in the Members' lobby of the Reichstag building, as are three books of remembrance honouring the memory of the murdered, imprisoned and persecuted Members of the Reichstag.

Düsseldorf-based artist Günther Uecker designed the Reflection and Prayer Room on the first floor of the Reichstag building, where a service of Christian worship is held at 8.40 a.m. on the Thursday and Friday of every sitting week. Its centrepiece is an altar of sand-blasted granite on which a simple cross lies and which is faced by 24 wooden chairs. The Reflection and Prayer Room is open to everyone and was intentionally designed as a multi-faith place of contemplation.

When the Red Army had captured Berlin in 1945, many Soviet soldiers wrote short messages on the walls of the Reichstag with pieces of charred wood. The Cyrillic graffiti first came to light again in 1995 during Norman Foster's reconstruction of the building. He wanted to preserve them as a sign of authenticity, which met with opposition from some Members, since some of the messages were not exactly complimentary. In the end it was agreed that names and places of origin would be preserved.

"The Bundestag conducts its business in public" – the visitors' level

The plenary chamber rises through all the upper storeys of the building to a height of 24 metres, where it meets the base of the dome. Above the back rows of Members' seats, six public galleries jut down into the chamber; these are part of the visitors' level. They contain seating for 470 visitors to plenary sittings as well as for press representatives, guests of the Bundestag and diplomats. These galleries are accessed from a mezzanine floor that was suspended at a level halfway up the walls of the chamber; information areas and lecture rooms are also located on this floor. The keynote colour on this level, which features primarily on the doors, is green.

The connecting walkways that encircle the plenary chamber on the visitors' level have more to offer than glimpses into the plenary chamber. On the northern and southern sides of the chamber the walkways pass beneath the old sandstone barrel vaulting with its elaborate ornamental carvings and reliefs; these artistic embellishments only came to light during the removal of the plasterboard cladding that had concealed the original fabric of the building since Paul Baumgarten's reconstruction in the early 1970s. Today's walkways afford a good view of this artistic stonemasonry.

Also visible are Cyrillic inscriptions and graffiti that were daubed on the walls by Red Army troops following the capture of the Reichstag building on 27 April 1945. The officers wrote with blue wax crayons, the other ranks with charcoal. Norman Foster was particularly keen to preserve some 200 items of this graffiti and make them, like the old ornamental stonework, accessible to visitors. In his own words, their preservation has created "a living museum of German history".

The presidential level, the parliamentary groups' level and the press lobby

The presidential level and the floor above it, the parliamentary groups' level, are not accessible by the public. As the name suggests, the presidential level, where burgundy is the keynote colour, houses the offices of the President and the senior staff of the Bundestag Administration. On this floor are facilities such as the protocol chamber, where the President receives guests, and the Council of Elders' meeting room; the lower half of the walls of these rooms is cladded in wooden panelling painted in a vibrant dark blue in accordance with Per Arnoldi's colour scheme. The meeting room, moreover, is characterised by its ring-shaped negotiating table, an appropriate item of furniture for a body seeking consensus solutions, and by the wall-mounted installation comprising sets of overlapping squares in various colours which was designed by Georg Karl Pfahler.

This page and preceding double page: Inside the Reichstag dome is a conical funnel or 'light sculptor', in which 30 rows of 12 mirrors guide refracted daylight into the plenary chamber ten metres below. A revolving sunshade tracks the sun and can shade the mirrors facing the sun when necessary to prevent direct reflection of the sun's rays. At the same time, the funnel draws spent air out of the chamber and expels it.

The identifying colour chosen for the parliamentary groups' level is grey, in which Sir Norman Foster had originally envisaged the whole interior of the building. The upper walls of the rooms for group meetings and for meetings of the group executive committees are generally in exposed brickwork, painted white; in the lower part, by contrast, Arnoldi has made bold statements with strongly coloured wooden panels. All of the rooms in the corner towers and the attic storey of the Wallot building, each of which is subject to a conservation order, are lit from above through roof glazing. In the interior part of this level, around the glazed area between the plenary chamber and the dome, is the press lobby.

From the press lobby, the eye is drawn to the lower end of the light sculptor located in the central axis of the dome; its 360 external mirrors catch the daylight passing through the glass of the dome and reflect it downwards into the plenary chamber, which considerably reduces lighting costs. Thanks to its conical shape, it works like a chimney, like a funnel in reverse, using the natural updraught to draw warm stale air out of the plenary chamber. Concealed inside the cone, moreover, is all the technology required for the ventilation of the chamber and for smoke extraction. The cone in the dome is part of the innovative and environment-friendly energy strategy developed by the experts from the office of Norman Foster, who himself has expressed passionate commitment to energy efficiency and environmental compatibility.

The dome of the Reichstag building that was for so long the subject of bitter controversy, of course, is not only part of the energy strategy but also and above all a visitor attraction and a tourist magnet.

If we consider that up to three million visitors a year regard the dome as an unmissable highlight of their stay in Berlin and that, for reasons of fire safety, only a limited number of people can be on the roof terrace and in the dome at any given time, we will have some inkling of the patience that casual visitors will need. The dome of the Reichstag building has taken its place alongside the Brandenburg Gate as the emblem of Berlin. An online travel guide to Berlin awards the Reichstag building top place out of more than twenty tourist attractions, even placing it ahead of the Brandenburg Gate. And why? "Because a visit to the spectacular dome is an absolute must".

Following double pages: Not only is the dome on the Reichstag building a tourist attraction that draws up to three million visitors a year, but it has also become an emblem of the federal capital itself, just like the Brandenburg Gate. What is more, it is part of the innovative and green energy strategy of the Reichstag building.

Architecture and parliamentary democracy in the Federal Republic of Germany

Gregor Mayntz

The palace of the Sun King in Versailles, St Peter's Basilica, seat of the Popes in Rome, and the pyramids of the Pharaohs in Giza are more than a residence, a place of worship or a final resting place. They also tell of authority, hierarchies and power structures set in stone. Moreover, architecture always expresses how the population of the time were supposed to view their leaders. And what of the politics of the Federal Republic? Quite apart from theoretical principles and the constitutional order, how does the political community present itself in reality on the ground, seven decades after the historic caesura and almost two decades after the move to Berlin? Where does the Bundestag stand, both literally and figuratively? How do the representatives of the people project themselves? What does the architectural landscape say about their daily political routine? Let us take a stroll through the parliamentary and governmental quarter to look for clues about power from two perspectives, namely how it is made publicly visible and how the players themselves experience it.

Backdrop for decision-making

Let us begin where the political world manifests itself every evening on the television news programmes, and let us consider the images that are transmitted with the news. "The Federal Cabinet has approved a bill that will …": we see a room with a long table at which the Chancellor sits, surrounded by ministers

Evening sunshine floods the Reichstag dome. Through its position above the plenary chamber and its glass construction, the dome also serves a symbolic function in that the people – represented by the visitors in the dome – are above their Members of Parliament and can keep a constant eye on them.

The Reichstag building, built in neo-Renaissance style to the plans of Paul Wallot between 1884 and 1894, was restructured and topped with a glazed dome by London-based architect Norman Foster before the Bundestag moved from Bonn to Berlin.

Following double page: View from the Paul Löbe Building towards the Federal Chancellery. The Chancellery was designed by Berlin-based architects Axel Schultes and Charlotte Frank when Helmut Kohl was still in office. The first sod was turned on 4 February 1997. The building took almost four years to complete, and on 2 May 2001, Gerhard Schröder became the first Chancellor to occupy the new seat of the government authority.

In the Bundesrat, the *Länder* – represented by members of their respective governments – are involved in federal legislation and administration and in matters concerning the European Union. More than half of the laws adopted by the Bundestag require the consent of the Bundesrat, which may also lodge an objection to any of the other laws. Each *Land* has three to six votes, depending on its size. Since 2000, the seat of the Bundesrat has been the former Prussian House of Lords in Berlin.

engaged in lively conversation. "The Opposition criticised the fact that ...": this scene shows people behind microphones, framed by partition screens bearing colourful party logos. "The Minister stressed...": a politician comes up a broad stairway and speaks in front of a blue wall; journalists sit opposite, taking notes. "There are some indications of problems in the Bundesrat. Criticism was voiced by the Minister-President of ...": here we see a politician standing next to the open door of a limousine.

Up to this point, the workings of federal politics have been contained within a meeting room or other indoor space. That changes when major projects or serious disputes are making news, and a reporter adds a summarising assessment. On such occasions, he rarely speaks from the neutral territory of a studio but often stands in front of the architectural structure in which the decision-making process is taking place. The favourite location is Willy-Brandt-Strasse with the Federal Chancellery in the background. Very often it is the Marschall Bridge, in which case the Bundestag forms the backdrop, and occasionally the reporter will stand in front of the Bundesrat on Leipziger Strasse.

What impressions are conjured up by these images? The view of the Chancellery is divisible into three parts. To the right and left are administrative buildings in the post-modern vernacular, and in the middle is the soaring central edifice, 36 metres high, which would tower above the standard building height for Berlin if such a restriction applied in this western part of the central Spreebogen district. Yet this government headquarters building, designed in the late 1990s by architects Axel Schultes and Charlotte Frank with an abundance of glass and clear geometrical shapes, stands in isolation – at least when viewed from the east. Compared with the villa character of the White House in Washington or the terraced-row charm of 10 Downing Street in London, the architecture of the Chancellery in Berlin resonates with aspirations to greatness. It is easy to see why the decision to adopt this design at the time of the removal from the Rhine to the Spree gave rise to discussions and to concerns that locating the capital in Berlin could change the politics of the Federal Republic. Was this singular building of monumental dimensions the harbinger of a new centralised state? Would the tried and tested federal system, in which the state was structured by the *Länder* and through the *Länder*, have been in safer hands if it had remained in tranquil Bonn? Especially as the modest three-storeyed Chancellery there was a prosaic functional building dating from the 1970s that seemed to have tucked itself away out of sight. We shall return later to this premise that the larger structure in Berlin is far more clearly 'integrated' than its predecessor in Bonn. A glance at the surroundings of the Berlin Chancellery, moreover, quickly puts those first impressions into perspective. To the north stands the new central railway station; its arched structures, though spreading outwards rather than soaring upwards, are nevertheless ten metres taller than the Chancellery. To the south rises the skyline of Potsdamer Platz with its office towers, and the Chancellery barely reaches a third of their height. In this setting, compared with Berlin's other architectural exclamation marks, the Chancellery even appears stunted.

"The Reichstag building is likewise taller than the Chancellery, although when the Reichstag serves as a backdrop for news reports, it rarely appears in the same shot as the government headquarters." Besides, the neo-Renaissance seat of Parliament, built by Paul Wallot from 1884 to 1894 and restructured by Norman Foster at the end of last century, shortly before the move to Berlin, is optically encased to the right by other towering constructions in the Parliamentary Quarter and to the left by an office tract constructed to the standard Berlin eaves height for tenement buildings. During evening and night hours, the light from the large glass dome radiates far across the Berlin sky; look closely, and you will see visitors moving up and down the spiralling walkways inside the dome. In this way, the

In the plenary chamber of the Bundesrat are 16 blocks – one for each of the federal states – arranged in a horseshoe formation; each block has six seats. In the front of the chamber is the platform for the Presidium, in front of which are the lectern and the shorthand writers' seats. Representatives of the Federal Government and staff of the Bundesrat are seated in front of the Presidium. The benches at the back and on the sides are for delegates from the *Länder* and the Federal Government. Above the chamber there are also press and visitors' galleries.

impression is always conveyed that neither Government nor Parliament is ultimately at the pinnacle. On the contrary, both of them look up to the people. And the latter look down on the seats of parliament and government. At the same time, the worldwide impression of extensive seclusion of parliamentary and governmental districts is replaced by a message of universal accessibility, of a Parliament opening itself to every casual passer-by.

Backdrop number three, the Bundesrat, likewise relies on a part of Berlin's historical architectural heritage. The representative chamber of the *Länder* moved into the former seat of the Prussian House of Lords, a building completed by Friedrich Schulze-Kolbitz ten years after the Reichstag building. Stemming from the historicist era of architecture and inspired by the Italian Renaissance, the building covers an area two and a half times that occupied by the Reichstag building and also exceeding the surface area of the Chancellery. Yet there is also a sense of the unassuming in the scene behind the reporter. Fronted by high railings, the building does comprise three four-storeyed wings and a strikingly ornate tympanum borne by six pillars, but the actual entrance beneath this portico is of rather average dimensions.

What other buildings form the backdrops to television news reports? If Members of the Bundestag are commenting on behalf of their parliamentary group, they will normally do so within the Reichstag building in front of the group meeting rooms, where large mobile partition screens with the colours and logos of the individual parliamentary groups are permanently stored for use in television shots to create an unmistakable link between individual speakers and the parliamentary group they represent. More of these background panels are to be found in the offices of the group chairpersons in the Bundestag office complex known as the Jakob Kaiser Building, which we shall examine later. If, on the other hand, politicians are speaking as representatives of their parties, they are generally filmed in front of or inside their respective party headquarters. Few of these are in the vicinity of the parliamentary and governmental quarter. The Alliance 90/The Greens party, for example, has its seat behind the facade of an ordinary residential building in Platz vor dem Neuen Tor, a square in the Mitte district. The Left Party has chosen a similarly rather inconspicuous piece of urban street architecture on Rosa-Luxemburg-Platz, near Alexanderplatz. Admittedly, that building, parts of which contain offices leased by other tenants, is the former headquarters of the German Communist Party, in which role it had a chequered history and was the scene of bitter confrontations. The Left Party has remained loyal to its roots by retaining the name Karl Liebknecht Building.

The headquarters of the other three parties are further away from the parliamentary quarter. The CDU has constructed its Konrad Adenauer Building on Klingelhöfer Straße behind the Tiergarten. Its eye-catching architecture fills the obtuse trapezoid shape of the building plot with spacious winter gardens, from which there rises a structure that is often likened to a glazed ship. The party headquarters of the SPD in the Kreuzberg district, the Willy Brandt Building, can also be seen as the bow of a ship. Like the CDU HQ, it adheres to the normal Berlin eaves height of 22 metres, and the extensive use of glass speaks of transparency and openness. Anyone seeking the CSU headquarters in Berlin will search in vain, for the sister party of the CDU stands for election in Bavaria only and has its Franz-Josef Strauss Building in Munich.

The Jakob Kaiser Building is a complex comprising eight six-storey buildings, which were designed in 1997 by four different architects' offices: buildings 1 and 2 by Schweger and Partners, buildings 3 and 7 by Busmann and Haberer, buildings 4 und 8 by Gerkan, Marg and Partners and buildings 5 and 6 by de Architekten Cie). Together they form the largest of the German parliamentary buildings. They are named after Jakob Kaiser, a politician from the Centre Party and CDU.

The seat of the *Bundespressekonferenz*, the Federal Press Association, in Schiffbauerdamm on the Spree. The building, designed by architects Johanne und Gernot Nalbach in 1998 and completed two years later, belongs to the Association, which brings together the accredited Berlin correspondents of the world's press.

The 'blue wall' that frequently features behind leading politicians on TV screens also contains the word *Bundespressekonferenz* (Federal Press Association) and belongs to neither the Bundestag nor the Federal Government nor the Bundesrat but to the capital's accredited journalists, who have formed an association of Berlin correspondents which holds its own press conferences. The journalists, in other words, are not the guests of politicians but their hosts and therefore lay down their own rules. The *Bundespressekonferenz* Building is located in the immediate vicinity of Parliament and of government headquarters, overlooking the River Spree, which means that both journalists, many of whom have their offices in this building, and politicians are within easy reach of each other. The facades of the eight-storey building are characterised by high windows, and a particularly prominent feature is the glazed facade of the conference hall, through which participants can see both the Federal Chancellery and the Bundestag buildings. The floor of the atrium inside the building, moreover, is crossed by a raised line, which marks the course of the former hinterland wall, the inner Berlin Wall.

Interplay of architecture and people

After this initial review of the scenes of decision-making, debate, deliberation, criticism and communication that are conveyed in televised images, we now come to the question how these places impact on the cityscape. If we consider how the players on these various stages interact, it very soon becomes apparent that, in the reality of a parliamentary democracy, it is not a matter of some only working here and others only working there. On the contrary, federal politics also entails frequent changes of location, which is also reflected to an extent in architecture and in where institutions choose to base themselves.

The Federal Chancellor, for example, has a desk in the Chancellery; in her role as chair of the CDU, she has an office in party headquarters, and as Head of Government she also has a permanent place on the government front bench in the Bundestag, where she likewise spends many hours. For brief working sessions and discussions she can also withdraw to an office of her own near the plenary chamber in the Reichstag building. Conversely, it is not only government ministers who regularly attend the Chancellery. Leading Members of Parliament from the coalition groups likewise have frequent appointments at Government HQ. The opposition leaders and sometimes policy specialists from the parliamentary groups are briefed there on matters of particular importance. The Minister-Presidents and numerous other ministers from the *Länder* also attend meetings at the Chancellery.

Norbert Lammert (CDU/CSU), President of the Bundestag, visiting the Federal Press Association. The registered association comprises full-time journalists, particularly Berlin correspondents. It holds its own press conferences and invites politicians for interviews.

Members of the Government, for their part, are regularly present in the Bundesrat when specific bills are reviewed there. The linkage between the state institutions is also reflected in the fact that members of both the Federal Government and the Bundesrat attend sittings of the Bundestag and can take part in the debates there. In the plenary chamber the government and Bundesrat representatives sit on either side of the podium, facing the Members of the House. In this way the interests of the individual regions always feature in deliberations on national policies. For the same reason there are many other locations between the Bundestag, the Federal Chancellery, the Bundesrat and the federal ministries where preparation and coordination take place, particularly the representations of the Länder, most of which are housed in the area between the Bundesrat and the Bundestag.

The Permanent Representations of the *Länder* are not only showcases for all the regions of Germany, nor are they merely places where people from other parts of Germany can experience their native culture during their stay in Berlin. They are the places where representatives of the *Länder* gather important information about every bill on the Bundestag agenda to enable their respective governments to form their own opinion, for the Bundesrat is, in principle, involved in the creation of every federal law. Each *Land* also uses its representation in Berlin to canvass nationally for majority support for its position. Moreover, for most Members of the Bundestag, the Permanent Representations serve as regular points of contact. During sitting weeks, *Land* groups, comprising the members of a parliamentary group from a particular *Land*, meet in their respective Representations to discuss how the interests of their home region will be affected by imminent decisions and where they should exert influence in order to guide the decision-making process in a favourable direction.

This particular feature of federalism in the capital has many diverse faces. No fewer than seven *Länder* decided to construct new buildings in the Ministergärten area between the Holocaust Memorial, Potsdamer Platz, the Tiergarten and Wilhelmstrasse. The name of the area was coined in the 19th century, when important ministries were established in Wilhelmstrasse, which meant that the private gardens previously known as *Palaisgärten* developed into "ministers' gardens". Schleswig-Holstein and Lower Saxony, as well as Mecklenburg-Western Pomerania and Brandenburg, have constructed shared buildings. In addition, Rhineland-Palatinate, Hesse and Saarland have their own structures, located halfway between the Bundestag and the Bundesrat. In the area south of the Tiergarten, where the embassies of various countries are located, Baden-Württemberg, North Rhine-Westphalia and Bremen have erected modern buildings, each with its own character. Thuringia constructed a new building at the corner of Mohrenstrasse and Mauerstrasse on the site of its former property that had been destroyed in the war, and a little further north, in Behrenstrasse, Bavaria redesigned the interior of a former bank building, creating a foyer in the former banking hall and a beer cellar in the old vaults. Hamburg opted for two buildings in Jägerstrasse dating from the Wilhelminian era, which had formerly served as rented accommodation and a

Schloss Bellevue, commissioned by Prince Augustus Ferdinand of Prussia and built from 1785 to 1786, became the secondary residence of the President of the Federal Republic and his Berlin seat in 1957. In 1994 it became the President's main official seat, and Roman Herzog became the first Federal President to take up residence there.

gentlemen's club, while Saxony-Anhalt chose a 19th-century bourgeois town house in Luisenstrasse, where the artists' club *Die Möwe* had been founded in 1946. Finally, the Permanent Representation of Saxony took shape within the walls of the historical offices of an insurance company in Brüderstrasse near the site of the City Palace in the oldest part of Berlin. Berlin itself initially moved its representation from Bonn to Wilhelmstrasse but then incorporated it into the competent directorate in the City Hall itself.

Other major players must also be mentioned in this overview. After all, no bill ever becomes law without the involvement of the Federal President, and the Federal Constitutional Court is often called upon to play its crucial remedial role. Neither of these players, however, is to be found in the immediate vicinity of the parliamentary and governmental quarter. The Head of State, however, can be reached quickly at his residence in Bellevue Palace at the far end of the Tiergarten whenever the President is required to act as the notary of the political process or as a stabilising influence in times of crisis. Since he is Germany's supreme representative abroad as well as being duty-bound to safeguard the cohesion of German society, proximity to the scene of the action enables him to invite major players for confidential talks at any time and to keep himself briefed by the Government on the facts behind the issues of the day. More than 500 kilometres, on the other hand, separate the Bundestag in Berlin from the Federal Constitutional Court in Karlsruhe. This distance reinforces the fact that the guardians of the Constitution who arbitrate in disputes between the organs of the Constitution can never be immersed in the operational legislative routine but are called on to assess adopted regulations from a distance in the sole light of the provisions of the Basic Law.

To sum up, then, the theatres of federal politics revolve around the Bundestag; the more intensive their operational links with Parliament, the closer they are located. The relatively greater distance of most party headquarters is not inconsistent with this finding. Although the parties are the recruiting grounds for policymakers in Government and Parliament, distinctions have to be made when politicians combine parliamentary, governmental and party roles. Although a Member's parliamentary work is based on a party programme, in everyday practice it breaks down into projects that are on the agenda or prescribed by the coalition agreement. Activities in the party HQs, which tend to be on the periphery of parliamentary business, are more fundamental in character and perform the role of an interface between parliamentary and governmental processes on the one hand and the involvement of the electorate and the party membership on the other. Even though a member of a party's federal executive and a member of a parliamentary group in the Bundestag are sometimes one and the same person, the debates they experience in these two bodies often have very different focal points and reflect very different lines of approach.

The Paul Löbe Building, opened in 2001, forms a single architectural entity with the Marie-Elisabeth Lüders Building on the opposite bank of the Spree, and the two buildings are linked by a bridge. Both were designed by the same architect, Stephan Braunfels. The foundation stone was laid on 28 April 1997 by Rita Süssmuth, who was President of the Bundestag at that time.

The 'Federal Ribbon' – symbolically binding divided Germany

Is this finding reflected in the architectural landscape too? The extent to which this is truly the case, particularly as regards the relationship between the Bundestag and Government HQ, is easily visible to viewers if they focus more sharply on the background when the television screen shows images of state visits, meetings in the Chancellery or the Chancellor's New Year address, for they will see that the Chancellery directly faces Parliament. It looks onto the place where, day after day, the Government has to convince the majority on which it depends and where the substance of policies takes shape. The special link between parliamentary work and the work of government manifests itself in the fundamentally similar design of the two workplaces, for both the Chancellery, where the detailed work on legislative bills is coordinated on the government side, and the Paul Löbe Building opposite, where these details and possible alternatives are discussed at length by parliamentary committees are characterised by office wings laid out in a comb structure.

Moreover, any aerial view shows clearly how the Bundestag structures and the Chancellery form a conspicuous ribbon of buildings – the 'Federal Ribbon' concept developed by Berlin architects Axel Schultes and Charlotte Frank, in which the Chancellery, the Paul Löbe Building and the Marie-Elisabeth Lüders Building form a single optical entity, which also symbolises the break with the criminal past as well as the binding of divided Germany. The continuation of the architecture across the Spree not only overcomes the river at that point but also replaces the Wall that once separated East and West there. At the same time, the 'Federal Ribbon' draws a line through the plans of the National Socialist regime, which had begun preparations for a north-south axis of monumental edifices and vast parade areas.

A committee meeting room in the Paul Löbe Building. The building has a total of 1,000 offices and more than 20 meeting rooms. When the building was designed, particular importance was placed on transparency and maximum openness. This is demonstrated by the eight open storeys with lateral walkways, the spectators' galleries, the glass lifts and, last but not least, the massive glazed facades.

This page and the following double page: The ribbon of federal buildings runs for about 900 metres from west to east. It is a series of buildings that stretches from the Chancellery Park to the Marie-Elisabeth Lüders Building. It symbolises the togetherness of East and West Germany as well as being a counter-design to Hitler's planned global capital *Germania* and its north-south axis. The overall architectural approach was set out by Berlin-based architects Axel Schultes and Charlotte Frank. The construction work began in 1997 and was temporarily concluded in 2003.

A break with the darker pages of German history was also made with the Reichstag building itself – which, incidentally, was never a stage on which the National Socialist dictatorship strutted, because it was burned out in 1933. Once the Wall was built, it found itself right next to the death strip. After the severely damaged building was made usable again in the early 1970s by Paul Baumgarten, who redesigned the interior in the modernist style, its merely served as a venue for meetings of parliamentary groups and committees and as the home of a permanent exhibition on German history. A few years before, when low-flying Soviet Air Force jets roared over the Broadcasting Tower in West Berlin, where the Federal Convention was meeting, the exclave problem as well as the issue of the West German presence in Berlin during the years of German division had been starkly highlighted. When the Wall fell, however, the Reichstag building assumed central importance once again. The international representatives who attended the unification celebrations watched them from its steps. There then followed eight months of intensive and passionate discussions that culminated in the Bundestag voting by a narrow majority of 338 to 320 to move its permanent seat to Berlin.

To prepare for this removal and create the conditions for a parliamentary and architectural new beginning, not only was the urban-planning concept of the 'Federal Ribbon' developed but the Reichstag building itself also underwent another thorough reconstruction. Although the robustly radical redesign at the end of the 1960s involved the preservation of numerous conference rooms and offices, these were primarily representative in character, reflecting the contemporary expectation of a sporadic and largely demonstrative presence in Berlin but not in any way designed for an easily walkable working parliament and, of course, with no aspirations to lead the way in climate-friendly, low-energy building use. Significant parts of the post-war building fabric, moreover, would have required dismantling to remove asbestos. Accordingly, the core of the building was gutted once again in the 1990s and brought more into line with the original architectural design without sacrificing the goal of exuding transparency, even through the thick solid masonry. Since then, the public have been able to look directly through the glazed western entrance, beneath the dedication *Dem deutschen Volke* ('To the German people').

The four corner towers of the Reichstag building were interpreted in an essay in the *Kunstgewerbeblatt* of 1895 as the four kingdoms within the German Empire that had been established in 1871, namely Prussia, Saxony, Bavaria and Württemberg. The towers are flanked by 16 allegorical sandstone sculptures representing, for example, statesmanship, agriculture, the army, viticulture, child-rearing, education, art and literature. This picture shows the north-eastern tower of the Reichstag building.

With a fresh pair of eyes

So how does a newly elected Member of the Bundestag experience everyday life in this architectural setting? Let us accompany one of them as he familiarises himself with his new surroundings. Before plunging into the stressful life of a politician in Berlin, our Member occasionally has a moment or two in which he can cast a curious glance to left or right and soak in the atmosphere. He has, after all, been elected and is therefore welcome in the offices of his parliamentary group, and his official pass enables him to look into all of the new parliamentary buildings. But since it takes 30 days until the new Bundestag is constituted, the old Bundestag remains in office, and during this transitional phase the outgoing Parliament, including its departing Members, remains on standby in case any important decisions have to be made at short notice.

That is unlikely to be happening when the new Member first arrives, and so he has arranged to meet his constituency predecessor first of all for a cup of coffee in the latter's office, which may soon be his. They then take the lift down to the cellar of the modern office building and follow an underground passage, where they encounter traces of German history. In the light-bathed passage stands a section of brick tunnel with a small plaque stating that this is a preserved section of the historical service tunnel that used to run between the Reichstag building, the Reichstag President's Palace and the heating station, the tunnel through which, rumour has it, Reichstag President Hermann Göring sent arsonists into the Reichstag on the evening of 27 February 1933. "But that is only a rumour", says the experienced Member. Although Dutchman Marinus van der Lubbe was arrested at the scene and made a confession, he says, he could not have laid the fire on his own, and so, by preserving this piece of the tunnel, the Bundestag is also commemorating the Dutchman as a victim of arbitrary National Socialist justice. Van der Lubbe was ultimately condemned to death on the basis of a law that had not even existed at the time of his alleged crime.

Space for art

No sooner have the two Members reached the cellar of the Reichstag building than they encounter the next place of remembrance, namely the Archive of German Members of Parliament. It is not an archive in the conventional sense but an artwork comprising ceiling-high walls of stacked rusted metal filing boxes, each bearing the name of one of the Members of the German Parliament who were democratically elected in the period from 1919 to 1999, the inauguration date of the reconstructed Reichstag building. In this way, French artist Christian Boltanski portrays the democratic foundations of every newly elected Bundestag. "So you will be here too?" the astounded newcomer asks. "Of course, look here." Crouching and taking out his mobile phone, the outgoing Member uses it in the dimly lit corridor to make the label legible on a box in one of the lowest rows. All of the Members are given equal status in this work, regardless of whether they served for only a year or had a hand on the tiller for decades.

"And why did the Bundestag commission a French artist to design this work?", the new Member wants to know; he is told that this was also a symbolic way of coming to terms with the history of the Reichstag building in a capital city that had been divided between the Soviet Union, the United States, Britain and France. "Hang on, and I'll show you another one", says the elder Member and goes up a few steps with his successor into the basement, then past a cloakroom, through a small connecting wing with sitting areas and round a corner towards the northern entrance of the Reichstag building. "This is the shortest route", he explains, "if you want to take some fresh air on your way from a meeting in the Paul Löbe Building to your speech in the Chamber". Then he points to another symbolic pillar of the Parliament building. "This here is by an American artist," he says, showing a column designed by US artist Jenny Holzer in which the wording of 447 speeches she selected from the records of the Reichstag and Bundestag, speeches delivered in the years from 1871 to 1999, are scrolled from the floor to the ceiling in a never-ending LED display, each of the four sides of the column showing a different speech on the same subject. Besides the ideas expressed in the parliamentary speeches, the main function of this structure is to illustrate another truth of parliamentarism, namely that there is never only one perspective and one solution.

A tunnel connects the Paul Löbe Building with the Marie-Elisabeth Lüders Building, the Jakob-Kaiser Building and the Reichstag building. Shown here is a section, displayed in the underground passage between the Reichstag and Jakob Kaiser Buildings, of the historical tunnel that once carried pipes between the Reichstag building, the residence of the Reichstag President and the heating works. Also in the photograph is an exhibition on the laying of the foundation stone for the Reichstag building.

The *Archive of German Members of Parliament* is not a real archive but a work by French artist Christian Boltanski, in which a wall of rusted metal boxes stacked ceiling-high runs along each side of a passage, every box bearing the name of a Member of Parliament. All Members who were democratically elected in the period between 1919 and 1999 are included.

U.S. artist Jenny Holzer's *Installation for the Reichstag building* is located in the north entrance hall of the building. The text of more than 440 speeches made by Reichstag and Bundestag Members in the period from 1871 to 1992 scrolls up the four faces of a stela, a slim upright column, in strips of digital LED lettering. They form a pillar of Parliament, as it were, symbolising its role as the home of the political speech.

The predecessor looks at his watch. "We still have a few minutes before the group meeting", he observes. "So I can also show you one of my favourite places". A few doors further along, he says, "This here is the reflection and prayer room. Impressed, the newcomer surveys the area designed by Düsseldorf-based artist Günther Uecker for quiet meditation, public worship and prayer. Members of every faith group can take time for reflection here and find references to diverse aspects of their faith. The high-backed wooden chairs, the fragmented indirect lighting, the large panels propped against the walls, containing countless protruding nails in shapes suggesting a cross and clouds, and other visual impressions create a sense of being in a very special place. "I can only recommend coming here if you need a couple of minutes to rewire when the going gets tough", is the older Member's advice to his young successor.

The mobile buzzes. "Yes, he has. But you can speak to him yourself; he is here with me", says the sitting Member and passes the smartphone to his successor. "Of course. Right now?", he asks, looking surprised. "The chairman of our *Land* group wants to meet me over a coffee right away", he explains. "In the cafeteria, I'll bet", says the older man and opens the door. "It's a good sign that he wants to get to know you. Who knows what jobs in the group are up for grabs at the moment?" The two politicians quickly take the lift to the first floor. They walk alongside a huge glazed wall through which they can see into the plenary chamber. A few metres further on, they pause in front of a grey wooden partition wall. "When voting cards are to be used in a vote, this compartment is opened, and that is where you find your card". Further on, the older Member points out a small podium on which stand a dark stool and two small spheres that are connected by wires to a little box on the stool. "Beuys", says the Member as they turn the corner. "And in a moment, next to the cafeteria, you will also see a genuine Heisig in the library. When you are waiting for colleagues to arrive, you can have a real visual tour of German history." For the time being, however, the younger of the two has no eyes for these things. What he hears during the conversation in the cafeteria sounds very promising, and then the two older Members need to have a private discussion about the next meeting of the party's federal executive.

History everywhere

And so our newcomer sets off on his own, wandering once round the outside of the plenary chamber, past the graffiti daubed on the walls by Soviet troops when they took Berlin in 1945, which came to light again during the reconstruction of the Reichstag building and was then conserved as a relic of that time. He enters the lift and ponders on the significance of the fact that, because of the mirrored walls on both sides of the lift, the traveller sees himself time and time again, gradually disappearing into infinity. He goes past the presidential level and alights on the level devoted to the parliamentary groups. Group staff are sitting at tables, handing Members their documentation packs and information brochures as they arrive. There is ample room in front of the group meeting rooms, and politicians are standing in clusters in the middle, around the windows through which they can look down into the Chamber. They can also look up at the visitors walking up or down the spiralling ramps inside the dome.

A firm pat on the back; our new Member turns round and greets his rival, with whom he tussled for several months in the electoral campaign in his home constituency. He congratulated her on her victory on election night. Now she is congratulating him for also making it into the Bundestag on the reserve list, albeit by a hair's breadth. So there will still be two Members from the constituency in Berlin, although only one of them was directly elected to represent it. She draws him over to a lateral passage, opens a door and goes outside with him. From a balustrade she points to the courtyard below. "Something from home is growing there", she says, indicating the nearest corner of a large framed bed of vegetation in which the words *Der Bevölkerung* ('To the population') are spelled out in neon lettering. Then she explains that the installation is an art project conceived by Hans Haacke, a Cologne-born artist based in New York. Years ago it was highly controversial, because some saw it as a provocation, a subversion of the inscription 'To the German people' above the main portal, while others regarded it as a logical consequence in a Parliament whose decisions not only impacted on people with German passports. Many colleagues, she said, had already brought earth from their constituencies, and she had made sure that the plastic bag with soil from her own municipality also contained corn-poppy seeds. "Well then, I'll see if we can have some sunflowers in the other corner next year", said the new Member, "because sunflower fields abound in the southern part of the constituency". "By the way," his colleague added, "anyone can check out this installation, because there are always updated photos of it on the Internet at derbevoelkerung.de.

Although the Reichstag building was scarcely ever used under the National Socialist regime, it was regarded in the Soviet Union as symbolising the birth of the Nazi dictatorship. After the Red Army had captured the building on 2 May 1945, many soldiers left messages or simply wrote their names. During the rebuilding, the graffiti was exposed again, and some of it was preserved.

In an installation designed by Hans Haacke, the words *Der Bevölkerung* ('To the Population') are spelled out in a seven-metre-wide and 21-metre-long bed enclosed within wooden edging; the lettering is legible from every floor. Changes in the wild biotope are documented by webcam and can be followed at www.derbevoelkerung.de.

Through the glazing they see arc lamps and flashlights outside one of the group meeting rooms. "If that's the boss arriving, I'd better go in too", she says. "Who knows?" replies her colleague. "After all the exploratory talks and coalition negotiations, she might become mine too." He follows her, passing a posse of journalists on his way to his own group meeting room on the opposite side of the building. Here too, numerous journalists are gathered round a man standing in front of a large partition screen bearing his party logo, the man whom our new Member will soon be helping to elect as group chairman. As the cameras roll, he explains the group's next projects and responds to journalists' questions. On entering the room, our new Member catches sight of many well-known smiling faces. A few friends give him a welcoming hug. From one row of seats his predecessor beckons him. "Here, I've kept a place for you". The parliamentary life of the new Member begins.

And the day does not end with the conclusion of the group meeting. "Are you coming over to the PG?", asks a colleague, who has heard about the policy area in which the newcomer could be asked to specialise and wants to talk through a few projects with him. New Members have to become familiar with the in-house abbreviations. 'PG' sounds like an abbreviation for *Parlamentarischer Geschäftsführer* – the parliamentary secretary or whip, who just gave a summary of the dates for Members' diaries in the period after the opening of the new term of Parliament. But he is abbreviated to 'PGF', and the 'PG' referred to in this case is the *Deutsche Parlamentarische Gesellschaft*, the German Parliamentary Association, whose premises are located opposite the eastern entrance to the Reichstag building. Anyone leaving the building to go to the PG, with its facilities for Members and their personal guests, follows the course of the old tunnel, which is marked in the floor and is illuminated at night. In the square between the two buildings, another significant line is traced in the paving cobbles, namely that of the Wall which once divided East and West and separated the Reichstag building from the former Reichstag President's Palace, where the PG now has its seat.

The Jakob Kaiser Building – a new entity behind an old facade

Visitors climb a marble stairway to reach the *bel étage*, the upstairs floor of the former Palace containing the reception rooms. The various club rooms and dining rooms on this floor can serve as venues for confidential discussions. For larger gatherings there is the *Kaisersaal* or Emperor Room, the inauguration of which in 1904 was attended by Emperor William II himself at the invitation of the President of the Reichstag. "Did I just see a brightly coloured boat there?", asks our new Member of Parliament as he looks through the glazing. What he sees is not the River Spree but the interior of the Jakob Kaiser Building. From his fellow party members, he learns that the former residence of the President of the Reichstag has been incorporated into a complex of eight other Bundestag structures ranged along both sides of Dorotheenstrasse and known collectively as the Jakob Kaiser Building. Many Members have their offices there, but the complex also houses several dozen small and large meeting rooms, a restaurant where Members can refresh themselves, a TV studio where they can explain their policies and a reference library where they can obtain essential reading material.

The marble stairway of the Reichstag President's Palace leads up to the *bel étage* or *piano nobile*, on which are situated various clubrooms and dining rooms that Members of Parliament like to use for confidential talks. Larger gatherings take place in the Emperor Room. After the Bundestag elections of 2005 and 2013, the CDU/CSU and the SPD conducted their exploratory coalition talks in the Palace.

The German Parliamentary Association has its seat in the Reichstag President's Palace, which was built between 1899 and 1904 to plans drawn by Paul Wallot. From 1961 the Berlin Wall ran directly between the Palace and the Reichstag building. In 1994 the building was placed under a conservation order, and it underwent restoration between 1997 and 1999.

The eight buildings forming the Jakob Kaiser Building complex house a total of 1,745 offices as well as two large meeting rooms that span two storeys each and include visitors' galleries. Within the complex, passages and raised walkways link the various parts of the buildings, and connecting footbridges also cross the street between buildings 2 and 6 and between buildings 4 and 8.

Externally, the Jakob Kaiser Building either uses the preserved facades of old buildings or follows their alignment. Even the historical entrance halls have been reconstituted in some of the buildings. Inside, however, the space has been completely reshaped, for the complex forms a single architectural entity, even though various different teams (Busmann and Haberer, De Architekten Cie, von Gerkan, Marg and Partners and Schweger and Partners) were involved in the design. This is explained in one of the brochures with which our new arrival now starts a brief tour in Building 1 next to the Palace. The Jakob Kaiser Building takes its name from a representative of the CDU, who had served in the Reichstag as a member of the Centre Party, belonged to the Christian resistance during the National Socialist era, was a co-founder of the Trade Union Federation and the Christian Democratic Union in the Soviet zone, spoke out against the subjection of all institutions to the control of the Socialist Unity Party and helped to shape the early years of the Federal Republic as a member of the Parliamentary Council and as Minister for All-German Affairs.

The part of the building closest to the Reichstag provides offices for the Vice-Presidents, who share with the President of the Bundestag the task of chairing parliamentary sittings and who must always be available at short notice. The large internal hall also contains the hovering *Racing Eights* designed by artist Christiane Möbus, one of which our Member saw from the PG. These four boats are suspended from the ceiling and bob up and down, each in its own rhythm, so that they constantly form new constellations like the boats on the capital city's many rivers and lakes and like political parties, parliamentary groups and Members of Parliament too. On his exploratory tour of the complex, the newcomer discovers that, while the interior of the structure reflects a high degree of interconnectedness, with a bewildering array of stairs, corridors and lifts – so much so that he is convinced he will lose his way several times in the course of the first few weeks – it is also noticeable, particularly in Building 2, that members of the various parliamentary groups are not accommodated *en bloc* within the individual buildings but on specific floors. At this point, only short flights of stairs separate the offices of the chairs of the CDU, CSU and SPD groups. When Grand Coalitions are in government, this will certainly make rapid coordination easier. The offices of the large parliamentary groups are scattered across most of the component buildings; members of each party are literally on the same level.

The fact that the complex is a fusion of diverse original buildings is reinforced by the great variety in the design of the internal and external courtyards. One is reminiscent of a birch grove, one of a rocky plateau, and another of the artistic designs even features a body of water. Many Members of Parliament and their staff have their offices here, each with 18 square metres of floor space. But there are also meeting rooms for group executive committees, press conferences, the whips' liaison group, study commissions and parliamentary committees. Once the Member has walked all the way from the entrance at the Reichstag end to the exit in Wilhelmstrasse opposite the Berlin studio of the ARD broadcasting corporation, he has covered more than 200 metres. He can then reach the other side of the Jakob Kaiser Building by turning right into Dorotheenstrasse, crossing the road and heading for the next entrance. He could also stay in the building, follow the signs leading to a footbridge and cross by one of two roofed and enclosed walkways joining the two building ranges that enable Members and staff to keep dry when moving between buildings on wet days – not to mention the underground connecting passages.

A meeting room in the old edifice forming part of building 7 of the Jakob Kaiser Building complex. While the eight buildings in the complex are very largely new structures, Haus Sommer at number 99 Dorotheenstrasse, erected between 1853 and 1857, was integrated into building 7. Originally designed by architect Friedrich Adler as prestigious flatted accommodation, the building was bought in 1901 by the Deutsche Hypothekenbank, which had it extended and reconstructed by Paul Schröder in 1910/1911. It later served as an office building for the Institute of Cultural Architecture. This new use involved complete restructuring of the interior, which was restored to its original condition when the edifice was incorporated into the Jakob Kaiser Building.

View of the Reichstag building from a consultation room in the Jakob Kaiser Building. The two large meeting rooms in the building complex are used by committees of inquiry as well as other parliamentary bodies.

Following double page: For his installation entitled *Stands and Falls*, British sculptor Antony Gormley completely flooded an internal courtyard of the Jakob Kaiser Building, a jetty being the only means of entering the courtyard. Affixed at right angles to the surrounding facades are five life-sized sculptures, all of which are identical casts from a mould that the artist produced of his own body. They are reflected in the pool; when visitors walk along the jetty, their own reflection joins those of the sculptures, and they themselves become part of the artwork.

In the internal courtyard of building 7 of the Jakob Kaiser complex is this brick three-storey sculpture by Danish artist Per Kirkeby.

In the internal courtyard of building 4 of the Jakob Kaiser complex, Hamburg-based landscape architects WES & Partners have designed this installation, entitled *Eindringendes Spreewasser* ('Spree water leak'). Pines have been planted on small islets in a rectangular pool of water as a reference to the landscape of the Brandenburg Marches around Berlin, while the granite slabs and the erratic boulders scattered about the installation are reminiscent of a Japanese garden. In addition, a monumental concrete sculpture in the form of a stairway is also part of the installation, although its steeply rising steps come to an abrupt halt, leading nowhere.

The rooms facing the internal courtyard in building 2 of the Jakob Kaiser complex have large glazed frontages overlooking the square-shaped light well, in which a grove of soaring birches stands. Its outer edge is formed by slabs of natural stone submerged in a shallow band of water.

In his work *Lichtschleife mit* Datumsgrenze ('Light Loop with the Dateline'), located in the external courtyard of the Paul Löbe Building, artist Jörg Herold deals with the perception of history. Each of the circular concrete slabs set in the soil shows the date of a historic event, many of which are rather less widely familiar. A round mirror mounted above the courtyard focuses the sunbeams on the concrete discs, and the changing position of the sun ensures that different dates are highlighted in the course of the day at different times of year.

Twilight view of the illuminated perspex cubes installed by artist Till Exit in the internal courtyard of the Paul Löbe Building. Through the structural elements inside the cubes and their semi-transparent surfaces, which also vary in texture, the sculptures convey entirely different optical impressions by day and by night.

The Jakob Kaiser Building complex, seen in the centre of this photograph, its component buildings grouped around the eight internal courtyards, was constructed between 1997 and 2002 on a site that was part of the historical Dorotheenstadt district to the south-east of the Reichstag building, an area that stood on the border between East and West Berlin until reunification. Three buildings under conservation orders were integrated into the new complex, namely the Reichstag President's Palace and the former headquarters of the Society of German Engineers and Haus Sommer in Dorotheenstrasse.

Our Member receives a mobile call from his predecessor. "No", he answers, "I haven't left yet. I've taken a hotel room for three days, and I intend to look for a small flat." The elder Member asks whether he has given some thought to his staff, saying that he will no doubt appreciate that his team is wondering what his plans are. It would be best if they could meet again shortly if he is still in the parliamentary precinct. "I'll show you something unusual", he adds, and gives the number of the room where he will be waiting; locating it will be a good test of the newcomer's ability to find his way about. The latter notes the number 6.556 and thinks to himself that the first digit does not stand for the building number but for the floor, so the office must be up on the sixth floor. The next digit is the building. He has been through buildings one to four on the other side of the street. He entered building 8 on this side, and now he is in number 7, so he must go all the way along to the Reichstag and Tiergarten end until he reaches building 5. Then up and up he goes, along to the end of the corridor, and there it is.

"Wow!", gasps the younger man when he sees his predecessor in the meeting room. Two sides comprise nothing but windows, through which the Tiergarten and the floodlit Reichstag building almost seem to be within touching distance. Moonlight shines in from above. "There are certainly some fine spots here, eh?", the older Member begins. A journalist once told him, he says, that, when Guido Westerwelle, chairman of the FDP group, was head of the Opposition, he held his weekly press conferences here, and for this reason the room had been dubbed *Café Guido*. Soon the two Members are deep in conversation about the challenges posed by the will of the electorate in terms of the allocation of office space by the Bundestag and by the commission appointed for that purpose by the Committee of Elders. Election winners need more space, losers need less, and so the spatial arrangements have to be flexible. Our newcomer also learns that he might not be given his predecessor's office at all. It depends in part, he is told, on his committee membership, because many Members are accommodated with their colleagues from other groups who belong to the same specialised committee. They may be in other office buildings, such as the one in the boulevard Unter den Linden, while many Members have their offices in the Paul Löbe Building. In the end, they agree that the new Member will very probably inherit his predecessor's private secretary, because it will be particularly important for him to have her knowledge and experience of procedures in the House and in the constituency, but that he should wait with the appointment of other staff until he knows what his policy specialisation will be in the coming years. He may need additional specific expertise in his office.

Paul Löbe Building – 'engine of the Republic'

The very next morning he calls the woman who is to take care of the routine tasks for him in Berlin and act as his early-warning system. May he invite her to a pleasant place for lunch, he asks, and she suggests the restaurant in the PLH below the *Europasaal*. 'PLH' stands for *Paul-Löbe-Haus*. That is the building which is aligned with the Federal Chancellery and which, with its huge projecting canopy, mirrors the selfsame architectural statement that reaches towards it from the Chancellery, thereby reinforcing the desired effect of a 'ribbon' of federal buildings. The new Member, meanwhile, is returning from a flat viewing in the West, from where he travelled back to Berlin Central Station on the suburban railway, the *S-Bahn*, before taking the new underground line U55 for one stop and alighting at the Bundestag station. Immediately in front of the exit stairway stands the imposing structure of the Paul Löbe Building with its huge glass facade covering the entire breadth and the entire seven-storey

On 8 August 2009, underground railway line U55 was opened. The new line runs from the Brandenburg Gate to Berlin Central Station, calling *en route* at the Bundestag station, which was opened on the same day. The line, also known as the *Kanzler U-Bahn* ('Chancellor's Tube'), covers a distance of only 1.8 kilometres as yet but is soon to be incorporated into line U5, which will then carry trains between Central Station and Alexanderplatz.

height of the building. The central part provides a view of the large internal hall, flanked to left and right by concrete walls on each of which a stairway is mounted, rising from floor to floor. Where the stairways reach each level, an entrance slit in the concrete walls draws the eye, as it were, into the interior of the building.

Our Member still has some time to spare, and so he does not go through the Members' entrance immediately but takes a walk round the building. A tourist guide has just stopped with his group and is talking about the 'eight cylinders', because on each side of the building, in the spaces between the jutting wing blocks with their office accommodation, are four glazed rotundas in which the committee meeting rooms are located – a total of eight meeting rooms, in other words, for 23 committees. The guide likens the structure of the building to an eight-cylinder engine. It is therefore known as the 'engine of the Republic', because it is here that the Bundestag functions as a 'working parliament', engaging in the real specialised deliberations away from the public sittings in the plenary chamber. The Paul Löbe Building, he says, contains more than 1,000 offices; it is named after the former editor-in-chief of the SPD newspaper *Volkswacht*, who was elected to the Weimar National Assembly in 1919, served as President of the Reichstag in the period from 1920 to 1932, was imprisoned by the Nazis, helped to rebuild the SPD after the war and was a member of the Parliamentary Council and of the first Bundestag, which he opened in his capacity as President by Age.

Artists, colours and shapes

"Why does the Bundestag have two domes now?" a little boy calls out. "What do you mean?" asks the tourist guide and explains that the Reichstag building still has only one dome. Another dome of sorts is now being added on the extension to the Marie-Elisabeth Lüders Building, he says, but you can't see both of them from here. "I do see them!", the child protests, pointing to the left towards the Spree to an elongated low blue structure looking like a ship that has docked near the Paul Löbe Building. On its roof there are indeed two domes to be seen. The expert corrects himself. "You are perfectly right. That is the Bundestag's day nursery, where staff can have their children looked after while they are at work", he explains. An Austrian architect, Gustav Peichl, designed this special feature of Parliament and evidently went about the task with a twinkle in his eye, for his architectural reference to the Reichstag comprises not just one but two domes.

The Member of Parliament smiles. He continues on his way and, as he turns the corner, has to smile again. What he saw yesterday when driving past here for the first time and took for an advertisement for window cleaners actually seems to be one of the Bundestag's Per Cent for Art projects. He will soon learn that this is the two-part sculpture by Leipzig-born artist Neo Rauch entitled *Man on a Ladder*. With his illuminated work that can be seen from far away at night, this artist also leaves scope for individual interpretations, ranging from people using ladders to look over the Wall, which stood not far from there, to politicians reaching for lofty goals, as indeed they actually do in this building. Our newcomer is taken aback when he realises that the two men, each about ten metres in height, are not side by side at all but affixed to opposite walls and even separated by a glazed wall. That is the extra twist – what is perceived as a second man is basically a third one, namely the mirror image of the second figure. "Clever!", he says to himself. But at the same time he starts to wonder why they are green. By putting two and two

Only a few metres away from the Reichstag building, the Paul Löbe Building with its postmodernist architecture makes its own statement. Its architect, Stephan Braunfels, designed the new eight-storey building with its five striking wing blocks on either side and eight distinctive glazed cylinders as an 'engine of the Republic'.

For the children of Bundestag staff, a day nursery on the bank of the Spree to the north of the Paul Löbe Building was opened in 1999. Its shape is suggestive of a ship that has docked alongside the ribbon of federal buildings. The two hemispheres on its roof contain little cave dwellings in which children can have their afternoon nap.

together, he hits on the idea that it might have something to do with the location "on the green beaches of the Spree", echoing the name of a novel and popular TV drama. He decides to ask the artist sometime whether he intended to allude to the novelist's examination of pre-war and post-war lifestyles in Germany, whether his work is a reflection on life, sited at the very place where the conditions of life are shaped.

And immediately he makes another connection as he enters the Paul Löbe Building, for set into the floor along the approximately 200-metre length of the internal hall are two quotations in aluminium lettering, the work of American artist Joseph Kosuth. They are lengthy passages from works by Thomas Mann and Ricarda Huch, both dealing with the question of what life is. Our new Member, meanwhile, has gone up a few floors in the lift and has walked the full length of the hall along a corridor leading past committee rooms and offices. Finding the direct route here is not so easy at all, he decides. On most floors of the building, in fact, the only way to move from east to west involves constantly following curving passages that wind round the various committee rotundas. When he looks back from the end of the building, the broad stacked drums with the narrow passages encircling them remind him of insulators in a huge electricity transformer station. The architect, Stephan Braunfels, had evidently guessed that Bundestag Members and staff were likely to be "highly charged" at many times. Recalling his physics lessons, our newcomer remembers that the purpose of such transformer stations is to establish a connection between differing voltage levels. At that time he would never have guessed that the principle could also be applied to parliamentary architecture.

It is time for lunch with his future private secretary. In the Members' restaurant, Cuban artist Jorge Pardo has come up with a very meaningful response to the predominance of grey concrete tones by suspending from the ceiling a shoal of crystal globes in green, blue, red, yellow and other colours. "Variety is the spice of life" springs to mind, and our Member's gaze then wanders from the ceiling to the Spree, which almost seems to be flowing past at floor level here. And the tables are as round as the committee rooms. He learns from his new secretary that numerous other artists responded to the Paul Löbe Building by using brightly coloured shapes. She mentions the huge rhombuses in red, black, blue and green that enliven the concrete walls facing the Chancellery with the dynamism conveyed by their slight asymmetry, which were christened *Diamond Shapes* by their American creator Ellsworth Kelly. And if he looks into the hall, she says, he will see how French artist François Morellet has hung red, yellow, green and blue garlands of neon light tubes from the ceiling; cutting across the longitudinal axis of the hall, these tubes also interplay with the shapes of the building.

The private secretary is a genuine art lover, and the next few minutes of their conversation are devoted entirely to other objects which passers-by might not even notice and of which the Member of Parliament was largely unaware during his first stroll round the building. She explains how individual artworks in the external courtyards, with their sculpted hedges, relate in either an abstract or a concrete way to the location and to German history. For example, the Teflon sculptures *German 1* and *German 2* created by artist duo Twin Gabriel give no clues at first sight, but then the shadows they cast reveal the profile of Goethe and that of a German shepherd dog. Or then there are the red

On the east facade of the Paul Löbe Building are two ten-metre-high neon light sculptures by Leipzig-based artist Neo Rauch. The outstretched arm of each of the two men, standing on ladders with their backs to the observer, is an allusion to the German culture of the democratic society.

and yellow metal formwork elements of the sort used to shape walls of poured concrete, which look as though they have been left standing after the construction work. These, says the secretary, have been arranged by artist Franka Hörnschemeyer to form a 'spatial labyrinth' in which it is not easy to keep sight of the whole picture. The artist uses the metal lattices to trace part of the course of the former border fortifications and the ground plan of the present-day Paul Löbe Building, overlapping these shapes. The neighbouring courtyard designed by Jörg Herold likewise reveals little at first sight. A number of disc-shaped stone slabs are inscribed with dates, some of which are very well known, such as 13 August 1961, when the building of the Berlin Wall began, while others are less familiar, like 2 July 1505, the day on which Martin Luther made his 'lightning decision' to become a monk, and some have been imaginatively developed by the artist, such as the arrival of the Huguenots on 8 November 1685, which she has labelled "Great Elector invents Green Card".

The secretary knows this from a leaflet containing a key to the inscribed dates, which she has brought along to this meeting with her future boss, having learned that he was very interested in art. For the same reason, she draws his attention to the fact that the Bundestag possesses an impressive art collection, from which Members can borrow exhibits to adorn their parliamentary offices. He is delighted to hear that.

The question regarding the location of his future office, she adds, is still unanswered. In his particular case he may end up with the UdL experts or near the committee room here in the PLH or else in the office vacated by his predecessor in the JKH. She suggests that they take a look at all of these places and has already taken the precaution of asking other private secretaries with whom she is acquainted whether she can pop in with him. Once he has memorised the abbreviations and now knows that 'UdL' stands for 'Unter den Linden', 'PLH' for the Paul Löbe Building and JKH for the Jakob Kaiser Building, they go over to one of the committee rooms, which are indeed perfectly circular with a corresponding circular seating plan. The secretary explains to him where the various parliamentary groups, the committee chairpersons, the Committee Service, the experts and government representatives sit and points out that, when meetings and hearings are conducted in public, interested spectators can follow proceedings from the tiered seats on the upper floor.

View into the restaurant in the Paul Löbe Building. Its spherical coloured glass lamps all over the ceiling are part of Jorge Pardo's artwork *Untitled Restaurant*, as are the furnishings, which were specially designed for the restaurant.

In the stairway on the west side of the Paul Löbe Building are the *Berlin Panels* produced by American artist Ellsworth Kelly. The four large-scale aluminium rhomboid panels in blue, black, red and green, with their emphatic colours and asymmetric positioning, create a contrast with the otherwise rigorous structure of the facade.

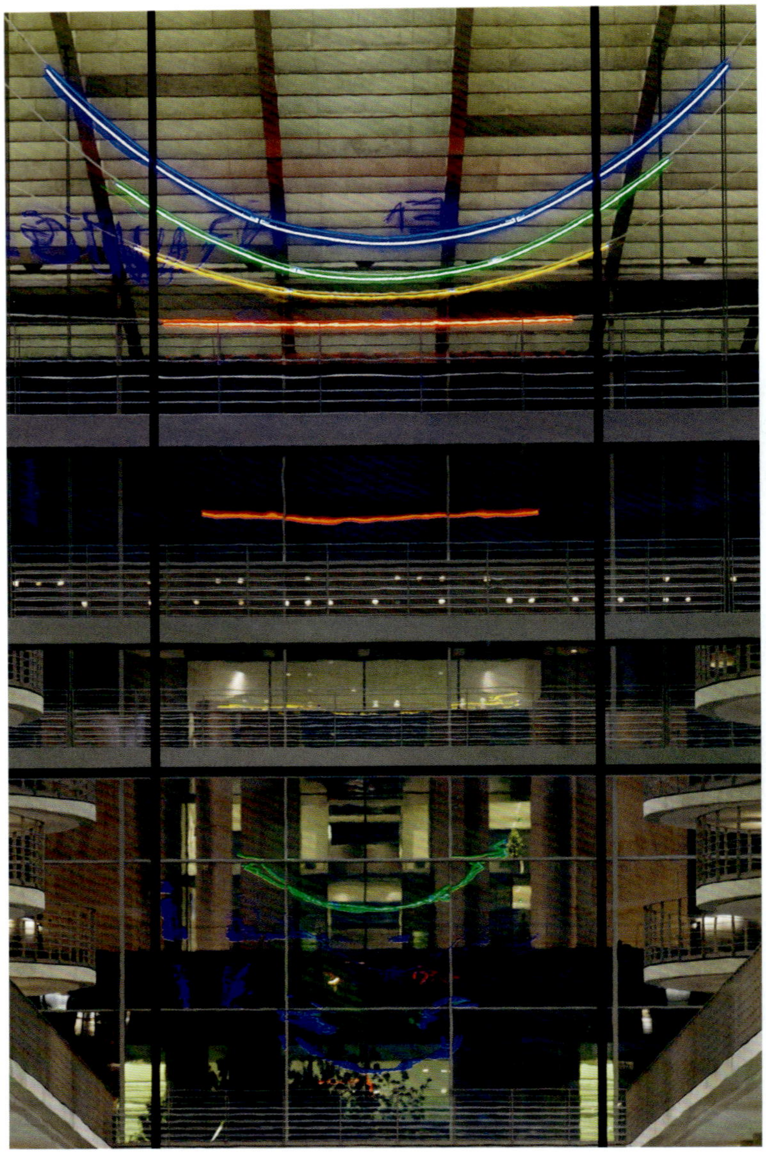

In the northern courtyard of the Paul Löbe Building between wings 2 and 3, Franka Hörnschemeyer used yellow and red lattice elements from formwork, the moulds that are used to build walls of poured concrete, to create an elaborate filigree spatial labyrinth. The arrangement of the lattices is based on the ground plans of sections of the Berlin Wall, buildings and GDR border guards' dog kennels that once lay to the east and on parts of the ground plan of the Paul Löbe Building, though these are not laid out separately but interlock with each other.

View from the Marie-Elisabeth Lüders Building into the Paul Löbe Building on the opposite river bank. The line of neon ribbons is an installation by artist François Morellet entitled *Haute et basse tension*. It begins with a straight, tightly stretched glowing red band, followed by a series of yellow, green and blue neon tubes that loop down from the ceiling.

A double-decked footbridge provides a high-level internal link between the Paul Löbe and Marie-Elisabeth Lüders Buildings as well as forming a symbolic bond between West and East. The lower deck is also accessible to the public and offers visitors a fine view of the Spree promenade. Architect Stephan Braunfels called it the 'leap over the Spree'.

Following double page: The ribbon of federal buildings that begins with the Federal Chancellery ends with the Marie-Elisabeth Lüders Building. The third of the new parliamentary buildings on the Spree was inaugurated with the ceremonial key presentation in December 2003; it was built over the original course of the inner or 'hinterland' Berlin Wall.

The Marie-Elisabeth Lüders Building – the Bundestag Library

Shortly afterwards, they are standing in the middle of the footbridge across the Spree. "You get splendid views here when you cross from the PLH to the MELH", says the private secretary, referring to the walkway that joins the Paul Löbe and Marie-Elisabeth Lüders Buildings, spanning the river high above the passing excursion boats. A few metres lower, the bridge has a second deck that arches from one bank to the other. It is clearly visible from here how the architecture that begins in the Chancellery with a large geometrical statement of intent is passed on from one edifice to the next, how the large circular opening on the end of the Marie-Elisabeth Lüders Building presents itself pointedly to the Spree like the first visiting card of that building, affording an interior view of a large hearing room. Here, as in the *Europasaal* across the river, many prominent figures have been questioned by committees of inquiry as witnesses in hearings that have generated huge media interest.

After turning only a few more corners, the new Member enters the rotunda where the Marie-Elisabeth Lüders Building performs its key function, that of the Bundestag Library, one of the world's largest parliamentary libraries. A band of blue neon letters with a circumference of more than 80 metres rotates just below the ceiling; this is the *Blue Ring* created by Italian artist Maurizio Nannucci. In two sentences penned by Hannah Arendt, it describes the tension inherent in the relationship between freedom and equality, which is central to the actions of Members of Parliament as well as being the subject of many of the volumes held by the library. The Marie-Elisabeth Lüders Building takes its name from a Free Democrat. The first woman in Germany to obtain a doctorate in political science, Marie-Elisabeth Lüders belonged to the constitutive National Assembly; as a Member of the Reichstag until 1930, she campaigned for equal rights for women and for better care of the unemployed. As President by Age, she opened the constituent sittings of the Bundestag in 1953 and 1957.

Our Member's mobile phone vibrates. He is able to make viewing appointments for two more flats in the early evening. "I'll soon be sitting down a lot and eating numerous working meals", he tells his future private secretary. "Are there any gyms near here where I can do a bit of physical training to redress the balance?" She gives him a few addresses but also walks a little way

with him towards the basement, where they soon reach a small sports hall. Then she tells him about the parliamentary sports club and about 'FC Bundestag', the Members' cross-party football team that plays matches against other teams. "I can see you are keen for some positive reinforcement", his secretary says knowingly. "Would you like me to ask about the next training session?" Our Member nods appreciatively.

The legislative process

A few steps further on is the 'memory' of the Bundestag, in other words the registry, where hundreds of thousands of documents with millions of pages document the legislative process and other parliamentary activities. This tour cannot end without a look at the extension currently being built, which will stretch the ribbon of federal buildings to Luisenstrasse and finalise it with a landmark tower, rising to a height of 40 metres. This is also earmarked as the new home for Bernhard Heiliger's sculpture *Kosmos 70*, which hovered for almost a quarter-century over the foyer of the old Reichstag building until the 1990s, interpreting the relationship between art, architecture and politics. In the street next to the building site, the new Member notices the numerous delivery vehicles heading towards the Marie-Elisabeth Lüders Building. The secretary does not know the exact details but has heard that the volume of supplies needed for a parliamentary estate with so many thousand employees would result in the surface entrances being blocked for half-days at a time if deliveries were to be taken through them. For this reason, she says, there is a tunnel system under the Spree through which all of the Bundestag buildings can be reached without any disruption of other operations. This is obviously the central access route. But there is more going on underground than might be supposed. There are, for example, storage aquifers in the bedrock under the Reichstag building in which the summer surplus of warm water can be stored for the cold months and additional cooling water can be stored in winter to be pumped up in summer. Even the spent air expelled from the plenary chamber, she says, is recycled to save energy.

On the way back towards the Spree bridge, they stop beside the Marie-Elisabeth Lüders Building, where the new Member takes a long, close look at a large equestrian sculpture that differs in a remarkable way from the various equestrian statues in the capital. This is not a proudly mounted monarch on horseback; after careful study of the shapes, it becomes clear that the rider in Marino Marini's *Miracolo – L'idea di un'immagine* can scarcely hold on to a rearing horse. Is it rearing in the face of virtually insurmountable threats?

Opposite page: The extension to the Marie-Elisabeth Lüders Building will take the ribbon of federal buildings all the way to Luisenstrasse, rounding it off with a 40-metre-high tower. Most of the building supplies are delivered through a system of tunnels below the River Spree.

The Marie-Elisabeth Lüders Building serves as the parliamentary memory bank of the Federal Republic. Press documentation, the parliamentary library and parliamentary documentation are all to be found here, as are the parliamentary archives, where hundreds of thousands of documents with millions of pages are stored. For the first time, all of these facilities have been brought together under one roof.

HEN / GLEICHHEIT IST DEN

Even from outside the building, Italian artist Maurizio Nannucci's installation entitled *Blue Ring* is visible through the glass facade of the library rotunda. The blue band of neon letters forms an eighty-metre circle just below the ceiling in the reading room of the library, displaying two consecutive sentences inspired by a passage from Hannah Arendt: "Liberty is conceivable as the possibility of action among equals"/"Equality is conceivable as the possibility of action for liberty".

Preserving and defending fundamental rights

From this sculpture, the eye is drawn to a vast external stairway, an equally inviting place to stop and linger, Mediterranean-style, as the similar layout of the riverside area on the opposite bank next to the Paul Löbe Building. Nothing appears more peaceful than this stretch of the Spree. Yet here, before the peaceful revolution, East German border guards had orders to fire on anyone fleeing from East to West, and many who tried to do so here paid with their lives. They are commemorated in a room below the stairway in which original fragments of the border fortifications rescued by Ben Wagin and incorporated into the building design by Stephan Braunfels record the course of the Wall in a harrowing way. Each fragment shows one of the years when the Wall divided Berlin and the number of deaths in that year. The nearby art room in the Marie-Elisabeth Lüders Building will be open to the public again once when the extension wing is completed but will then be accessed from Luisenstrasse. Our Member naturally makes a mental note to keep an eye open for forthcoming exhibitions here.

Three weeks later, the newcomer experiences the core architecture from a very special perspective. The Bundestag holds its constituent sitting, and he is one of the two Members acting as secretaries who, taking turn about, read out the names of all Members of the German Parliament. He is seated above the rostrum from which Members address the House, next to the President by Age, who opened the sitting and will shortly give way to the newly elected President (Speaker) of the Bundestag. In front of him, with their backs to him, are the shorthand writers. On his left, the Parliamentary Commissioner for the Armed Forces has just occupied a vacant seat. The Commissioner is the only Member of the House who is already in his post, because his period of office extends beyond the legislative term, which serves to underline his independence. In the neighbouring rows for Members of the Bundesrat, only a few of the seats are occupied. On the opposite side of the Presiding Committee is an entirely vacant block of seats. These are the government benches, which will not be reoccupied until the coalition negotiations have been completed, the House has elected a Chancellor and he or she has brought the members of the Cabinet to be sworn in following their appointment by the President of the Federal Republic.

Vestiges of the Berlin Wall that divided the city from 1961 to 1989 are exhibited today as a memorial in a room which is open to the public in the Marie-Elisabeth Lüders Building. The fragments were marked by artist Ben Wargin with figures showing each year of the Wall's existence and the number of known Wall victims in that year. The architect, Stephan Braunfels, arranged the segments in such a way that they retrace the course of the Wall and cut through and divide the circular room.

The plenary chamber is the centrepiece of the German Bundestag. The seats are arranged in a fixed pattern. From the President's perspective, the Members belonging to the CDU/CSU parliamentary group sit, in principle, on the right of the hemicycle, those in the group of Alliance 90/The Greens sit in the centre, and the Members from the SPD and Left Party groups sit on the left.

Artikel 3
(1) Alle Menschen sind vor dem Gesetz gleich. (2) Män-
ner und Frauen sind gleichberechtigt. (3) Niemand darf
wegen seines Geschlechtes, seiner Abstammung, seiner
Rasse, seiner Sprache, seiner Heimat und Herkunft, seines
Glaubens, seiner religiösen oder politischen Anschauun-
gen benachteiligt oder bevorzugt werden.

The newcomer looks round the large semicircular plenary chamber, which is full. The seating layout has been altered since the previous Parliament. One parliamentary group now has a broader block of seats, another has a slimmer block – just as the electorate has decreed. Many well-known faces that he had only ever seen on television are sitting in the front rows and looking at him expectantly. Spectators are watching the constitution of the Bundestag from the large galleries that extend far down into the chamber. Diagonally to the left above him he recognises the President of the Federal Republic as well as a number of former Federal Presidents and other distinguished parliamentary veterans. Up there to his right, his wife and children are also watching his first day in the chamber.

He has arranged to meet them in a few hours' time by the Spree near Friedrichstrasse station. The children have been promised a sightseeing cruise on the river. He is almost late when he goes to meet them, because he stops on the way at a glass partition in front of one of the external courtyards of the Jakob Kaiser Building, where the Bill of Rights from the Basic Law in its original wording of 1949 is engraved into the glass. . So simply, so imposingly and so decisively they identify those to whom all the work and all the architecture in this place is dedicated. As for our Member, he is still uncertain as to his future role, nor does he know yet whether his office will be here, there or elsewhere. But after studying the sentences engraved on these glass panels, he is sure of one thing – that there is much to preserve, much to defend and still a great deal of work to do.

In front of one of the external courtyards of the Jakob Kaiser Building, Israeli artist Dani Karavan installed the artwork *Grundgesetz 49* ('Basic Law 49'). On glass panels it displays the original text of the 19 articles containing the fundamental rights enshrined in the Basic Law for the Federal Republic of Germany. The second photograph shows the glass panel with Article 3.

Manfred Görtemaker

Professor Manfred Görtemacher was born in 1951. He studied history, political science and media and communications in Münster and Berlin. From 1975 to 1980 he was a research assistant and from 1983 to 1989 an assistant professor at the Free University of Berlin. From 1980 to 1981 he was a John F. Kennedy Memorial Fellow at Harvard University. From 1982 to 1983 he was Visiting Assistant Professor of Overseas Studies at Stanford University. From 1989 to 1990 he was a Krupp Foundation Senior Associate at the Institute for East-West Security Studies in New York. Since 1992, he has been Professor of Modern History at the University of Potsdam. From 1994 to 1995 he was deputy vice-chancellor, and from 2001 to 2004 chairman of the Senate of Potsdam University. Since 2014 he has again been a member of the University Senate. He is an adviser of studies for the Fulbright Commission.

In 1995 he was a visiting scholar at Duke University in Durham, North Carolina. In 1999 he was a visiting scholar at Dartmouth College in Hanover, New Hampshire. From 2002 to 2003 he was a Visiting Fellow in St Antony's College at the University of Oxford. In 2005 and 2008 and from 2010 to 2012 he was a visiting scholar in the Department of Politics, Institutions and History at the University of Bologna, where he was also a visiting scholar in the Department of Political and Social Sciences from 2013 to 2015.

From 1992 to 1994 he was a member of the academic advisory board for the restoration of the historic parts of Cecilienhof Palace. From 1996 to 2004 he was on the academic advisory board of the Centre for Contemporary History in Potsdam. From 2005 to 2011 he was a member of the academic advisory board of the Human Rights Centre of the University of Potsdam. From 2006 to 2010 he served on the academic advisory board of Memorium Nuremberg Trials. From 2009 to 2015 he was on the academic advisory board of the Point Alpha Memorial Foundation. Since 1998 he has chaired the academic advisory board of the Bundeswehr Centre for Military History and Social Sciences and the academic advisory board of the Bundeswehr for museum matters. Since 2012, he has been on the board of trustees of the Ernst Reuter Archive Foundation in the Berlin *Land* Archives. Since 2015, he has been a member of the academic advisory board for the extension of Memorium Nuremberg Trials.

Since 2012 he and Professor Christoph Safferling have been joint heads of the Independent Academic Commission at the Federal Ministry of Justice for the Critical Study of the National Socialist Past.

About the authors

Everhard Holtmann

Professor Everhard Holtmann, born in 1946, held the chair of systems analysis and comparative politics at the Martin Luther University of Halle-Wittenberg until 1992, is a member of the Editorial Advisory Board of *German Politics* and, from 2007 to 2012, was the spokesman for DFG Collaborative Research Centre 580, involving the Universities of Jena and Halle and devoted to the study of post-unification social developments; since 2012 he has been Director of Research at the Halle Centre for Social Research of the Martin Luther University of Halle-Wittenberg.

Publications (selection): Everhard Holtmann and Anne Köhler, *Wiedervereinigung vor dem Mauerfall. Einstellungen der Bevölkerung der DDR im Spiegel geheimer westlicher Meinungsumfragen*, Frankfurt and New York, 2015; with Oscar W. Gabriel *et al.*, *Deutschland 25. Gesellschaftliche Trends und politische Einstellungen,* Bonn, 2015; Everhard Holtmann, *Der Parteienstaat in Deutschland. Erklärungen, Entwicklungen, Erscheinungsbilder,* Bonn 2012; Heinrich Best and Everhard Holtmann (eds.), *Aufbruch der entsicherten Gesellschaft. Deutschland nach der Wiedervereinigung*, Frankfurt and New York, 2012; Everhard Holtmann and Marion Reiser (eds.), *Farewell to the Party Model? Independent Local Lists in East and West European Countries*, Wiesbaden, 2008; Everhard Holtmann, Kerstin Völkl, Kai-Uwe Schnapp and Oscar W. Gabriel (eds.), *Wähler und Landtagswahlen in der Bundesrepublik Deutschland*, Baden-Baden, 2008; Everhard Holtmann, Hans Braun and Uta Gerhardt (eds.), *Die lange Stunde Null. Gelenkter sozialer Wandel in Westdeutschland nach 1945*, Baden-Baden, 2007.

Wolfgang Ismayr

Wolfgang Ismayr, Dr. phil., Dr. rer. pol. habil., was born in Munich in 1942; since 1995 he has been a professor in the Department of Political Science in the Faculty of Arts at the Technical University of Dresden; since becoming an emeritus professor in 2008, he has headed the University's Research Centre for Parliamentarianism. He studied political science, modern history, philosophy and German and obtained his doctorate from the Ludwig Maximilian University of Munich in 1972 and his post-doctoral lecturing qualification (*Habilitation*) from the University of Bamberg in 1994. From 1972 to 1993 he was a research assistant and academic director at the University of Bamberg; from 1993 to 1995, he was an acting professor at the University of Passau.

In 1993, he was awarded the Bundestag Research Prize for Outstanding Works on Parliamentarianism.

Publications (selection): *Das politische Theater in Westdeutschland*, second edition, Königstein, 1985; *Parlamentarische Kommunikation und Abgeordnetenfreiheit*, Frankfurt am Main, 1982; *Der Deutsche Bundestag. Funktionen, Willensbildung, Reformansätze*, Opladen, 1992; *Ausschüsse*, second updated edition, Berlin, 2004 (new edition pending); *Bundestagspräsident und Präsidium*, third updated edition, Berlin, 2004; (ed.) *Die politischen Systeme Westeuropas*, fourth updated and revised edition, Wiesbaden, 2009; (ed.) *Die politischen Systeme Osteuropas*, third updated and expanded edition, Wiesbaden, 2010; (ed.) *Gesetzgebung in Westeuropa. EU-Staaten und Europäische Union*, Wiesbaden, 2008; *Der Deutsche Bundestag*, third entirely revised and updated edition, Wiesbaden 2012, (the first and second editions appeared in 2000 and 2001 as a volume in the UTB (University Paperbacks) series under the title *Der Deutsche Bundestag im politischen System der Bundesrepublik Deutschland*).

Hans Wilderotter

Professor Hans Wilderotter was born in 1949. He studied ethnology, history and philosophy at the Free University of Berlin from 1969 to 1973 and worked from 1974 to 1979 as a research assistant in the Institute of Ethnology of the Free University of Berlin. From 1979 to 1981 he lectured at Berlin School of the Arts and the Free University of Berlin, and from 1982 to 1995 was a freelance exhibition curator, working in Berlin, Bonn, Dessau, Dortmund, Dresden, Frankfurt am Main, Munich, Paris, Potsdam and Weimar. From 1995 to 2015 he lectured in museum studies and museum communication as a professor at Berlin University of Applied Sciences; from 2010 to 2013 he was also a visiting scholar in Abu Dhabi.

From 2000 to 2010 he was a member of the academic advisory board of the Documentation Centre on the Everyday Culture of the German Democratic Republic in Eisenhüttenstadt, from 2000 to 2001 he chaired the academic advisory board for the Prussia 2001 exhibition in Potsdam, in 2003 he served on the academic advisory board for the Albert Einstein exhibition in Ulm, and from 2003 to 2005 he was chairman of the academic advisory board for the projected exhibition on the Anhalt region in Dessau. Since 2009, he has chaired the academic advisory board for the House of Brandenburg-Prussian History in Potsdam.

Gregor Mayntz

Dr Gregor Mayntz, born in 1960, is the political editor in the parliamentary editorial team at the *Rheinische Post* newspaper. He comes from Oedt in the Lower Rhineland and wrote his first piece for the *Rheinische Post* at the age of 15. Moving from the Kempen local news office to the editorial headquarters in Düsseldorf, he was then transferred in 1997 to the capital office of the *Rheinische Post* in Bonn and moved with Parliament and the Government to Berlin in 1999.

After attending the Thomaeum senior secondary school in Kempen, he did his national service in the army and in the Ministry of Defence and studied politics, modern history and administrative law in Bonn, where he also obtained his doctorate with a thesis on parliamentary journalism.

As for voluntary activity, since 2011 Gregor Mayntz has chaired the Federal Press Association (*Bundespressekonferenz*), an association of more than 900 accredited Berlin correspondents. This work has made him put his photographic hobby on the back burner for the time being.

Cover, top Deutscher Bundestag (DBT)/Axel Hartmann; bottom DBT/Werner Schüring; p. 2 DBT/Thomas Trutschel/photothek.net.

Chapter 1: pp. 6/7, pp. 10--12, pp. 14–18, pp. 20–21, pp. 25–28, p. 31, p. 35 top, p. 41, pp. 45–46 picture alliance/akg-images; p. 9 picture alliance/Heritage Images, Fine Art Images; p. 13 bpk/Hermann Buresch; p. 19 akg-images; pp 22–23, pp. 29–30, p. 32, p. 33 bottom, p. 34, p. 38, p. 40, p. 42 bottom bpk; p. 33 top picture alliance/Federal Archives; p. 35 bottom bpk/Dietmar Katz; p. 36 picture alliance/dpa-Zentralbild/Stefan Sauer; p. 37 picture alliance/dpa-Zentralbild/Berliner Verlag/Archives; p. 39 top bpk/H. Louis Held; p. 39 bottom dpa – Bild-archiv; p. 42 top bpk/Kunstbibliothek, SMB, Photothek Willy Römer/Willy Römer; p. 43 bpk/Carl Weinrother; p. 44 picture alliance/akg/Alfred Hennig.

Chapter 2: pp. 48/49 DBT/Ute Grabowsky/photothek.net; p. 50 Federal Government/Puck-Archiv; p. 51, p. 53, p. 56 right, p. 63, p. 86, p. 89 bottom left picture-alliance/akg-images; p. 52 bpk (in spite of our investigations, we were unable to identify the legal successor; the latter's legitimate claims may therefore be settled retrospectively); p. 54, p. 92 top dpa–Bildarchiv; p. 56 left picture alliance/dpa-Zentralbild/Deutsche Fotothek; p. 57 Federal Archives/Allgemeiner Deutscher Nachrichtendienst (ADN) Zentralbild, Fotograf Igel, image reference 183-S88849; p. 58 Federal Archives, ADN Zentralbild, Agentur Illus, image reference 183-2005-1017-513; p. 59 top dpa – Report/dpa DENA; p. 59 bottom, p. 85 bpk; p. 60 DBT/Sylvia Bohn; p. 61 DBT/Junophoto/Julia Nowak-Katz; p. 62 picture alliance/AP images; p. 64 top dpa image archive/UPI; p. 64 bottom, p. 65 Federal Government; p. 67 Federal Government/Lothar Schaack; p. 69 picture alliance/AP Images/Kreusch; p. 70 picture alliance/AP Images; p. 71 Federal Government/Egon Steiner; p. 73, p. 88 picture alliance/Kurt Rohwedder; p. 74 Federal Government/Gerhard Heisler; p. 77 picture alliance/AP Photo/Markus Schreiber; p. 82 Federal Government/Marvin Ibo Güngör; pp. 83–84 DBT/Achim Melde; p. 89 top, p. 91, p. 92 bottom left, pp. 96–97, p. 110 left Federal Government/Engelbert Reineke; p. 89 bottom right Federal Government/Jens Gathmann; p. 90 dpa image archive/Rapp; p. 92 bottom right Federal Government/Ludwig Wegmann; p. 93 bottom left picture alliance/dpa/Reinhard Kemmether; p. 93 bottom right, p. 94 picture alliance/dpa-Zentralbild; p. 95, pp. 102–103 Federal Government/Klaus Lehnartz; pp. 98-99 ullstein bild/ADN image archive; p. 100 picture-alliance/dpa image archive/Roland Holschneider; p. 101 picture alliance/dpa-Zentralbild/Paul Glaser; p. 104 picture alliance/AP Images/Roberto Pfeil; p. 105 Federal Government/Arne Schambeck; pp. 106–109 DBT/Presse-Service Steponaitis; p. 110 right ullstein bild/Christian Bach; p. 112 dpa/Lusa Inacio Rosa; p. 115 picture-alliance/Ulrich Baumgarten.

Chapter 3: pp. 116-117 DBT/Jörg F. Müller; artwork: © VG Bild-Kunst, Bonn, 2016; p. 119 DBT/Thomas Trutschel/photothek.net; artwork: © VG Bild-Kunst, Bonn 2016; p. 122 DBT/Junophoto/Julia Nowak; p. 123 The Federal Returning Officer, Wiesbaden, 2015; p. 126 dpa/Jens Büttner; p. 127 Werner Schüring; p. 128 dpa/Maurizio Gambarini; p. 129, p. 143 bottom right, p. 157, p. 184 DBT/Achim Melde; p. 133 top left, top centre, bottom left, bottom centre DBT/Stella von Saldern; p. 133 top right DBT/Inga Haar; p. 133 bottom right The Left Party in the Bundestag; p. 136 top DBT/Marc-Steffen Unger; p. 136 bottom DBT/Simone M. Neumann; pp. 190191 DBT/Simone M. Neumann, © VG Bild-Kunst, Bonn 2016; p. 137 top, p. 148 DBT/Thomas Imo/photothek.net; p. 137 bottom, p. 194 DBT/Ute Grabowsky/photothek.net; p. 139 DBT/Hermann J. Müller; artwork: © VG Bild-Kunst, Bonn, 2016; pp. 140–141, p. 156, p. 179 DBT/Werner Schüring; p. 142 top left Federal Government/AP; p. 142 top centre Federal Government; p. 142 top right Federal Government/Renate Patzek; p. 142 bottom left Federal Government/Richard Schulze-Vorberg; p. 142 bottom centre, p. 143 top right, p. 143 bottom left Federal Government/Ulrich Wienke; p. 142 bottom right, p. 143 top left Federal Government/Engelbert Reineke; p. 143 top centre Federal Government/Georg Bauer; p. 143 bottom centre Federal Government/Bernd Kühler; p. 145 sources: Peter Schindler, Datenhandbuch zur Geschichte des Deutschen Bundestages 1949–1999, Baden-Baden, 1999, pp. 862 et seq., and Michael F. Feldkamp, Datenhandbuch zur Geschichte des Deutschen Bundestages 1990 bis 2010, Baden-Baden, 2011, pp. 410 et seq. (accessible as updated at www.bundestag.de); p. 146, p. 153, pp. 170–171, p. 176 DBT/Thomas Trutschel/photothek.net; p. 147 source: www.bundestag.de (last updated: May 2014); p. 150 sources: Feldkamp, op. cit., p. 945, and Datenhandbuch at www.bundestag.de, chapter 8.7; p. 158 DBT/Lichtblick/Achim Melde p. 164 sources: Schindler, op. cit., pp. 2394 et seq., and Feldkamp, op. cit., pp. 1154 et seq. (Stand der Gesetzgebung des Bundes/GESTA, Abschlussbände 8. bis 15. Wahlperiode, German Bundestag, Parliamentary Documentation Division); p. 165 sources: Schindler, op. cit., pp. 2394 et seq., and Feldkamp, op. cit., pp. 1154 et seq. (Stand der Gesetzgebung des Bundes/GESTA, Abschlussbände 8. bis 15. Wahlperiode; German Bundestag, Parliamentary Documentation) and Datenhandbuch at www.bundestag.de (last updated 10 September 2014); p. 168 DBT/Sylvia Bohn; p. 174 sources: Schindler, op. cit.; pp. 2638 et seq., and pp. 4378–4379, and Feldkamp, op. cit., pp. 1237 et seq. (German Bundestag, Parliamentary Documentation Division); p. 177 DBT/Marco Urban; p. 178 sources: Schindler, op. cit., pp. 1189 et seq., and Feldkamp, op. cit., pp. 573 et seq.; pp. 185–187 sources: Schindler, op. cit., pp. 2188 et seq., p. 4375, Feldkamp, op. cit., pp. 1036 et seq. (accessible as updated at www.bundestag.de) and author's additions; p. 192 DBT; p. 195 sources: Schindler, op. cit., pp. 3159 et seq., Feldkamp, op. cit., pp. 1444 et seq., and author's additions; p. 197 DBT/Anke Jacob; pp. 198–201 sources: Schindler, op. cit., pp. 2252 et seq., Feldkamp, op. cit., pp. 1069 et seq., and Datenhandbuch at www.bundestag.de.

Chapter 4: pp. 204-205 bpk/adoc-photos; p. 206, p. 219 bpk; p. 207 bpk/Dietmar Katz; p. 209 bpk/Staatsbibliothek zu Berlin/F. Albert Schwartz; p. 210 bpk/Hermann Buresch; p. 212, p. 216, p. 218, pp. 220–224, pp. 234–235 picture alliance/akg-images; p. 215 dpa-Report/dpa-Zentralbild/Stefan Sauer; pp. 228–229 ullstein bild; p. 230 bpk/Luftbild Berlin GmbH; p. 231 picture alliance/Süddeutsche Zeitung Photo; p. 232 picture alliance/dpa, Gregor Fischer; p. 233 picture alliance/RIA Nowosti; p. 236, pp. 238–239 DBT/Parliamentary Archives; p. 237 picture alliance/akg-images/Gert Schuetz; pp. 241–242 Christo and Jeanne-Claude, Wrapped Reichstag, Berlin, 1971-95, Germany; photo: Wolfgang Volz/laif; p. 244 dpa/picture alliance/ZB/Hubert Link; p. 245 picture alliance/ZB – Fotoreport/Computerfoto; pp. 246/247 DBT/Thomas Trutschel/photothek.net; p. 249 DBT/Achim Melde; artwork: © VG Bild-Kunst, Bonn, 2016; p. 250 DBT/Thomas Trutschel/photothek.net; artwork: © VG Bild-Kunst, Bonn, 2016; p. 251 Federal Government/Bernd Kühler; artwork: © VG Bild-Kunst, Bonn, 2016; p. 252 DBT/Werner Huthmacher, © VG-Bild-Kunst, Bonn, 2016; p. 253 left DBT/studio kohlmeier; p. 253 right DBT/Julia Kummerow; p. 254/255 DBT/Jan Pauls; p. 256 DBT/Axel Hartmann; p. 257 DBT/Stephan Klonk; pp. 258–259 DBT/Axel Hartmann.

Chapter 5: pp. 260–261, p. 268, pp. 274–275 top, p. 290 bottom, p. 291, p. 294 bottom DBT/Linus Lintner Fotografie; p. 262: DBT/Thomas Trutschel/photothek.net; p. 263, p. 275 bottom DBT/Axel Hartmann; pp. 264–265 DBT/Jörg F. Müller; artwork: © Zabalaga-Leku/VG Bild-Kunst, Bonn, 2016; pp 266–267 Bundesrat; p. 269, p. 290 top, p. 304 right DBT/Jörg F. Müller; artwork: © VG Bild-Kunst, Bonn, 2016; p. 270 DBT/Sylvia Bohn; p. 271 DBT/Lichtblick/Achim Melde; p. 273 Federal Government/Steffen Kugler; p. 276, p. 288, p. 293, p. 303, p. 314 DBT/Simone M. Neumann; pp. 277–279 DBT/BSF Swissphoto; pp. 281–282, p. 294 top left DBT/Jörg F. Müller; p. 283 DBT/Katrin Neuhauser; artwork: © VG-Bild-Kunst, Bonn, 2016; p. 284 DBT/Johannes Backes; artwork: © VG-Bild-Kunst, Bonn, 2016; p. 286 DBT/Anke Jacob; p. 287 DBT/Stephan Klonk; artwork: © VG-Bild-Kunst, Bonn;

Picture credits

p. 289 DBT/Siegfried Büker; p. 292 DBT/Hans Grunert; p. 294 top right DBT/Junophoto/Julia Nowak; p. 295 bottom right, p. 295 bottom left DBT/Junophoto/Julia Nowak; artwork: © VG-Bild-Kunst, Bonn 2016; p. 295 top DBT/Jörg F. Müller; artwork: © courtesy of Galerie EIGEN + ART, Leipzig and Berlin/VG-Bild-Kunst, Bonn, 2016; p. 296 DBT/Arndt Oehmichen; p. 297 DBT/Julia Kummerow; p. 298 top Linus Lintner Fotografie; artwork: © VG-Bild-Kunst, Bonn, 2016; p. 298 bottom DBT/Fritz Reiss; p. 300 DBT/Jörg Seiler; artwork: © courtesy of Galerie EIGEN + ART, Leipzig and Berlin, and of Zwirner, New York and London, and VG Bild-Kunst, Bonn, 2016; p. 302 DBT/Edgar Zippel; artwork: Jorge Pardo, courtesy of neugerriemschneider; p. 304 left DBT/Stephan Erfurt; artwork: © VG Bild-Kunst, Bonn, 2016; p. 305, pp. 306–307 bottom DBT/Jan Pauls; pp. 306–307 top, p. 312 DBT/Jörg F. Müller; p. 308 DBT/Johannes Backes; p. 309 DBT/studio kohlmeier; p. 310/311 DBT/Axel Hartmann; p. 313 DBT/Jörg F. Müller; artwork: © VG Bild-Kunst, Bonn 2016.

Rear cover: top left DBT/Sylvia Bohn; top centre picture-alliance/akg-images; top right DBT/Ute Grabowsky/photothek.net; bottom left picture alliance/akg-images; bottom centre DBT/Julia Kummerow; bottom right Federal Government/Gerhard Heisler.

Bibliographical information from the German National Library:
The German National Library has catalogued this publication in the German National Bibliography; the catalogued details may be accessed on the following website: http://dnb.ddb.de.

First edition, September 2016

Published by: German Bundestag, Berlin
Head of publication project: Rainer Maucher, Verlagsbüro Wais & Partner, Stuttgart
Edited by: Thomas Grimpe and Tina Steinhilber, Verlagsbüro Wais & Partner, Stuttgart
Translated by: Language Service of the German Bundestag, in cooperation with Raymond Kerr
Design: Tanja Krichel, Verlagsbüro Wais & Partner, Stuttgart
Federal eagle: Created by Professor Ludwig Gies, revised in 2008 by büro uebele, Stuttgart
Image processing: D\D\S Digital Data Service Lenhard, Stuttgart
Printed and bound by: appl, Wemding

Language versions of this edition:
German (original): ISBN 978-3-86764-619-2
English: ISBN 978-3-86764-732-8
French: ISBN 978-3-86764-733-5
Spanish: ISBN 978-3-86764-734-2

UVK Verlagsgesellschaft mbH, Schützenstrasse 24, 78462 Konstanz, www.uvk.de

FSC www.fsc.org MIX Paper from responsible sources FSC® C004592